SEARCHING FOR GOD IN BRITAIN AND BEYOND

# Searching for God in Britain and Beyond

## Reading Letters to Malcolm Muggeridge, 1966–1982

DAVID G. REAGLES

McGill-Queen's University Press

Montreal & Kingston • London • Chicago

ISBN 978-0-2280-0881-1 (cloth)
ISBN 978-0-2280-1007-4 (ePDF)
ISBN 978-0-2280-1008-1 (ePUB)

Legal deposit fourth quarter 2021
Bibliothèque nationale du Québec

Printed in Canada on acid-free paper that is 100% ancient forest free
(100% post-consumer recycled), processed chlorine free

We acknowledge the support of the Canada Council for the Arts.

Nous remercions le Conseil des arts du Canada de son soutien.

---

**Library and Archives Canada Cataloguing in Publication**

Title: Searching for God in Britain and beyond : reading letters to Malcolm
    Muggeridge, 1966–1982 / David G. Reagles.
Names: Reagles, David G., author.
Description: Includes bibliographical references and index.
Identifiers: Canadiana (print) 20210286733 | Canadiana (ebook) 20210286857
    | ISBN 9780228008811 (cloth) | ISBN 9780228010074 (ePDF) | ISBN 9780228010081
    (ePUB)
Subjects: LCSH: Muggeridge, Malcolm, 1903-1990—Religion. | LCSH: Muggeridge,
    Malcolm, 1903-1990—Correspondence. | LCSH: Christians—Great Britain—
    Correspondence. | LCSH: Christian life—Great Britain—History—20th century.
    | LCSH: Authors and readers—Great Britain—History—20th century.
    | LCSH: Great Britain—Religious life and customs.
Classification: LCC BR743.3 .R43 2021 | DDC 274.2—dc23

---

This book was typeset by True to Type in 10.5/13 Sabon

# Contents

# Tables

# Acknowledgments

A long list of scholars, librarians, archivists, and colleagues helped make this book a reality. Keith Call, David Osielski, Katherine Graybar, and the rest of the staff at the Wheaton College Archives and the Billy Graham Center Archives provided wonderful assistance and good cheer throughout the research process. They were so hospitable and helpful that it is tempting to choose future projects simply by delving into whatever collections happen to be in their care. Additionally, the library staffs at Drew University and Bethany Lutheran College provided considerable support. Special thanks must be extended to Alyssa Inniger, Ramsey Turner, Annie Williams, and Jessie Zimmerman, who facilitated many interlibrary loan requests. Without their help, this project would have slowed to a crawl. I am also grateful for the help of my research assistants, David Evans and Julia Abreu-Siufi.

Jonathan Rose, Jesse Mann, Darrell Cole, and Alister Chapman each read through the manuscript when it was still a fledgling graduate thesis, and their comments and critiques during the first stages of its life greatly improved it. Kyla Madden and the anonymous readers from McGill-Queen's University Press provided helpful critiques and suggestions that substantially shaped its revision, and Correy Baldwin's keen eye prevented many errors during the copy-editing stage. Drew University, the Mid-Atlantic Conference on British Studies, the Antiquarian Booksellers' Association, and Bethany Lutheran College provided the financial support and time needed to complete this project. An earlier version of chapter 3 was published in the *Journal of Religious History*, and I am grateful to its editors for the permission to include the material in this book. Permission to quote unpublished documents was kindly granted by the Malcolm Muggeridge literary estate and the Ruth Graham Literary Trust.

I must also thank many friends and colleagues who provided stimulating conversation and sound advice. In no particular order, I owe a great deal to Ryan MacPherson, Erling Teigen, John Boubel (and the rest of the close-knit faculty and staff at Bethany Lutheran College), Timothy Larsen, Jennifer McNutt, Edward Baring, Sloane Drayson-Knigge (and the many other profound scholars at Wheaton College and Drew University), Reba Soffer (through the North American Conference on British Studies Mentorship Program), and countless others who shaped this project in unexpected ways, and in ways I haven't realized.

Even harder to forget is family, and I am blessed with a large one: five siblings, nine siblings-in-law, and thirty-one nieces and nephews, who all bring a great deal of happiness to my life. My father- and mother-in-law, Lee and Linette, have been a mainstay of wisdom, and have provided a sense of much-needed perspective whilst I was enveloped in a singular topic of study for multiple years. My wife, Karla, has been a source of abundant love, patience, and inspiration for more than a decade now, and our three children, Isaiah, Gregory, and Felicity, bring more joy to life than we thought possible.

Finally, I must thank my parents, Steve and Patti. They have given unwavering love and support my entire life. This book is dedicated to them.

# SEARCHING FOR GOD IN BRITAIN AND BEYOND

# Introduction

"I have also received a very large number of letters, many of them of quite overwhelming sweetness and charity ... I have put all these letters – some thousands of them in a large metal box in the hope that after I am dead someone may go through them. They reveal, I think more fully than any public opinion poll or other so-called scientific investigation, the extraordinary spiritual hunger which prevails today among all classes and conditions of people, from the most illiterate to the most educated, from the most lowly to the most eminent."

Malcolm Muggeridge, *Jesus Rediscovered*, 1969

"Despite the warnings that you have thousands of letters in a large metal box, perhaps, you may find room for one more."

J. Milson to Malcolm Muggeridge, 8 September 1969

R.J. Slyfield could not sleep no matter how hard she tried. A severe head cold – or perhaps, she feared, the flu – roused her at an "unearthly hour" one Tuesday evening in November. Over the past few days, she had been reading Malcolm Muggeridge's two-volume autobiography, *Chronicles of Wasted Time*, and without any intention of wasting her own, decided to occupy the restless night with a letter to Muggeridge recounting her busy thoughts:

I have been reading your books ... eating sleeping Muggeridge for the last few days and this night dreaming Muggeridge, your words and observations going over and over in my head. For a number of years now I have had imaginary conversations with you. Whenever I get a bee in my bonnet about something, I wonder what you would have to say about it – then off we go.[1]

Reading Muggeridge was different from her experience with other books. It did not matter that they were separated by a thirty-year age gap and what felt like an equally wide cultural distance. Despite having never met him personally, Slyfield sensed they were "alike in so many ways," and she wanted him to know why. In sixteen handwritten pages, Slyfield crafted a story of her life. She began with her birth and working-class upbringing outside Manchester as a mechanic's daughter, an otherwise happy childhood that was violently disrupted by the terror of the Blitz, then described the postwar anxiety she felt after moving to Sheffield, finding her dream job as a nurse, falling in love and getting married, and, most recently, a transatlantic move to Toronto. She went on to describe in detail her current religious practices, the great difficulty of finding a church she liked, and, especially, her most recent encounter with a local Baptist preacher. He had given her the "heebie-jeebies," and seemed to emanate a stolid self-righteousness that felt altogether emotionless and divisive. For weeks she had tried different denominations, but they always left her somehow unfulfilled. Her lack of spiritual contentment seemed to reflect her life in general, as she confided in Muggeridge: "I have never felt that I belong anywhere." Listlessly, she felt as though she were "always searching and wandering." But reading Muggeridge seemed to offer balm to her weary soul. No church gave her the same sense of spiritual contentment as his books. It was he who crystalized her thoughts so well, and whose spiritual journey seemed to parallel her own. Slyfield closed her letter with not just one "P.S.," but three. The letter must have taken all night to compose because by the last page she reported to be half listening to a live radio show discuss Muggeridge's most recent work, *Something Beautiful for God*, which she had every intention to purchase. Her only concern was that the letter would be lost among the multitude Muggeridge received, and would find its end swiftly in the bin.[2]

Slyfield's letter is rich not for its uniqueness, but because it expresses many of the themes that characterized Muggeridge's readers as a whole. Like so many others, she drew parallels between her life and Muggeridge's in the attempt to form a cohesive and sustainable self-narrative in a context rife with dynamic change. Paul Ricœur once remarked that constructing a self-narrative is "life in search of its own history," and that is exactly what Slyfield's letter did.[3] Through the acts of reading and writing, she formed a deep connection with someone she never met and felt compelled to provide an utterance of her life, complete with its fears and anxieties, its joys and hopes. The emotional experience of reading, to borrow a phrase from Janice Radway, was like "a peculiar act of transubstantiation," where she seemingly became something different from before through the crystallization of once inchoate thoughts.[4] Reading and writing were not passive experiences; on the contrary, Slyfield actively used Muggeridge's books and her writing of a letter in the small hours of the morning to wrestle with matters of faith and doubt in a rapidly changing religious climate.

This book recovers the lived experience of readers like Slyfield. It considers nearly 2,000 letters from like-minded fans who described the effect Muggeridge's spiritual and autobiographical writings had on them.[5] This began in 1966 when Muggeridge publicly converted to a doctrinally loose form of Christianity just as it seemed inevitable that honest faith was in irreversible decline. He immediately had access to a niche market. In addition to his being a familiar figure in the British media, the reading public by the mid-1960s and 1970s was purchasing fewer dense theological works than ever before and was increasingly gravitating towards "literature which prioritised a questioning, eclectic 'spirituality.'"[6] Muggeridge provided just that. His spirituality was shaped not by the church, but by his own storied experience and personal reading of works by figures like Søren Kierkegaard, Simone Weil, Fyodor Dostoevsky, John Bunyan, William Blake, and Blaise Pascal. For the next fifteen years, he became a symbol of anti-institutional Christianity with whom readers felt a deep affinity as their trust in conventional religion declined. This status was crucial for maintaining his following, and it continued even as Muggeridge aligned more closely with creedal Christianity throughout the 1970s. However, the passion of his fans cooled (and the number of fan letters dropped significantly) when he unexpectedly joined the Roman Catholic Church in 1982.[7] These letters offer a glimpse into how ordinary readers responded to, and came to terms with, the transformations of religious culture between those years. Cultural revolution undoubtedly began before and continued after, but the long 1970s are central for understanding how these changes were felt at the ground level. Regardless of social setting, readers interacted with Muggeridge's religious works autobiographically. In so doing, they transformed their fan letters

into something much more than superficial signalling of popularity.[8] The letters allow for a history of audiences that reveals how people from locales as disparate as the British Isles, North America, and
Australasia each responded to parallel changes.

Muggeridge and his readers were embedded in similar religious
contexts, shared the same concerns, and addressed them through the
mutually reinforcing acts of reading and writing. Through the media,
and confirmed by their own lived experience, these fans became
aware of churches struggling to maintain social significance as attendance plummeted, membership rolls thinned, Sunday school rosters
shrunk, marriages fractured, and baptisms dried up. They also learned
of declining clergy numbers, both in Protestant and Catholic
churches alike, just as divisions deepened within churches as they
adapted theology and practice to progressive social mores. Even as
they wrestled with these internal issues, they grew cognizant of the
proliferation of religious diversity that underscored, in Charles
Taylor's words, that Christianity was merely "understood to be one
option among others."[9] Indeed, as people became more vocal in their
rejections of religious dogma and ecclesiastical authority, they began
to think less and less of their nation as definitively "Christian."[10]

Ever since the 1960s, scholars have commonly invoked some varia-
tion of the secularization thesis to explain these changes. This was a
narrative Muggeridge and his fans largely took for granted. In its classic formulation, secularization occurs because of a necessary link
between modernization (urbanization, class consciousness, increasing rationality, political economy, and bureaucratization) and religious decline. It characterizes this connection as so deeply
entrenched within the logic of modernity that religious decline is
assumed to be inexorable or, at the very least, unlikely to reverse. Statistics and anecdotal biographical evidence of the nineteenth and
twentieth centuries suggest a common sense story of linear decline
in categories of believing, behaving, and belonging.[11] This literature
depends heavily on survey data and commonly shares an assumption
that religious change is understood primarily through social class,
which, in some cases, judges religious activity as a cloak over more
fundamental structures of class consciousness, or in other cases, as a
force for social control.[12]

This standard account argues the cultural foment of the 1960s was
thus merely a natural fruition of decades, even centuries, of social
development. It was a revolution of the masses, which, accelerated by

unprecedented affluence, chiselled away at traditional practices and institutions while expanding tolerance for alternative moral frameworks. Free of the overbearing tutelage of the church, people welcomed a permissive environment with newfound allowances for sexual liberation. There was a thirst for cultural exchange with other nations, a preoccupation with cutting-edge fashion, and great interest in intellectual originality in philosophy that each worked to weaken inherited religious frameworks.[13] The sixties may have been the result of a "vast number of innovative activates taking place simultaneously, by unprecedented interaction and acceleration,"[14] but they were a long time coming. These innovations, disseminated through advancements in media and transportation technology, popularized the values and ideas of youth subcultures already underway in regional locales like the Cavern Club in Liverpool or the Crawdaddy Club in London. Variations of this narrative have remained a basic premise of religious studies and religious history for decades.

Yet, as Margaret McGuire has noted, "researchers sometimes discover that assumptions, embedded in their field's basic definitions, get in the way of understanding the phenomenon they are observing."[15] Historians have had these blinders, too. The last few decades have witnessed a considerable challenge to the conventional narratives of religious decline and scholars have begun to historicize the secularization thesis itself.[16] As it turns out, there was considerable continuity in religious belief and practice between the nineteenth century and the early 1960s. Youth cultures were not nearly as cohesive or necessarily anti-church as once thought. Immigration and the sexual revolution were significant social developments, but not really until the 1970s. Moreover, affluence in the 1960s could and did result in a radical individualism that damaged honest faith, but there were plenty of exceptions to this trend.[17]

While certainly not denying the real existence of religious crisis in the postwar context, this revisionist scholarship insists that religious decline did not result from some inherent logic of modernity. Rather, it de-emphasizes socio-structural explanations, and instead centralizes the stories people internalized as being more fundamental to the development of religious belief and practice.[18] Narratives are important for historical change because they link the personal with the public through multilayered accounts that shape and guide the free choices people make. Internalized narratives give "meaning to an event by implying what has come before and what ought to come after, identifying the relevant characters and their relation to each other as well as pointing to the bundle of practices that constitute possible 'strategies of action.'"[19] In this vein, Sam Brewitt-Taylor has argued that religious revolution in the 1960s occurred because of the rapid and successful promotion of an "alternative paradigm" that reframed how people understood the conditions of belief and the future health of Christianity in society. Departing from the assumption that Britain was a Christian nation, this novel characterization of society "insisted that humanity's future was radically individualist, expressive, anti-authoritarian, sexually libertarian, global, and, above all, secular."[20] Christian intellectuals were on the forefront of developing and accepting this view, in some cases to articulate a spirituality more suitable for modern life, or in others as an accurate depiction of what threatened conventional Christianity. This view gained currency just as opinion polls recorded that over 80 per cent of respondents thought Britain was or ought to be a predominantly "Christian country."[21] Alister Chapman, for example, showed that once evangelical leaders like John Stott became aware of sociological work on secularization, they worked to "buck the trend" through a revitalized evangelism. In this way, "the theory became a part of the story it was trying to tell."[22] Matthew Grimley's analysis of the 1957 Wolfenden Report makes a corollary argument, finding that the Church of England's changing position on homosexuality was a deliberate reaction to accommodate, and stay relevant for, an increasingly secular society. He found that even though "this wider secularisation was perhaps more imagined than real," it nevertheless "informed the clergy's decisions."[23] This "invention" of secularity may have begun in the circles of worrisome clergymen, but it was rapidly promulgated in the early 1960s by highbrow broadcasts on the BBC, which provided a mouthpiece for "death of god" theologians who fundamentally shaped the public conversation.[24] The result was, in the words of Hugh McLeod and of Simon Green, a "revolution of people's perceptions of their society and the place of religion within it," which seemed to have happen "almost overnight."[25] Once this paradigm of secularity was internalized and taken for granted, it legitimized, normalized, and then actually caused the "seismic social transformation that occurred during the 1970s, 1980s and 1990s."[26] Christianity has often brooded on its own decline, but what made the cultural revolution of the 1960s different was the consensus that secularization was inevitable, irreversible, and embedded within the very logic of history.

If the secularization story was an alternative paradigm that, as a cultural artefact, resulted in real social changes, then we need evidence of how ordinary people absorbed it.[27] So far, the use of cultural-historical methods to understand postwar religious change has focused almost exclusively on elites.[28] This is crucial, but incomplete. One may surmise that John Stott's flock, students participating in the British Christian Student Movement, or listeners of highbrow BBC religious programming surely must have accepted arguments about secularization, but how, exactly, did they respond? How did the "invention" of a secular society enter into the lived religion of rank-and-file Christians?[29] This is especially important to gauge in the 1970s and thereafter when this narrative set in motion actual social changes. Ordinary people, including Muggeridge's readers, who internalized the "invention," then witnessed its realization. Yet as we will see, they were not passive casualties of the 1960s and 1970s. On the contrary, they actively crafted their religious identity even as they situated their own lived histories within the metanarrative about the inevitably secular character of modern history.

*Searching for God* addresses these issues by considering how the books people read shaped their religious lives. Even though "most reading acts in history remain unrecorded, unmarked, or forgotten," book historians have innovated methods to recover, describe, and explain what people read, and how and why they read. This depends entirely on the self-description of readers' inner lives, drawn from wide-ranging but "inchoate" source material in a field "still in its infancy," with a current "paucity of extant research for the topic of reading" in the twentieth century.[30] These challenges notwithstanding, recovering the experiences of ordinary readers allows us to steer a course between the narrow focus on elites and the macroscopic analysis of survey data detailing in broad strokes such areas as "believing," "behaving," and "belonging." Scholarship has demonstrated that religious decline was not gradual and linear, but rapid, sporadic, inconsistent, and supremely disorienting. This was the case not least of all for Muggeridge's readers, many of whom, until very recently, had thought of their society as a Christian one. By the time Muggeridge converted to Christianity the real social changes resulting from the cultural revolution had begun to take shape. Students, homemakers, secretaries, farmers, auto mechanics, and shopkeepers tried to make sense of both the secularization story and the actual changes that resulted from it, in their own ways. They did so by picking up the writings of a recent Christian convert, reading them closely, and then jotting down their thoughts as they came to terms with what it all meant. In the act of reading, Ricœur reminds us, the "world of the text" encounters the "world of the reader" and results in "effective action"[31] – in the case of these readers, this manifested in writing a fan letter to a minor celebrity.

With few exceptions, however,[32] historians have passed over fan mail in favour of other entry points into the history of reading, making especially good use of autobiographies and published memoirs.[33] There is admittedly good reason for this. Much of the fan mail available is disjointed, disorganized, superficial, or incomplete. For many authors, fan mail was not worth its postage. Authors commonly burned,[34] selectively kept,[35] or disdained their fan letters as the most "irrational and annoying aspect of the outside world that is always infringing on a writer's life."[36] Muggeridge's mailbag does not have many of these limitations. First, Muggeridge treasured his fan mail and saved it. It bears the residue of his keen engagement; coffee stains, underlined words, date stamps, check marks, exclamation points, question marks, carbon copies of personalized responses, follow-up letters from fans, and occasional references to his fan mail throughout his published works give testament to his love for fan mail. He even hired personal assistants to organize his letters and went so far as to glue some of them into his diary.[37] When Muggeridge received fan mail while travelling, he stowed them away in his luggage so that he could file them away in the "large metal box" at his home in Robertsbridge, just south of London. So moved was Muggeridge by his fans that he welcomed them into his personal residence when they asked, so long as he had an open schedule. A quick cross-reference between fan letters and his date book reveals instances when he pencilled in visits from people he had only met by interaction of ink and paper. Sometimes the invitation to tea was Muggeridge's idea and not a shot in the dark from a fan pressing her luck. What emerges looks more like a fruitful exchange between mentor and mentee than it does a "weak feedback loop" between producer and consumer.[38] Thus, these letters were not similar to those sent to newspaper editors that David Paul Nord analyzed in *Communities of Journalism*. Muggeridge was not there just "to listen"; he responded, too.[39] In this way, his readers were joint-participants in a textual community whose members were unaware of each other's existence. Fans did not treat Muggeridge as an abstraction, and so neither should their letters be seen as placeholders for lost social space in the public sphere, as Barbara Ryan has recently suggested.[40] Letter writing is a social practice that is eminently inter-personal. They felt they *knew* Muggeridge and they used letters to "narrate experiences, dispute points, describe situations, offer expla-nations, give instructions, and so on."[41] More than this, they used them as a place for prayer, exhortation, benediction, poetry, and hymn writ-ing. Each of these religious practices were prompted by the experience of reading Muggeridge's books.

Thus, fan mail offers particular opportunities into the history of reading. While autobiographies undoubtedly offer a more in-depth portrait of ordinary readers' intellectual lives, they were, among com-mon readers, decidedly uncommon projects that required consider-able discipline and perseverance. Additionally, creators of these sources are susceptible to post-hoc rationalizations while making sense of choices they made and experiences they'd had decades earlier. As E.H. Carr reminds us, history is an "unending dialogue between the past and the present" that is shaped by the selection of facts directed by contemporary values and concerns.[42] Writing a personal history in the form of autobiography is no different. By contrast, fan letters took considerably less time to write, and were not infrequently impulsive in their creation. There was a close immediacy between the act of reading and the recording thereof in the fan letters that readers sent to Muggeridge. Indeed, readers regularly wrote while working through a book, amidst discussion in a book club, or having only just finished a text. There was B. Meisenbach, who began his letter with the confession, "I was seized by the impulse … to write a letter, the let-ter being my only means of literary expression, and being a genre of sufficient lack of magnitude, the letter form is most nearly commen-surate with my ability."[43] Or, from that same year, there was D. Hunt, a British journalist living in Zimbabwe just before its independence, who explained the pretext for his letter: "I felt, when I first read *Jesus Rediscovered* in 1976, impelled to write thanking you for addressing to me in language that I could accept what I so deeply needed to under-stand. But I resisted the impulse for fear of burdening you with yet another of an imagined flood of letters. Then, very recently, I re-read the book. This time, I could not resist."[44] Many others wrote of being "compelled to write,"[45] of being "so moved that I felt I must write,"[46] or that they "cannot refrain from writing"[47] because of the effect read-ing had on them. The impulsive nature of fan mail, the dynamic con-text of social change, and the mental disquiet of wrestling with faith and doubt made letter writing a social practice fraught with feeling.

Thus, the following pages cannot ignore those feelings if they are to reconstruct this community of readers. The "emotional turn" over the past few decades has developed a rich vocabulary for exploring the cultural mediation of emotions as well as the specific ways they act as agents of change.[48] Following Monique Scheer, we can situate the activities of Muggeridge's fans as part of this.[49] For them, reading and letter writing were self-reflexive performances that used linguistic forms requiring particular material artifacts and social space to make sense of complex circumstances. Books and letters were not merely receptacles into which readers dumped feelings they could no longer contain; on the contrary, reading and writing were emotional prac-tices with spiritual dimensions that mobilized, named, communi-cated, and regulated feeling.[50] There is a fixed connection between belief and practice, and these fans illustrate how their lived religion was embodied in and through reading and writing. Fans mobilized emotions when they picked up one of Muggeridge's texts and medi-tated on it in an almost ritualistic fashion, which they followed with writing letters to confess sins or to ask for spiritual guidance. They also wrote letters to organize inchoate emotions into a coherent nar-rative, thereby naming their feelings in order to make them "available to experience."[51] In other cases, they knew exactly what they were feel-ing and wrote instead as a communicative performance, sometimes to complain or to accost Muggeridge, but more often than not to lament some tragedy: the death of a child, the loss of a job, or being evicted from a home. Finally, Muggeridge's readers regulated their emotions because the very act of letter writing itself was a practice with "emo-tion norms."[52] There were demands for "social etiquette" in the con-ventions of letter writing by which readers had to manage how they expressed themselves.[53] Those conventions were constituted by "the embodied effect of our ties to other people," which, in the case of Muggeridge's fans, was first imagined, then realized through episto-lary exchange. For them, reading and writing were emotional acts that created a "network of relationships" – often imagined and distant, but nonetheless present as readers fashioned their religious lives.[54] Think-ing and emoting were thus not analytically separate phenomena, but occurred as mutually dependent, even synonymous activities within a specific social context by individuals adapting to changing cultural circumstances. These practices, far from merely reflecting emotional realities, actually conditioned and gave shape to them.

Because emotions are embodied practices, they are no less transient and hidden than the cognitive experience of reading that has moved book historians to write histories once thought impossible.[55] The same sources that reveal the "lair of the skull"[56] also open to us the realm of the heart. Indelible traces of feeling remain in marginalia, in diaries, and – for the present purpose – in fan mail. While this study is not a history of particular emotions, it nonetheless takes seriously the roles emotions played in the lived religion of Muggeridge's readers.[57] In most cases, they were explicit in detailing specific instantiations of their attempt to recalibrate what it meant to have faith in a secular age. But some did not. Take Lancashire native J.M. Raby. We know little about him. He identified as a Christian, but he chose not share his age, occupation, family background, or socio-economic status. His letters were never more than a few short lines, and they offered scant detail about the precise ways Muggeridge's books shaped his life. But they *must* have meant a great deal to him, because he sent eleven letters over the course of a decade recounting his ongoing engagement with Muggeridge's works. We learn from these brief missives that he read *Jesus Rediscovered* ten separate times, *Jesus: The Man Who Lives* six times, and *Chronicles of Wasted Time*, *A Third Testament*, and *Things Past* each once.[58] Raby's letters may not say much about his intellectual life, but they exhibit the sustained emotional connection he formed with Muggeridge's person and writings. An inability or lack of desire to communicate precision of feeling should in no way suggest an absence of emotional intensity. What we are left with are opaque snapshots of feeling from a faithful reader who was compelled, repeatedly, to form a meaningful connection with someone whose writings affected him. Behind the raw statistics of readership resides a profound display of complex emotives, and this was no less true when reading became entangled within the religious dynamics of the 1960s and 1970s. The secularization story, complete with its own teleology, norms of behaviour, styles of belief, and modes of belonging, could not but function as a kind of emotional framework through which Muggeridge's readers navigated. Fan mail shows the paths they took.

Bringing these letters to bear on postwar historiography also addresses simultaneously a general lack of attention to Muggeridge's significance as a historical figure. Literature on Muggeridge fits into three camps. In the first, small religious presses have made something of a cottage industry out of reprinting his religious works for contemporary devotional use. Some of these include sketches of Muggeridge's life that frame him as a Christian example. Because the primary purpose of this literature is not historical, and verges towards the hagiographical, it is limited as a source for understanding the times in which Muggeridge lived. The second includes a small number of concentrated studies on his long and illustrious career as an author, journalist, and television personality. The most important of these include biographies written by Ian Hunter, Richard Ingrams, and Gregory Wolfe, as well as a short study on Muggeridge's moral philosophy by Paul Philips.[59] Finally, Muggeridge occasionally receives brief mention within the broader study of twentieth-century Britain, usually as a wellspring of snarky quotes. Indeed, precisely how he influenced people around the world has been a subject entirely ignored until now, and this despite being "a perennial figure on the small screen in the late 1960s and 1970s"[60] and "one of the most successful communicators of his time."[61] With the exception of a few (brief) mentions in studies such as Noel Annan's *Our Age* and Julia Stapleton's *Political Intellectuals*, Muggeridge has not been recognized as a public intellectual.[62] For example, Dominic Sandbrook's comprehensive survey of postwar Britain gives scant attention to Muggeridge by painting him as a somewhat solitary, idiosyncratic figure whose conversion was just the first step "on his long, lonely march towards greater conservatism and, eventually, Catholicism."[63] Such broad strokes miss the mark because his readers between 1966 and 1982 never imagined he would join institutional Christianity, least of all the Roman Catholic Church. For them he was a surrogate cleric whose writings formed, in some cases, the single most important source for their spiritual self-fashioning. Moreover, as this study shows, he was not only attractive to conservative Christians. He appealed to a diverse group of people representing a wide array of political, religious, and ideological perspectives. A close reading of these fan letters offers a corrective to the claim that Muggeridge "was not a theologian and certainly not an intellectual."[64] In fact, his readers saw him as both of these and more. Whether by phone calls, written replies, or welcoming personal visits, Muggeridge went to great lengths to meet his fans. The unique personal connection he formed with readers around the world gave him a special status. In this way, he became not just a public intellectual that pontificated from the airwaves, but also a personal intellectual who took the time to respond to readers' letters on any variety of issues they felt they needed help with. The fact is, readers saw a mirror image of their own journey of faith in the life and work of Malcolm Muggeridge. As readers became dissatisfied with their churches and felt increasingly alienated from the society they inhabited, they sought to form close, personal connections with Muggeridge.

Indeed, community was something Muggeridge understood from an early age. Philips has argued that between the competing visions of *Gemeinschaft* and *Gesellschaft*, Muggeridge unreservedly aligned with the former.[65] Muggeridge had a storied life. He was born in 1903 to a lower-middle-class family in a suburb just a few miles south of London. His father, Henry Thomas Muggeridge, was a Labour politician with strongly socialist sympathies. Even though his mother, Annie Booler, had Methodist roots, his father's agnosticism had the more significant impact on Muggeridge's early religious development. Jesus Christ was a premier example of pious living, but not, as Muggeridge later confessed, the "Incarnate God" whose coming "into the world is the most stupendous event in human history."[66] Muggeridge won a competitive scholarship to study at Selwyn College, Cambridge, where he formed a close friendship with Alec Vidler, who became among the most important spiritual influences in his life. There Muggeridge dabbled with high-church Anglicanism, but soon became disillusioned with institutional Christianity in general. After graduating in 1924, Muggeridge had short-term positions teaching English literature in India and, after marrying Kitty Dobbs, at Cairo University. From there Muggeridge began his illustrious career in journalism. He remained committed to socialism until the 1930s, when a trip to Moscow and first-hand encounter with Communism inspired a turn away from the political left. For the next fifty years, Muggeridge was ubiquitous in the British media. He wrote for the *Manchester Guardian*, the *Statesman*, the *Evening Standard*, and the *Daily Telegraph*. He worked for the Ministry of Information and MI6 during the Second World War, was editor of *Punch* magazine from 1953 to 1957, appeared regularly on the BBC as a talk show host, and even produced a handful of documentaries. Muggeridge developed the reputation of an iconoclast who relentlessly lampooned just about anyone or anything, especially the political and ecclesiastical establishments. He remained agnostic into the 1960s, even as his literary output focused increasingly on criticizing religious personalities and institutions. Much like the highbrow media and church official, Muggeridge began to speak of the inexorable decline of Christianity due to secularist forces from without, and secularizing clergy within.[67]

Muggeridge was a prescient critic who recognized early in the postwar context the reality of Britain's transforming religious character. While still an agnostic, he joined with those elites who "successfully normalized a whole new set of metanarratives for thinking about the modern world."[68] That is why his conversion to Christianity came at such a surprise in the mid-1960s. Muggeridge dedicated the last decades of his life promoting the faith he had satirized. Yet Muggeridge's conversion did not mean an immediate rejection of secularization. On the contrary, he continued to promote it earnestly in word and deed. Muggeridge adamantly avoided joining a church for nearly twenty years and continued to excoriate the institutional church and its actions. As a Christian, he still saw the churches as among the primary causes for permissiveness in society and religion's decline. Muggeridge, by contrast, defined his religiosity outside of the conventional parameters of Christian practice by expressing his newfound faith in authoring spiritual books and articles, speaking on religious issues, and producing faith-based documentaries and programs. Thus, at once Christian apologist and social gadfly, Muggeridge came to symbolize an alternative way of expressing authentic faith in an age his readers accepted as secular. He "authoritatively proclaimed" the irrefutable reality of Britain's religious decline, but instead of celebrating it, he challenged his readers to practise their spirituality in spite of the secularity they took for granted.[69] Muggeridge was certain that secularization meant "The end of Christendom, but not of Christ."[70]

The close relationships between Muggeridge and his fans – resembling the bond that can exist between a minister and parishioner – created the conditions for his writings to influence profoundly his readers' religious lives. Fans used his books as they wrestled with spiritual questionings about ecclesiastical authority and the nature of the church, and how they perceived the current and future health of Christianity, and even used them as they redefined patterns of religious behaviour. In some cases, this bred despair, but in others, it inspired hopeful anticipation of how religion might itself be transformed by its interaction with a secular society. Muggeridge was of the unusual combination of being both anti-establishment and socially

Table 0.1
Malcolm Muggeridge's letter writers by sex[1]

| | Male | Female | Unspecified |
|---|---|---|---|
| 1966 | 61 | 29 | 11 |
| 1967 | 38 | 15 (16) | 8 |
| 1968 | 24 (25) | 25 | 5 |
| 1969 | 53 (55) | 66 | 17 |
| 1970 | 63 (67) | 71 | 13 |
| 1971 | 49 (51) | 77 (82) | 8 |
| 1972 | 63 (66) | 76 (78) | 6 |
| 1973 | 56 (58) | 61 (64) | 7 |
| 1974 | 57 (64) | 38 (41) | 8 |
| 1975 | 42 (47) | 39 (46) | 5 |
| 1976 | 60 (70) | 64 (65) | 3 |
| 1977 | 53 (58) | 67 (70) | 7 |
| 1978 | 36 (41) | 43 | 2 |
| 1979 | 29 (32) | 25 (27) | 4 |
| 1980 | 51 (54) | 36 (41) | 1 |
| 1981 | 81 (86) | 59 (71) | 8 |
| 1982 | 58 (63) | 49 (61) | 0 |
| Unspecified Year | 3 | 2 | 1 |
| Total (1833) | 877 | 842 | 114 |

[1] Unparenthesized figures count only individual fans and exclude subsequent letters. Parenthesized figures include readers who sent multiple letters.

conservative, yet who nevertheless insisted that he was a "man of the left."[71] He thus attracted letters from a wide spectrum of political, religious, social and cultural perspectives.

## MUGGERIDGE'S READERS

Despite the diverse demographic backgrounds of Muggeridge's fans, their reading experience was not particularly coloured by their class, age, or sex. The common ground was religious discontent. Unsatisfied with institutional Christianity, they saw Muggeridge as a spiritual guide, were anxious about the shrinking role of religion in their societies, and were inspired toward social activism. What bound them together was the shared experience of reorienting themselves to new terrains of religious culture.

Table 0.2
Religious identification of Malcolm Muggeridge's letter writers

|  | Number | Percentage |
|---|---|---|
| Unspecified Christian | 1,077 | 59 |
| Roman Catholic | 281 | 15 |
| Anglican | 105 | 6 |
| Methodist | 12 | 1 |
| Presbyterian | 11 | 1 |
| Other Specified, Christian[1] | 58 | 3 |
| Agnostic | 19 | 1 |
| Atheist | 13 | 1 |
| Other Specified, Not Christian[2] | 52 | 3 |
| Unspecified | 205 | 11 |
| Total | 1,833 | 100 |

[1] "Other Specified, Christian" includes Baptist (nine), Swedenborgian (seven), Evangelical Christian (seven), Christian Fundamentalist (four), Pentecostal Christian (four), Quaker (three), Christian Scientist (three), Jehovah's Witness, Christian spiritualism, the Salvation Army, Lutheran, Christedelphian, the United Church of Christ (two each), and Unitarian, Christian Universalism, Church of Jesus Christ of Latter-day Saints, Christian (Open) Brethren, Plymouth Brethren, Russian Orthodox-in-Exile, Christian Mysticism, the Order of the Cross, and the Jesus Freaks (one each).
[2] "Other Specified, Not Christian" includes readers who thought of themselves as spiritual, but who had rejected Christianity (nineteen), Jews (eight), Bahá'í (seven), Transcendental Meditation (three), Hindu (three), Buddhist (two), and Muslim, Sikh, Psychic, Scientologist, Spiritualist, Baba lover, Raja Yoga, Deist, humanist and self-identified gnostic (one each).

The 1,833 people who wrote the 1,935 fan letters provide a decent, though not comprehensive, picture of the religious affiliation, sex, age, occupation, and geographical distribution of Muggeridge's readership. We know readers were almost evenly split between male (877) and female (842),[72] and, taken together, represented at least forty-five different religious persuasions or worldviews (see tables 0.1 and 0.2). His youngest letter writer was eleven years old; the oldest was ninety-three.[73] The average and median age was forty-nine. Just under 30 per cent (543) of Muggeridge's readers gave some sense of their occupations. While nearly 40 per cent of these were religious workers,[74] readers also attended universities or taught at them,[75] worked in the press,[76] or served as medical doctors.[77] His readers were also blue collar. They were construction workers, auto mechanics, homemakers, farmers, factory workers, bartenders, lawn mower contractors, soldiers, manufacturers, painters, and transit workers.

Most readers included a return address on their letters, though 106 evidently wrote theirs on an envelope that was soon discarded. These readers hailed from forty-seven different countries across six continents, though most came from Anglophone societies (see table 0.3).[78] A majority shared a common cultural background in that they experienced many of the fundamental transformations that characterized Western societies in the 1960s and after. Of course, this is not very surprising. Muggeridge's fame resulted from his familiarity on television and radio outlets that were mostly accessible in places like the British Isles, North America, and Australasia. It was in these locations where Muggeridge also went on his many speaking tours or lived for extended periods. True, Muggeridge had readers in parts of Africa, Asia, and South America, but many of these learned of him because of their Anglophone background or exposure to English-language media. It is telling that some of Muggeridge's bilingual fans wrote to offer their translating services *so that* his books would reach a wider audience.[79]

Between 1966 and 1982, fans wrote about their experience of reading *Jesus Rediscovered* more than any other book (table 0.4). As Muggeridge's first major book-length religious work, it remained widely available throughout the period of this study. Readers simply had more opportunity to get their hands on it than those books he published later, such as *The End of Christendom* (1978) or *Like It Was* (1982). The other three books that attracted the most fan mail were *Something Beautiful for God* (378 mentions), *Chronicles of Wasted Time* (294 mentions), and *Jesus: The Man Who Lives* (204 mentions). Muggeridge's fans wrote to him about ten of his other works as well, which together amounted to 241 mentions. There were 244 letters that did not mention any specific writing by name, but intertextual evidence suggests the letter was prompted by reading. Fans commonly said things like "having read your many publications,"[80] "I have most of your books,"[81] or "recently I read some of your writings,"[82] or referenced in general "all those books of yours that I have read."[83] In these cases, it is rather difficult to tell exactly which writings or books they were talking about – they very well may have been thinking of several works simultaneously. Muggeridge also liked to return to the same themes in multiple publications, so even a detailed cross-reference between the date of their letters and Muggeridge's various publications would not make us any wiser about what they were reading.

In any case, what is popular is not necessarily most meaningful. Every fan who was inspired to write a letter was moved in some way

Table 0.3
Geographic distribution of Malcolm Muggeridge's letter writers

| Continent | Country | Number |
|---|---|---|
| Europe (57 per cent) | Austria | 1 |
| | Denmark | 1 |
| | England | 876 |
| | Finland | 2 |
| | France | 3 |
| | Germany | 10 |
| | Hungary | 1 |
| | Republic of Ireland | 39 |
| | Italy | 5 |
| | Netherlands | 3 |
| | Northern Ireland | 13 |
| | Norway | 3 |
| | Portugal | 1 |
| | Scotland | 49 |
| | Spain | 2 |
| | Sweden | 2 |
| | Switzerland | 7 |
| | Vatican City | 1 |
| | Wales | 32 |
| North America (24 per cent) | Bahamas | 1 |
| | Canada | 134 |
| | Mexico | 1 |
| | United States | 300 |
| Australasia (9 per cent) | Australia | 119 |
| | Fiji | 1 |
| | New Zealand | 47 |
| Africa (2 per cent) | Cameroon | 2 |
| | Democratic Republic of the Congo | 2 |
| | Gambia | 1 |
| | Ivory Coast | 1 |
| | Kenya | 3 |
| | Lesotho | 1 |
| | Nigeria | 1 |
| | Rhodesia (Zimbabwe) | 5 |
| | South Africa | 16 |
| | Tanzania | 1 |
| | Tonga | 1 |
| | Uganda | 1 |
| | Zambia | 1 |
| Asia (2 per cent) | India | 16 |
| | Israel | 1 |
| | Japan | 3 |

Table 0.3 (*continued*)

| Continent | Country | Number |
|---|---|---|
| | Philippines | 1 |
| | Singapore | 11 |
| | Sri Lanka | 3 |
| South America (<1 per cent) | Argentina | 1 |
| | Peru | 1 |
| Unspecified (6 per cent) | | 106 |
| Total (100 per cent) | | 1,833 |

by the books they read. We can't place *Jesus Rediscovered* on a hierarchy and conclude it was Muggeridge's most important book just because it was mentioned most often. Muggeridge's fans would likely disagree among themselves about that very question. Their letters reveal that the circumstances in which they read determined this or that book's relative meaning and importance. The peculiar social context of reading is crucial for its ability to mobilize emotions. Take *Things Past*. Receiving only 2 per cent of all mentions makes it among Muggeridge's less popular books. Yet, R. Nathan, a sixty-year-old man from Queensland, Australia, wrote to express just how much it meant:

> This book, now read, is beside me, and I know quite positively, that it will be till I die … and … if I thought there were a purpose to do so, it would be buried or burned with me … This copy, given to me with love, will remain in my mind and heart and back and forth between hand and shelf in the same as, and beside, the Gospels.[84]

One senses from Nathan's letter that yes, he very well may have thought the text was insightful, well written, etc., but what really made it matter was that it served to embody the connection of a loved one. His reading (or, perhaps, just the ownership) was a practice of object association whereby the book itself transformed into a source for emotional mobilization. Nathan's letter reminds us that that statistics from book sales (or, in this case, the number of times a book is mentioned in fan mail) say nothing about the specific meanings certain books have for readers. The text's importance is inseparable from

Table 0.4
Publication by number of mentions

| Publication | Male | Female | Unspecified | Total mentions | Per cent of total mentions |
|---|---|---|---|---|---|
| Jesus Rediscovered | 310 | 298 | 45 | 653 | 32 |
| Something Beautiful for God | 119 | 242 | 17 | 378 | 18 |
| The Chronicles of Wasted Time | 179 | 101 | 14 | 294 | 14 |
| Articles later republished in a book | 126 | 72 | 23 | 221 | 11 |
| Jesus: The Man Who Lives | 94 | 106 | 4 | 204 | 10 |
| A Third Testament | 32 | 19 | 5 | 56 | 3 |
| Things Past | 22 | 16 | 0 | 38 | 2 |
| Paul: Envoy Extraordinary | 19 | 16 | 2 | 37 | 2 |
| A Twentieth Century Testimony | 20 | 15 | 1 | 36 | 2 |
| Tread Softly Because You Tread on My Jokes | 28 | 6 | 0 | 34 | 2 |
| Christ and the Media | 22 | 5 | 1 | 28 | 1 |
| The End of Christendom | 15 | 2 | 0 | 17 | 1 |
| Muggeridge: Ancient and Modern | 7 | 8 | 1 | 16 | 1 |
| The Thirties | 12 | 2 | 0 | 14 | 1 |
| Muggeridge through the Microphone | 7 | 4 | 0 | 11 | 1 |
| Like It Was | 9 | 1 | 0 | 10 | 1 |
| In the Valley of a Restless Mind | 4 | 4 | 1 | 9 | <1 |
| Winter in Moscow | 5 | 0 | 0 | 5 | <1 |
| Affairs of the Heart | 4 | 0 | 0 | 4 | <1 |
| Three Flats | 1 | 0 | 0 | 1 | <1 |
| | | | | 2,066 | 100 |

Table 0.5
Number of letters prompted by reading, 1966–82

| 1966 | 1967 | 1968 | 1969 | 1970 | 1971 | 1972 | 1973 | 1974 | 1975 | 1976 | 1977 | 1978 | 1979 | 1980 | 1981 | 1982 | No date | Total |
|---|---|---|---|---|---|---|---|---|---|---|---|---|---|---|---|---|---|---|
| 101 | 68 | 54 | 138 | 151 | 139 | 149 | 128 | 110 | 97 | 138 | 133 | 76 | 63 | 96 | 165 | 123 | 6 | 1,935 |

the physical object itself, which readers keep close for comfort and may even seek to carry with them to the grave.

How often did fans send letters? Did they all arrive infrequently, but in high quantities? Or did they arrive gradually? Depending on how one looks at it, we could say both. On average, per year, Muggeridge received 114 letters that detailed reading practices. If we counted *every* fan letter he received (including those inspired by a television or film appearance), the number jumps to approximately 1,250 per year. Thus, between 1966 and 1982, just under one out of every ten letters was prompted by reading. He certainly produced enough material for fans to write about. Muggeridge published a new book almost every year during the 1970s, not to mention the dozens of impressions, new editions, and translations that were printed throughout his later career. His books followed what was likely a typical market pattern in that they generated significantly higher interest (and therefore fan mail) in the first years following publication, and then slowly tapered off as the buzz died down. Yet, as soon as one of his books began to lose popularity, another would hit the shelves. For example, of the 653 letters prompted by *Jesus Rediscovered*, 255 of them arrived within the first two years of publication. After that initial spike, the number dropped significantly. Between 1971 and 1982, readers sent roughly thirty-two letters each year. Just as fan mail inspired by *Jesus Rediscovered* began to dip, he released in 1971 what ended up becoming another solid-selling book, *Something Beautiful for God*, which received just under 400 mentions. His other books followed a similar pattern. Of the 204 letters that mentioned *Jesus: The Man Who Lives*, eighty-nine of them arrived during the first two years after publication, with an average of about nineteen coming in each year after that. Again, just as fan mail mentioning *Jesus: The Man Who Lives* slowed to a trickle, Muggeridge published both *A Third Testament* and *Christ and the Media*. The rate of new publications appearing in the 1960s and 1970s also had the simultaneous effect of inspiring new fans to search his corpus for other reading material. Therefore, it was not uncommon for someone to learn of Muggeridge for the first time in the late 1970s by seeing him on shows such as William Buckley's *The Firing Line*, only then to seek out and read books he had published years and perhaps decades before. Indeed, *Jesus Rediscovered* prompted the last fan letter considered in this study, written when the book was more than twelve years old.

We therefore can make at least a few statistical generalizations about Muggeridge's readers. Taken at random they were probably English, generally Christian, middle aged, and were reading *Jesus Rediscovered*. This should therefore revise Richard Ingram's assumption that Muggeridge's theological tone "did not endear him to British audiences," while it was "more appreciated on the other side of the Atlantic – in the USA and Canada."[85] The fact that the majority of his fan mail was written by British Christians who did appreciate his theology may perhaps indicate instead that they liked it every bit as much as Americans. Perhaps the difference was that they chose to express their appreciation in more subdued form, like a private letter.

Muggeridge claimed to love receiving fan letters, and we know that some fans even sent him letters in the first place *because* they thought that was true. But how often did he actually respond? How do we know if he did not just throw them away and use the sentiment to produce good will among his customers? For that matter, how could he have possibly tended to each of the tens of thousands of letters he received? It would seem Muggeridge cared enough about his fans that he made sure that one of the jobs of his personal assistant, Marian E. Williams, was to make sure they were accounted for. None of Muggeridge's biographers mentions her. Unfortunately, she did not leave any memoirs, and the textual evidence she left behind is limited. However, it is possible to partially reconstruct her important role for the study of Muggeridge's fan mail.

It would seem he hired her to care for his letters mostly while he was away travelling. She indicates as much in at least a couple of responses that she sent to admiring fans. There is evidence that she also helped him stay organized even while he was at home. The system they used to keep track of letters was simple, but irregular. Depending on who opened the envelope, either she or Muggeridge would indicate on the letter whether a response had been sent. This would vary from a check mark with a date or a note saying something like "Replied on," followed by the date. Most of these were written in Williams' hand, but there are a few in the chicken scratch that was Muggeridge's handwriting. If we count *just* the letters with the indications that a response was sent, then replies were sent to just over half of all the letters he received. That is a conservative estimate, however. Some letters without marginalia still have textual evidence of responses. For example, no marginalia appears on the six letters Muggeridge received from E. Wilson over the course of about four years, but we know that he *did* respond from the fact that she quoted from letters she had received from him.[86] Most fans, as we have seen, did not send follow-up letters. It is entirely possible that fans received a response without Muggeridge or Williams leaving any record of it happening.

Is it possible to know if the only response they received was from Muggeridge's personal assistant, Marian Williams? Not entirely, but some clues are available. Since Muggeridge was oftentimes preoccupied with writing, appearing on television, giving public lectures, producing documentaries, and travelling abroad, more often than not it was she who first received the letters. But if we consider those letters Muggeridge received while aboard, Williams does not appear to have sent responses in his name. What she did instead was send a short note to fans explaining his absence, and that Muggeridge would read it once he returned. We know that Muggeridge followed through on her promise, even if it was months afterwards. H. Fern sent his fan letter about having read *Chronicles of Wasted Time* on 18 December 1972.[87] The margin of the letter includes two dates. The first says, "Keep, Forward 21.12.72," which may indicate that she forwarded Muggeridge's fan mail to wherever his current address was while travelling. It might also mean that she saved it for him to peruse once he got back home. The latter is probably more likely, because the letter's second time stamp, "20.4.73," was also written in Williams' hand.[88] In either case, it likely indicates Muggeridge did, in fact, read and send personal responses to letters he had received months prior. This example, at least, suggests that Williams' main role was logistical in that she was tasked with receiving, organizing, and keeping track of the hundreds of letters that Muggeridge would receive during the time he was away from home. It would seem that they even had conversations with each other on the letters themselves regarding logistical issues. When a fan living in a Sydney suburb asked when *Jesus Rediscovered* would finally appear on Australian shelves, Muggeridge wrote in the margin: "?When will Jesus Rediscovered be on sale in Aust?" Williams wrote back in the margin: "on sale now Fontana books."[89] Evidently, Muggeridge had every intention of responding to a fan halfway around the world, took the time to get the information, and depended on his personal assistant for it.

In some cases, Williams took the liberty of filing the letter away without responding. Thirty-four letters have "No Reply" written at the top. This might have been due to letter writers having neglected to include a return address, but sometimes not responding was deliberate. When K. Downes sent one of her several letters in November of 1972, Williams noted on the margin (perhaps in annoyance), "No Reply She Writes Every Other Week."[90] Again, it was possible that Muggeridge still read these, but without marginalia, carbon copy of responses, or follow-up letters from fans, we can only guess. Yet, given what we know about what Muggeridge thought about his fan mail, it is very likely that he did glance through them, even if a reply was not sent.

One gets the sense that Williams became quite invested in the problems fans shared as she organized the letters for Muggeridge's later view. When one anonymous fan wrote a four-page letter without an address in handwriting that was, frankly, illegible, Williams took the time to decipher each word by rewriting the letter between the lines. She included a note for Muggeridge: "Do Read This."[91] These letters were an end in and of themselves, even when they were difficult to read or when it would have been impossible to send a reply. After twenty-four-year-old R. Stark, who read *Jesus Rediscovered* three times, wrote for advice on whether or not he should enter the priesthood, Williams included a special plea for Muggeridge: "Can you help this eager beaver?"[92] On this letter (as many others), there are two time stamps ten days apart. The first probably refers to when Williams acknowledged receipt of the letter while the second was the record of Muggeridge's personal reply. Examples like these seem to confirm that she probably did not ghostwrite his responses, but did take it upon herself to nudge him when the letters she screened touched her emotionally.

A few letters show the kind of editorial liberties Williams took. One Australian fan, A. Crawford, had read *Jesus Rediscovered*, which inspired him to send a fan letter to Muggeridge as he struggled with the classic philosophical problem of the existence of evil. Muggeridge was travelling when the letter arrived, so Williams took it upon herself to send him a two-page letter with a long quotation of something Muggeridge had said about suffering in a recent BBC program, *The Question Why*: "Why Suffering." After mailing the response, she then wrote a little note for Muggeridge on the top of Crawford's letter, "hope this is okay," with the carbon copy attached.[93] Here, then, is another component of their system. Muggeridge trusted Williams to respond on his behalf, even to the point of editing a reply of what she thought Muggeridge would say to whatever issue a fan was writing about. The note on the letter itself not only indicates that Muggeridge took the time to read the stack of letters that piled up while travelling, it shows that he was invested enough that Williams knew he would want to know exactly what she was communicating to his fans, perhaps especially if it was constructed from Muggeridge's own words. In another case, after reading a six-page letter, Williams wrote "lots of questions" in the margin. Her initial reply encouraged the writer to purchase *Jesus Rediscovered* because she believed it would serve to answer his questions with as much success as a personal response from Muggeridge would. Muggeridge often sent his books to fans free of charge if he felt they would benefit from them and faced financial hardship. Williams evidently knew this, so she included a note on the carbon copy of her reply saying, "He trains horses so he can afford to buy it."[94] Whether she was right is another matter, but this short note sheds some additional light on the system that Muggeridge and Williams had for responding to fans.

This book is a history of these personal connections that, assembled together, reveal the interworking of a textual community spanning the Anglophone world. By analyzing its key characteristics and central preoccupations, this book argues that the bond readers formed with Muggeridge through reading and writing was means for their spiritual self-fashioning. These emotional practices were conditioned by the emergence of the popular individualism that became a dominant cultural script beginning in earnest by the late 1960s. In this context, fans saw Muggeridge as a guru who crystalized their otherwise nebulous thoughts and feelings on matters of faith. He thereby became an authentic spiritual authority readers sought for guidance as their trust in conventional religion weakened. This process continued even as they internalized narratives of religious decline – increasingly dominant in the 1960s – that proclaimed the definitively secular nature of society and the inevitable death of Christianity as they knew it. Muggeridge's texts, their social acts of writing, and the replies they received each served to mediate their understanding of religious realities and to shape the practices they pursued in response.

But Muggeridge's readers did not despair at these challenges and then write as a form of escapism. They were also inspired to change the world around them. Even as the rise of the welfare state witnessed a concomitant decline of Christian voluntarism, Muggeridge's books invigorated his readers to donate money, volunteer their time in impoverished neighbourhoods, embark on missionary trips, and even change career paths. Muggeridge's readership was broad, and its character reflected the increasing religious diversity in the Anglophone world. His religiously plural readership included Buddhists, Muslims, Jews, agnostics, atheists, and more. Muggeridge kept his hate mail, but these readers did not add to it. They certainly had significant qualms with the theological vision Muggeridge promoted, but just like his Christian readers, they also turned to him for guidance as they wrestled with spiritual issues in their lives.

Together these letters reveal the profound and sometimes unexpected ways fans used reading and letter writing to make sense of the religious crisis of the 1960s and 1970s. This book is thus just one contribution to the need for historians to include voices from below, in order to illustrate the cultural manifestations of religious change. These readers may have passively accepted that Christianity as they knew it was declining, but they were not hapless victims caught in circumstances beyond their control. They actively participated in this history by redefining how they practised faith in a secular age.

# Reading and Writing as Self-Discovery

You have compelled me to recognise the religious, mystical and philosophical impulses in myself and also to attempt to act on them. Don't consider me a "fan" or a disciple – maybe a "kindred spirit."

Fleur B. to Malcolm Muggeridge, 26 June 1982

We do not know much about K. Williams from Surrey. Her fan letter to Muggeridge had fewer than two hundred words and included no personal details apart from her name and return address. She just wanted him to know one thing after reading *Jesus Rediscovered*: "I feel I know you through your book and also love you for revealing and unfolding your thoughts. *It has served to unfold my own*."[1] Williams' short letter signals what so moved Muggeridge's fans to write after reading. As this chapter demonstrates, fans formed a close personal relationship with Muggeridge through the emotional practice of naming. In so doing, they saw him as a friend and kindred spirit whose life was a mirror image of their own. This perception proved fundamental for Muggeridge's lasting influence on their lives of faith. As Monique Scheer, building on William Reddy's theory of emotives, explains, "every emotion is unique and gets put into a category – is typified – only through naming."[2] This is what happened to Williams and it reoccurred with striking regularity among other readers who described how his books had crystalized the nebulous thoughts and emotions they struggled to put into words. Though Muggeridge did not write "self-help" books, his writings nevertheless were a source for the self. In this way, his books functioned in a similar fashion to those "industries dedicated to improving 'emotional intelligence'"; that is, he helped their "work of signifying and resignifying emotions."[3] If typifying feeling into concrete linguistic forms is how emotions become available to experience, and emotions are an embodied engagement with the world, then the emotional practice of naming is fundamental to historical change. As Scheer continues, naming only occurs in the "meaningful intersection of socially situated concepts and bodies."[4] It is a learned behaviour, "meaning that feelings are transferred between people ... through socializing processes." Muggeridge's fans expressed these processes in the form of reading and writing, which "unfolded" thoughts and feelings into coherent and accessible forms. But what did this actually look like among Muggeridge's readers? Why did it matter, and what difference did it make for their religious lives? As we will see, it made all the difference because it connected people in a kind of imagined community that granted affirmation and recognition to the fashioning of their reflexive selves.

By the time Muggeridge had publicly converted to Christianity, the "invention" of the 1960s as a secular, progressive, and anti-authoritarian era was well established. At the heart of these dynamics was the emergence of a "popular individualism" that caused pervasive "dealignment" along traditional categories of class, gender, and religious persuasion. It was characterized chiefly by a desire for "greater personal autonomy and self-determination" that was expressed by an unprecedented departure from inherited attitudes, customs, habits, and cultural meanings.[5] People used the growing freedom they experienced from rising affluence, the welfare state, and the expansion of educational opportunities to redefine themselves in new and creative ways. Anthony Giddens has described this context – that of "late modernity" – as one in which the crafting of one's identity develops as a "reflexive project."[6] Individuals made and remade themselves as they faced the myriad of choices that comprised the conditions of their experience. Once people turned away from traditional cycles to define the practices of everyday life, their personal identity needed to be "routinely created and sustained in the reflexive activities of the individual" in order to negotiate a sustainable "biographical narrative" in response to a culture they took to be in constant flux. Ultimately, the reflexive project is a means to thrive within a society that was contingent and unpredictable. As Giddens describes this project,

> The narrative of self-identity has to be shaped, altered and reflexively sustained in relation to rapidly changing circumstances of social life, on a local and global scale. The individual must inte-

grate information deriving from a diversity of mediated experiences with local involvements in such a way as to connect future projects with past experiences in a reasonably coherent fashion.[7]

"Popular individualism" and the reflexive project were both aspects of the cultural script that dominated the late 1960s and 1970s encouraging personal refiguration in response to the perception of social change.[8] Television and print media play a central role in late modernity because they link the local with the global, mediating multiple visions of social change as individuals reflexively craft and recraft the self in response.

According to Giddens, the principle of "authenticity" gives shape and direction to the self-reflexive project at an individual level. Authenticity is a tricky concept to define precisely because it became such an amorphous term during the 1960s and 1970s. Consumer practice had democratized cultural authority, and so what counted as "authentic" became fragmented by individual preference. This process mirrored politics, which witnessed a decline in the influence of class identity on voting choice. People "made up their minds for themselves more often, changed their views more frequently, and weighed issues more carefully."[9] Much more than merely "being true to oneself," authenticity in the 1960s and 1970s was defined by the trust fostered within personal relationships. People who wished to remain Christian, but nevertheless wished to disassociate from institutional Christianity, began to seek out alternative sources of "authenticity" as they carried out their self-reflexive projects. The popular individualism of the 1960s and 1970s expressed "multiple valences," which included some who exhibited serious doubt and uncertainty. Those who had anxiety and uncertainty about their identity – religious or otherwise – sought out guides who had achieved, in Giddens' term, "self-mastery" of who they were. Self-mastery, in effect, occurs by successfully overcoming the "doubt" that "permeates into everyday life."[10]

Muggeridge's readers recognized him as possessing both the authenticity and self-mastery that would help them to carry out their self-reflexive projects. He earned this status because he appeared to have so successfully worked through the problem of individualism that they struggled with. Remaining outside of Christianity's traditional structures, Muggeridge practised to a mystically informed Christianity characterized by personal devotions, private contemplation, and moral activism. He thereby served as a public and outspoken counterpoint to internalized narratives of religious decline. Muggeridge modelled how his readers could maintain Christianity as an essential component of their "biographical narrative" without remaining committed to inherited structures like the institutional churches. Muggeridge's conversion to Christianity was less as an atavistic reaction to the popular individualism of the 1960s and 1970s than it was a religious expression of it. This helps to explain why fan letters to Muggeridge were so autobiographical in their scope and content. The dual processes of reading and writing served as an exercise through which they worked through and came to terms with those challenges.[11] Their self-reflexive projects made use of emotional practices. Recrafting self-identity required recalibrated emotives, by which readers translated internal feelings into expressible form amidst newly recognized cultural and social norms.[12] It is no coincidence that popular individualism became a definitive feature of late modernity just as institutional Christianity witnessed declining numbers and dwindling social influence.[13] As traditional frameworks that had given British (and by extension, Western) society cohesion began to decay, people came to believe it was necessary to make sense of their religious identity apart from inherited institutional frameworks. Reading Muggeridge's books, writing him fan letters, and sometimes receiving personalized responses helped to foster trust, which established the conditions in which fans could strive for self-mastery in their own lives.

### KINDRED SPIRITS

This kind of relationship that resulted in fans recognizing Muggeridge as a kindred spirit crossed geographic, social, cultural, religious, and in some cases even linguistic distances. V. Gargano, a Franciscan monk living on Lake Como, must have been among the first to read *Christos Riscoperto* (*Jesus Rediscovered*) because his letter was sent mere months after *Jesus Rediscovered* was translated into Italian.[14] He felt enough "affinity with [Muggeridge's] spirit" after reading that he opened his letter with "Dear Friend and brother."[15] Londoner Victoria I. felt the same. After receiving a previous letter from her some months earlier, Muggeridge decided to give her a copy of *Jesus: The Man Who Lives*. Her thank-you letter expressed a desire for genuine friendship when she addressed him as "Dear Malcolm," because it made her "somehow feel nearer ... than Mr. Muggeridge."[16]

Thirty-two-year-old G. Flax felt the same. She was a busy mother of three young boys who stopped reading *Jesus Rediscovered* "reluctantly, on page 50 in order to get on with my day's work."[17] Like Muggeridge, she was a recent convert herself who felt somewhat alone because her husband did not share her newfound convictions. Moreover, she evidently was not taken all that seriously when she became a Christian, because, as she described it, her friends wrote it off as her being "merely off on another kick, much like trying a new hair style." For that reason, she felt a special connection to a fellow convert who, at least from his books, seemed like he would understand where she was coming from. Reading Muggeridge's books felt like "an introduction to a friend, and now a brother."[18] She hoped that one day she could meet him and discuss more fully all the ideas flooding into her mind. Until then, she promised that her daily prayers at such sacred altars as the "sink or the stack of diapers" would include a supplication or two on Muggeridge's behalf.

What was it about his books that so often inspired his readers to see him as a friend or kindred spirit? The most common reason his readers indicated was his blunt and genuine openness. Readers saw Muggeridge's typical candour – so often expressed in the form of derisive satire – transformed into honest, if hesitant, reflection in his religious writings. It seemed as if they were granted special access to his real personality, and not some manufactured product for consumption. In Gidden's definition of the term, Muggeridge had "authenticity."[19] This was the thought of R. Groening, a student at the University of Winnipeg pursuing degrees in history and theology. His interest in those subjects stimulated his summer reading of Muggeridge's biography, *Chronicles of Wasted Time*. Groening was deeply touched when he finished, and wrote, "You shared yourself so openly and completely that you reached your hand across the ocean and gave a bit of yourself to everyone."[20] It was a combination of Muggeridge's "strength of personality" and willingness to reveal his true self that made his autobiography come across as authentic; Muggeridge himself and the people he discussed were "mortal and prone to error."[21] In short, they were human.

Muggeridge's quite personal replies to fans validated his reputation for being authentic. Montreal native J. Ford, for example, wanted Muggeridge to know he was her "spiritual friend" and that she agreed with "practically every one" of his "feelings and reactions."[22] That said, she took serious issue with his overtly conservative stance on contraception and overpopulation. When she was reading *Jesus Rediscovered*, she must have come across the half-dozen times when Muggeridge condemned contraception and wrote off related fears concerning overpopulation. Though Muggeridge did not appear to make any actual argument about legislating morality through the apparatus of the state or church, Ford nevertheless suspected that was what he really meant. As she saw it, external restraints on sexual behaviour were counterproductive. Not only were state-backed abstinence policies impractical, she felt they were downright "anti-life" by preventing people from learning through their sexual experimentation why such self-control was important and necessary. Repressing those desires would only make matters worse. She implored Muggeridge to look to William Blake as an authority on the matter, and recognize that the "Garden of Love" was spoiled when authorities like the church tried to bind with shackles of briar individual freedom and happiness.[23] Muggeridge appeared to have felt Ford misunderstood his meaning, and so jotted down his thoughts in the margin of her February letter, which was typed out and mailed to Ford within the week:

> I loved your letter. It's the greatest comfort to me to know that my words reach someone like you. I don't regard abstinence, any more than contraception, as the answer to the so-called population explosion. What's needed is to see that we have such abundance now that, if we truly loved our neighbour, there [could] never be too many people in the world. Regarding abstinence – it's something each individual has to work out. Only, I utterly disbelieve the contemporary notion that satiety is the answer. No one [would] suggest one [could] eat one's way out of gluttony. No more can one fornicate one's way out of lechery.[24]

However much Ford misunderstood *Jesus Rediscovered*, or whatever wishful thinking Muggeridge may have had on the subject, the exchange nevertheless illustrates the kind of relationship that was typical between Muggeridge and his fans. Fans expressed sincere attachment to him after reading his books, imagining him as a friend and kindred spirit, even in the face of quite contentious disagreements about human freedom and social goods. Sometimes he would rifle out a standard template that, whatever the intention, anyone could have written. But in many cases, Muggeridge took the extra time to send his readers a copy of one of his books, honour requests for an autograph or personal photo, or even invite them into his home.

This was G. Evans' experience. Not much is known about her other than that she was from London, enjoyed reading Muggeridge's books, and sent him a letter on 25 July 1977 asking to meet in person when she would be near Robertsbridge at the end of August.[25] Muggeridge sent a prompt reply four days later, obliging her request with a date for afternoon tea when she came to the area.[26] Muggeridge appears to have intended to keep the meeting: his calendar for 23 August 1977 has "*Tea Time*, 400, [G.] Evans" penned in as the only appointment.[27] This clearly was not an isolated incident. One week after Evans sent her letter, D. Baker, a young Roman Catholic priest working in the Hertford Parish also sent Muggeridge a request to visit him. He learned that "many visitors often call upon you at Robertsbridge, and I wondered if I might do so at some date convenient to you."[28] He had read *Jesus Rediscovered*, *Chronicles of Wasted Time*, and *Jesus: The Man Who Lives*, but a fan letter did not seem like enough. He preferred to share his reactions with Muggeridge in person. Muggeridge responded two days later much as he had to Evans, asking Baker to contact him via his unlisted number to confirm before arriving.[29] Baker's name was recorded in his datebook, too. Like most readers, Baker and Evans found they would rather speak in person about what they read, and, for that reason, their fan letters were more like a prelude to a tête-à-tête that reverberated into silence at Robertsbridge. It is impossible to know just how many of his fans who wanted to meet actually did. His datebooks are riddled with similar-looking entries, with just a name and time. Given the regular replies from Muggeridge to his fans, there is good reason to suggest the examples of Evans and Baker were not isolated occurrences.[30]

Others were quite happy pouring out in almost diary-like form the unfiltered thoughts that entered their mind while reading. This was what D. Murphy did. While most fan letters exhibit an impulsive character, Murphy wrote her 1977 letter in three separately dated sections that spanned the course of twelve days as she worked through *Jesus Rediscovered*. The header of the typed-out note states that parts of the letter were "copied over from my notebook." She shared her immediate reaction to reading, as well as how she thought about these written responses after digesting her own comments. Murphy's note, first written while sitting alone in a theater in Muskegon, Michigan, drips with emotion:

Just now, I have finished reading, for the first time, your book, *Jesus Rediscovered*. If you were here right now, I would run to you, and embrace you to say, "Oh, *thank you* for sharing *so much* of yourself so *honestly*!" ... Sitting here, with your book in my lap, I feel almost suspended in time ... Your book has given me tears, and goose-bumps, and skips in the heart. Please, I don't want to take away from the depth of your insights and experiences, but everything there, in some very real way, I too am groping with. It means so *very*, very much to be able to reach out to someone else who has gone through this ... Just WHY, when wandering into the bookstore at the corner, looking for something to read, my glance should meet your photo and then the title and then your name ... [It] was enough to urge buying the book.[31]

Reading Muggeridge inspired her to pick up Leo Tolstoy's works. She began with *Childhood*, *Boyhood*, and *Youth*, and spent the next two pages comparing Tolstoy with Muggeridge. Their books became united in her mind in a seamless, intertextual discourse. On her reading they were both essentially the same because they were animated by an internal conflict between the "Puritan and Epicurean." The conflict between pursuing moral rectitude and physical pleasures was one she saw in herself, too. Recognizing a common struggle in people like Muggeridge gave her confidence to stay the course on her own religious journey.

The final section of her diary-like letter is considerably less animated, largely because, as she described it, "Your book has settled more within me."[32] Reading, as this letter shows all too clearly, is subject to temporal mediation that often eludes the researcher's attempts to pinpoint a singular "reading experience." For reading, as Ricœur argues, is a point of contact where preconceived notions enter into negotiation with unfamiliar textual terrains, which then can serve to mediate a reconfiguration of how reality and self-identity interact.[33] For D. Murphy, this process was ongoing for weeks after finishing *Jesus Rediscovered*, and was further mediated by the other books she read. Thus, she thought about Muggeridge in conjunction with Tolstoy's quasi-autobiographical work, and even imagined them as experiencing the same struggle – a struggle she also described having. When she continued the letter twelve days later and realized *Jesus Rediscovered* had "settled" in her, it can be seen as a way of admitting a full internalization of the text. She was then ready to move on to Tolstoy's *Resurrection*, and, since her exposure was shaped by her interaction with Muggeridge's writings, it is probable that she would continue to link them indelibly in her mind. Muggeridge never responded to D. Murphy because she did not leave a return address. She wrote that if her letter never got to him, or if his secretary opened it and read it, she would rather not know out of regret or embarrassment.

But if Muggeridge never had the chance to respond to fans like D. Murphy, he had plenty of opportunity with T. Farquharson. In comparison with most of Muggeridge's fan letters, Farquharson's are less informative about his reading experience and much more informative of his everyday life and experiences, complete with their troubles, joys, and discoveries. Yet he is a particularly good example illustrating the common theme of Muggeridge's fan mail: his readers saw him as much more than just the author of the books they read, but as a kindred spirit and friend with whom they would share just about anything. This was the case with R.J. Slyfield, J. Ford, R. Groening, Rev. D. Baker, D. Murphy, and thousands of others. What makes Farquharson of particular interest is that he was a mental patient in his fifties or sixties for several years during the 1970s at Bangour Village Hospital, just outside Edinburgh.[34]

His exact mental diagnosis is not disclosed in his letters, which are scattered throughout the Muggeridge Papers and span the course of about a decade. Whatever his mental condition, it did not prohibit him from writing lengthy letters detailing his active intellectual pursuits. He read broadly, receiving many works through various book clubs, including the History Guild Book Club. He had read Darwin's *Origin of Species*, biographies of Florence Nightingale and Madame de Pompadour – a "sort of mythical name I heard of so often yet remained shrouded in mystery."[35] Of all that he read, however, he thought, "Russian novelists were in a class by themselves." He shared with Muggeridge a particularly deep love for Tolstoy and Dostoevsky, having read both *War and Peace* and *Anna Karenina*. Now he was just about to crack open Nikolai Gogol's *Collected Tales*. He had even made some Ukrainian friends at the hospital, from whom he tried his hand at learning some Russian. He also dedicated his energies to learning German. He procured several German textbooks, and was ambitious enough to seek out a German-born patient for additional assistance on grammar and pronunciation.[36]

Institutionalization at a mental hospital would in no way inhibit the joy of intellectual discovery.

Muggeridge was impressed enough with Farquharson's intellectual life that he sent him *Chronicles of Wasted Time*. To a certain degree – as with so many fan letters – the letters are frustratingly one-sided, since Muggeridge did not always include a carbon copy of his response, nor did he always jot his thoughts in the margin before sending them off. The only marginalia on Farquharson's letter in which he discussed his reading habits said, only, "Book sent, 8.8.74."[37] Farquharson did not waste any time at all. His thank-you letter was dated 14 August, and in it he remarked just how much the gift meant to him, and that he had "been devouring the first chapter ... and could hardly put the book down to take up my pen and scribble this note of thanks for the very great humour you have done me."[38] It moved him enough that he included two photographs of himself with his fourteen-page letter. Meeting Muggeridge in person was unlikely, so lengthy letters and some photos were the next best thing. In the end, it is perhaps less important for the present discussion to know every twist and turn of Farquharson's life than it is to recognize that he felt Muggeridge should. This kind of connection was forged in the crucible of thought, and was based only on Muggeridge's books and whatever letters he received in return.

## UNFOLDING THOUGHTS

Recognizing Muggeridge as a kindred spirit through the acts of reading and writing gave coherence to fans' nebulous thoughts in ways they did not anticipate, and left them feeling as if the words remained their own. The Irishman A. Moriarty is a case in point. In a brief letter, he wrote:

> I have just finished reading your book "Jesus Rediscovered." *Within those pages you have crystalised for me many of the rather disjointed thoughts I had on the Spiritual side of man's nature.* I know what you have communicated to me in your book to be true ... I was brought up a Roman Catholic and was happy in that faith until I became familiar with the Doctrines of Darwin and Freud, etc., as a result my spiritual Barque became unstable. I experienced many

dark nights of the Soul. It was you through your writings more than anyone else who gave me light in that darkness.[39]

Moriarty's experience fits the classic "crisis of faith" motif that, until recently, was a caricature of how religious decline occurred from the Victorian era well into the twentieth century.[40] It does not appear Moriarty lost his faith, but he did enter into an existential crisis that precipitated crippling doubts – a more common feature of modernity.[41] This sort of experience – that of forming a close, personal relationship with Muggeridge through his writings – occurred regardless of sex, age, religious denomination, or geographic locality. It speaks to the emergence of a distinct textual community whose members were unaware of their shared intuition. Arthur Marwick, Adrian Hastings, Hugh McLeod, and Callum Brown have each pointed to parallel cultural and religious developments occurring in multiple Western contexts during the 1960s and 1970s.[42] For this reason, it should not be surprising that readers across the Anglophone world experienced uncannily similar "ideas, thoughts, and feelings ... which until now have only existed in the most nebulous of forms."[43]

The experience of having one's thoughts crystalized served a double function. As indicated above, it left Muggeridge's readers to feel like he was their friend. Additionally, and more significantly, it left them with the sense that he was a seer of their own mind's eye. There is perhaps no better sign of influence than someone feeling as though the words were taken right out of their mouth. After reading *Jesus: The Man Who Lives*, M.J. Kett thanked Muggeridge for "putting into words the many thoughts that 'flash through the mind' but never find pen and paper."[44] Her only criticism of Muggeridge was that he ought to take Holy Communion, which, indeed, prior to his 1982 entrance into Roman Catholicism, he rarely, if ever, did. Half a dozen references later to what Muggeridge had written on the subject (with equally as many Biblical proof-texts), she nevertheless held that it was a blessing when he "put into bound cover" his thoughts for readers like her to imbibe.[45]

M.J. Kett and J. Ford[46] illustrate what was true for many readers: although they felt Muggeridge was a kindred spirit who had the ability to articulate their incoherent and unrealized thoughts, their reading was not of passive approval of every position Muggeridge advocated. Book historians have long recognized that the production, dissemination, and reception of information are rarely monodirectional,[47] meaning creation in the act of reading is a negotiation between readers and authors within particular contexts and material circumstances.[48] Understanding how and why people read books in certain ways should thus include – when available – the various aspects of a reader's life that shaped their interpretation. Thinking about readers as implied, assumed, imagined, inferred, or inscribed will not serve to uncover the individual idiosyncrasies of everyday life.[49]

Such an approach is helpful for understanding twenty-three-year-old C. Hall, who found Muggeridge and his works much too orthodox. Writing from a Sydney suburb, she wanted Muggeridge to know "that I have gained strength from your words and that many of your questionings have crystallized my own thoughts."[50] *Jesus Rediscovered* had "cast an important light on a seemingly unseeing world," but it did not go quite far enough, as her life story testified. She described her upbringing as a heart-on-fire Methodist, but once she entered adulthood, her faith in the atonement and Trinitarianism had cooled. She believed the former had dangerous implications for an effective theodicy ("how could a God of love be thought of as angry & unforgiving"), while the latter was a blatant logical paradox ("how could there be three Gods?"). It was reading Emanuel Swedenborg's self-published works, and adopting a few of his core ideas, that solved these dilemmas for her. She thought that maybe they might assist Muggeridge, too, as he seemed to have some uncertainties and doubts of his own. Her reading experience underscores the much broader development in the religious history of these years, in which people became increasingly eclectic about their beliefs.[51] This development was informed by criticisms towards religious authority and institutionalized Christianity.[52] People grew increasingly comfortable with appropriating elements from various theological traditions both inside and outside of Christianity to personalize religious experience. Or, in Hall's case, she was open to eclecticism as a way to solve troubling theological dilemmas.

A. Brandow, self-described "housewife & very bad typist," expressed a similar sentiment, though her Christianity was more mainstream than Hall's.[53] Brandow had coincidently seen Muggeridge in person at a talk he gave at Queen's University, in Kingston, while on a speaking tour in Canada, just as she was reading *Jesus Rediscovered*. She found that it had "opened many new avenues of thought for me and

served to crystalise some ideas of my own." But after seeing Muggeridge speak, she admonished him to be more gracious with the
youth. She felt he spent the entire Q&A session tearing the students
down and decrying the inevitable decline of the world. "Would it not
be wise," she asked, "to throw them a life line once in a while? Perhaps
you feel that they should work out their own answers ... but I feel
they are crying out for a little gentler understanding." After all, there
was so much misinformation and "waves of fact and fiction" from the
news media that finding truth, meaning, and purpose was difficult
enough without the likes of Muggeridge frustrating that effort.[54]
What they really needed was a caring role model to give them encouragement and direction.

The timing of her letter is important. When scholars of the 1960s
and 1970s talk about youth culture, they describe it as affluent, materialistic, trendy, and progressive. While recent scholarship has noted
that youth culture was not a monolithic entity necessarily inclined
towards rebellion,[55] there was still the reality of countercultural movements among the youths that posed a direct challenge to churches.
Prosperity meant that youth groups and church functions had to
compete with movies and dancehalls. Participation in the former
dropped like a rock while it increased in the latter.[56] Growing anti-
authoritarian attitudes and cultural commercialization were enough
to degrade the kind of influence various religious denominations had
in the past on steering the youth away from secular pursuits. Confes-
sional subcultures, whether doctrinal or social, became increasingly
difficult to maintain. The knee-jerk reaction for many of the older
generation was to accommodate change to avoid alienating the youth.
Adrian Hastings describes the religious mood of the 1960s as one
resembling a "flight of lemmings," in which just about anything theologically rigid or old-fashioned was seen as absurd.[57] If the clergy
were not convinced about the strictures of their church body's official
theological and social positions, ecclesiastical discipline for not adher-
ing to those precepts would lax. These insecurities were felt at the
local level, where active church members like Brandow feared that
disciplining the youth on religious matters would drive them away.
The older generation treaded softly where they felt most insecure, and
interaction with the youth was where they were most insecure of all.[58]

Muggeridge had developed a reputation of being uncompromis-
ing with youth culture. Brandow's letter was written not long after
Muggeridge had resigned his post as the rector of Edinburgh Uni-

versity two years earlier. The events surrounding his resignation
became something of a minor headline. The campus newspaper, *The
Student*, had lobbied the university administration to provide free
contraceptives through the campus health services. Muggeridge's
views towards contraception and abortion were well known by this
point. He characteristically dug his heels in, declined their request,
and chose to resign rather than remain for a fight. He announced his
resignation, perhaps symbolically, in a sermon address that was soon
thereafter published in *Jesus Rediscovered*. Part of that sermon was
spent accusing the students of squandering their education for cheap
thrills: "All is prepared for a marvellous release of youthful creativity;
we await the great works of art, the high-spirited venturing into new
fields of perception and understanding – and what do we get? The
resort of any old slobbering debauchee anywhere in the world at any
time – Dope and Bed."[59] Brandow's observation of his talk at Queen's
University alongside her reading of this sermon confirmed to her, at
least, his reputation as a stodgy and disagreeable gadfly, particularly
with the young.

Yet, if Brandow gives the impression that Muggeridge's derisive per-
sona alienated him from college-aged youths, it is only partially true.
Generational differences were important for shaping the ethos of the
1960s and 1970s, but that should not obscure important exceptions.
Twenty-one-year-old A. Lacey, for instance, at first thought Muggeridge was "a rather boring old man who talked about religion a
lot."[60] But when he came across *Muggeridge: Ancient and Modern*, he
"suddenly realised that you were talking about things which meant a
great deal to me, in the sense that you were verbalising and brought
into focus, feelings and impressions in myself which were then buried
and indistinct." These indistinct feelings largely centred on observing
what he saw as a materialistic and pleasure-seeking culture at Lough-
borough University, where he was pursuing a degree in history. What
he thought was supposed to be a "temple of reason" seemed much
more an excuse for reckless hedonism. His disagreement with this
"fantasy" of modern life, that pleasure is its highest pursuit, made him
feel as though he were "a displaced person" from the rest of society.
Muggeridge seemed to change that for him by putting his observations in a spiritual perspective: "Thank you for letting me know that
I am not mad, that somebody else of greater intelligence and infi-
nitely greater experience than I, has also seen the joke of this world,

and realised what our true purpose of life, and the true meaning of life, really is."[61]

## PARALLEL LIVES
## AND PERSONAL REFIGURATION

Recognition of Muggeridge as a kindred spirit who crystalized nebulous thoughts was foundational to the ways readers used his writings to reshape their self-identity. Readers who might have been decades or continents apart constructed parallels between their own lives and Muggeridge's, even if these parallels were superficial at best.[62] Readers juxtaposed the personalities, events, localities, and experiences they read about alongside their own memories as they refigured the narratives of their lives. Muggeridge's books, in the words of Londoner D. Raymond, "leave you not quite the same as you were before."[63] Her transformative reading of Muggeridge reflects Ricœur's argument that reading functions mimetically, in that it effects fundamental transformation in how a reader sees the world.

L.M. Wallace, a retired army major from Beckenham in Kent, read Muggeridge's autobiography three times. He had just moved on to his published diary, *Like It Was*, when he typed out a short letter. He could not help but think of his own life as "a (very pale) reflection of yours, not materially ... but in attitudes to life, including thoughts of suicide at about the same age."[64] Trust begins with shared life experiences, and it is fostered by mutual care and concern for the other. Letters were traces of the connectedness readers felt and evidence of the trust they wished to foster between themselves and Muggeridge. One American reader, Mary B., drew many parallels between herself and Muggeridge. For one, they were the same age, and both had the rare experience of serving as spies during the Second World War – he in Africa and she in Europe. Yearning to learn about a fellow veteran's war stories, Mary's reading was wistfully impulsive.

In a review of your books, I saw your wartime activities mentioned and so in a moment of nostalgia, decided to read what you had been up to. Well, I read that chapter about the liberation of Paris, picked up the phone and ordered "The Green Stick," cancelled all my engagements, shoved my own manuscript aside and just lay on my bed for those five enchanted days and nights ... I

assume I must have eaten and possibly slept, but have no recollec-
tion of such mundane pursuits. And it has taken me at least ten
days to reach a point where I can write you a letter a hundred
times shorter than I would like to! ... I am exactly your age. *But
this means that we "experienced," if that is the word, many of the same
things even if in different forms.*[65]

Same, but different. Mary made herself comfortable in the foreign
terrains of Muggeridge's life and conflated their circumstances. Just
as Muggeridge had attempted to drown himself in a moment of
inebriated despair, Mary admitted that she also had attempted suicide – though for her it occurred not in India, but off the coast of
Florida when she was a teenager. Unlike Muggeridge, however, her
change of heart resulted not from a quasi-spiritual epiphany, but by
the uncomfortable realization that she was treading shark-infested
waters. Suicide is always a matter to take seriously, but if Christopher Hitchens was right that Muggeridge's sincerity was suspect,
perhaps she and Muggeridge had more in common than she
lets on.[66] In any case, readers like Mary B. recurrently saw their
own life's idiosyncrasies reflected in Muggeridge's, however general
they were.

It was more common that readers saw Muggeridge as an archetypi-
cal figure who encapsulated better than anyone the general experience of modern life. M. Hardcastle might as well have been speaking
for hundreds of Muggeridge's fans when he said, "I feel in many ways
that your literary pilgrimage is a microcosm of us all; that in an articulated form you have expressed so well the dilemma of most of us in
the twentieth century." The problem Hardcastle was referring to was
that of maintaining adherence to Christianity in a context in which,
by any quantifiable measure, it had lost considerable social and cultural significance.[67] Since Muggeridge's conversion to Christianity cut
against both this trend and the narrative of inevitable religious
decline, his life story gave confidence to many readers concerned with
either their own faith, or with the general state of Christianity in society. It provided a sense of comfort for readers to draw parallels
between their lived religion and Muggeridge's.

Late-life converts to Christianity found in Muggeridge a particularly strong parallel and source of self-reflection. K. Crawford and E.
Kemp are two such examples. The first time Crawford remembered
reading the Bible he was in his twenties. At the time of his letter, he

had been a Christian for many years, but reading *Chronicles of Wasted Time* reanimated the confusion, uncertainty, and guilt he remembered from his youth:

> Here I was quietly reading through your autobiography, studiously noting passages of interest, when, suddenly, on page 81 ... I found myself back in the days of my youth, vainly striving to piece together the jigsaw puzzle of human relationships. Sex! Lust! Platonic friendships! Love: all-embracing and yet somehow empty! Where did the pieces fit: all colours seemed blurred, all shapes contorted beyond visible recognition; even the straight pieces appeared to have rounded corners! Finding no solution, I abandoned myself to that "nausea of overindulgence," which seemed to plague every other student at the University of Aston at the time, to such an extent that I reached the point of complete saturation.[68]

During this time of his life, Crawford had sparked a heated affair with the "nymphomaniac fiancée" of a young Austrian who, after learning of it, "soundly thrashed" him. The beating was evidently enough to bruise more than just the body, because he afterwards voluntarily enrolled in a sexual addiction rehabilitation course. Since his conversion to Christianity, he had desired to document his journey so that others might benefit, and it was reading *Chronicles of Wasted Time* that gave him the inspiration to begin that project.

Like Crawford, Kemp's reading of Muggeridge caused her to look back on her life with regret. Kemp had spent much of her life in Wales, "without too much concern about religion – or the mysteries of existence."[69] It was only after retiring from teaching in 1958 that she became increasingly interested in spiritual questions. She spent the next twelve years looking for answers, and though she "gained much help" reading authors like Søren Kierkegaard and Simone Weil,

> It was not until I got your "Jesus Rediscovered" that I was brought up starkly against something. I have never written to a "famous" person before, and I am really unable to explain now, why your book stands out ... Your book made me look back on my own life as a failure. I know now I should have done a much better job in school, if I had your picture of Christ before me in all I said and did. It is now alas too late.[70]

These emotions were facilitated by comparing her past life with Muggeridge's. His writings may have helped her to answer questions she had wrestled with for over a decade, but the restructuring of her worldview came at the expense of the integrity of her own past.

In addition to reconverts, readers of a variety of theological commitments – whether fundamentalist or liberal – recognized in Muggeridge a parallel life. Fifty-one-year-old E. Vellacott was a member of the conservative Christian Brethren. He was rather old school in seeing his membership in the Labour party as an "extension" of his Christian faith, and not at all as a distinct expression of a secular, political consciousness. He read *Jesus Rediscovered* and found that not only did he agree with Muggeridge ("your views very largely happen to be my own"), but, more significantly, he saw "rather piquant parallels between your development and my own."[71] That said, he still took issue with some of Muggeridge's positions. Included in his letter were several pages of notes that he had taken while reading *Jesus Rediscovered*, which paint the picture of a deeply conservative Christian who thought Muggeridge was much too liberal dogmatically. The chief problem in his view was that Muggeridge's attitude to Scripture was much too vague, especially for a work of "Christian propaganda" that was supposed to convince people of the truth of Christianity.[72] Vellacott did not share Muggeridge's distrust of institutions, either. He saw the harsh criticisms of the institutional church and its clergy that were peppered throughout *Jesus Rediscovered* as crass and sacrilegious hyperbole. Together these issues led him to question if Muggeridge had actually rediscovered Jesus. He wondered: how could one be fully in the body of Christ if he refused to support its members and institutions?

Like Vellacott, Mrs. J. Thiel of Lafayette, Indiana, thought that Muggeridge's life "parallels my own experience so much; and there is always joy to discover one is not alone."[73] Her career as a social worker, however, had led her to much different conclusions on a variety of issues, especially regarding his "constant sniping at efforts to control the world's population." His go-to solution of choosing to "withdraw from the world and its problems" confirmed that he was entirely out of touch with actual people.

Go into the streets, meet and talk with the people, especially the poor and uneducated, the mentally and physically ill. Talk with the children, watch their reactions; get acquainted with the homeless teen-agers; and then dare to tell your public about morality and continence and following rules. Christ would not withdraw from these people.[74]

It could be argued that the time Muggeridge took to read and respond to his thousands of fan letters, and sometimes even meeting with those who wrote them, was his way of engaging with real people – including the poor, uneducated, and mentally ill, and children and teenagers. The old adage that actions speak louder than words is cliché only because it is so often right. It would be difficult to argue decades of consistent replies, gift giving, and invitations to tea are in some way not actions. Then again, neither Theil nor anyone else knew that Muggeridge was so dedicated to responding to his fan mail.

In both of these cases, of Vellacott and Thiel, themselves representing quite different positions theologically and socially, still saw meaningful parallels between their lives and Muggeridge's. It was because of that affinity, and not despite it, that they each went to such lengths to admonish and direct Muggeridge onto what they saw as the straight and narrow.[75] Their criticisms were more so cast in a spirit of correcting an erring brother than they were the vociferations of hate mail. Ideological disagreement did not preclude meaningful self-reflection.

It also served to inspire hope that they might overcome a similar spiritual dilemma that Muggeridge had. For the global evangelist Ruth Graham, Muggeridge's life meant hope for her and Billy's youngest son, Nelson:

When I first saw *Chronicles of Wasted Time*, I thought, "Why should I waste my time reading how he wasted his?" Then I started and couldn't put it down – both books. You see, I have followed you with fury and fascination since way-back-when. But I kept listening and reading and it was as if I could hear the Hound of Heaven baying in the distance. Something was happening, and we who were out there alternately pulling our hair and/or praying, realized God would win. But I like your writing about yourself better than Ian Hunter's book. In fact, I gave up on page 225 ... because of all the un-likable traits he brings out. In fact, I stopped at one point and listed all those traits you had as a young man. And one evening I read them aloud to Bill ... and without betraying you, asked him whom they described. Without hesitation he said, "Ned." Now Ned is our fifth and youngest. He, too, has been on his spiritual pilgrimage, camping leisurely along the way. But progressing. Seeing how God did finally reach you, I realized again, "Nobody's hopeless!" Our Ned will never be a Malcolm Muggeridge, but God has a spot for him to fill.[76]

Indeed, like Ruth Graham, Christian readers regularly situated their reading of Muggeridge's books, his life, and their own in a broader scheme of divine providential will. Graham's trust that Ned would reach his spiritual destination safely was confirmed by drawing a parallel between his life and Muggeridge's. In so doing, Graham collapsed time, space, and circumstance to discern meaning and purpose behind contexts, which for other observers might have remained imperceptible.

H. Fern of Birmingham, England, expressed something similar about his life in a letter to Muggeridge. After reading both volumes of *Chronicles of Wasted Time*, he found therein a reflection of his own life, despite the events of Muggeridge's occurring years before his own: "I have formed much satisfaction in reading your book; for, in terms of intellectual and spiritual experience, you have trodden a path which, in its general direction, I have myself travelled. You, however, traveled the turning points along the way ten to fifteen years sooner than I did."[77] S. Morgan also thought of herself as a fellow traveller after years of reading Muggeridge. She was seventy-five at the time of her letter and had lived in the same farmhouse outside Bailey, North Carolina, for over fifty years. Members of her family had lived there since the eighteenth century. She had first learned of Muggeridge because her daughter had given her *Something Beautiful for God* and *Chronicles of Wasted Time* as Christmas presents, and she had just received *Jesus: The Man Who Lives*. She appreciated enough of what he wrote in those books to admit, "I am very glad that I am sojourning here at the same time that you are; for I have been made richer by insights gleaned from sublime thoughts that you have put down on paper."[78] Like Bunyan's "traveller" in *The Pilgrim's Progress*, Morgan was guided by the counsel of another – that of Muggeridge. But she also understood her interaction with Muggeridge as providentially sanctioned. Reflecting on her life and the influence Muggeridge had had on it, she thought: "I am among the most blessed of all people. Looking back, I can see how the strands of life were being woven into the fabric that is now me. Without a guiding Light, all would be darkness. I wish I knew you and Kitty. I feel like I do. I am glad you are still here."[79]

B. Moss formed a similar conclusion to that of Morgan, though hers developed out of an internal crisis. Moss provided Muggeridge with a short narrative of her life to illustrate "just how very ordinary I am."[80] Emphasizing the ordinariness of her background magnified the significance she placed on her interaction with his books. They were the catalysts that changed her life. She thought of herself as an introvert, partly because she had never lived more than ten miles from Bolton, where she grew up in a religious household. She attended Catholic school until age sixteen, when she obtained a job as an office assistant. Shortly thereafter, she married an agnostic man, though she remained an active member of her church. At the time of the letter, she was in her mid-thirties and had a seven-year-old son and a five-year-old daughter.

Three years before writing to Muggeridge, "her world turned upside down" when she fell in love with another man. Though her letter states that an affair never occurred, the description of her internal conflict is cast in stronger language than that in the letter by K. Crawford, who actually did have an affair – and a messy one at that. However melodramatic Moss's writing was in comparison, her clandestine affair of the heart caused her a great deal of guilt. She was not comfortable sharing this internal problem with anyone in person, so she first sought out answers at the local library, where she checked out anything she could find on the philosophy of love. During her study, she came across the writings of Richard Wurmbrand.[81] Learning about Wurmbrand's imprisonment and torture in Communist Hungary for his faith was enough to put her own problems into proper perspective. She resolved that her sin was not that she'd had romantic feelings for someone else, but rather that these feelings were an expression of her own pride and self-centredness. Her journey of self-discovery led her to reading several of Muggeridge's works, beginning with *Jesus Rediscovered* and *Paul: Envoy Extraordinary*. These books forced the realization that "this event in my life had thrust me out of my comfortable cocoon into real-life ... If I was ever going to mature, now was the time."[82] The spiritual maturity she had in mind was to place the transient worries of mortal life into eternal perspective, which, as we have seen, was perhaps *the* central tenet of Muggeridge's theology. Self-abnegation, she resolved, was the path to emotional and spiritual tranquility. She then delved into the classics of Christian mysticism that Muggeridge had quoted and referenced so liberally in the telling of his own religious journey, including St Augustine, William Blake, Blaise Pascal, and John Donne. In other words, Moss was describing the central role that Muggeridge played in her own reflexive project. Her crisis may not have been caused (as far as we can tell) by the conditions of late modernity, but she nonetheless had a personal dilemma that struck her to the core. It caused a serious internal conflict that commenced a three-year study that led her to reading Muggeridge, recognizing his authenticity, and refiguring herself in response. At the close of her letter, Moss summed up in ancient metaphor, so loved by the mystics, the recognition at which she had finally arrived over the past three years: "I have found that thread of gold or silver which has run down the ages since time began and you have been part of my thread."[83]

## CONCLUSION

The popular individualism that began in the late 1960s and peaked in the 1970s fragmented traditional communities of belonging. The growth in autonomy and self-determination resulted in wide-scale redefinitions of personal identity. Malcolm Muggeridge's readers participated in this as they, too, negotiated their religious identity in response to social change. Fundamental to their self-reflexive projects was the personal relationship they forged with Muggeridge through the mutually reinforcing acts of reading, writing, and even face-to-face visits. Their reading and letter writing were emotional practices through which they used Muggeridge's texts to give coherence to the nebulous thoughts and feelings elicited by cultural, religious, and social change. The result was a deep recognition of Muggeridge as a friend and kindred spirit whose spiritual journey ran parallel to their own.

This dynamic of reading, writing, and identity formation had several important implications. First, even though the religious crisis of the 1960s and 1970s resulted in the weakening of collective identities, Muggeridge's readers illustrate how individuals sought out new modes of belonging. Scholarship has long recognized how ideas that had been in circulation for generations gained new currency in counterculture through underground media outlets. Just as a "Generation of Seekers"[84] had accreted eclectic belief systems by borrowing from New Age, Transcendental Meditation, or ecumenical forms of Christianity, the fans of Muggeridge forged their religious lives through their close reading of a fellow seeker. Theirs was a textual community with collectively shared emotions across felt distances.[85] Second, by seeing Muggeridge as a Christian whose spiritual authenticity was worthy of emulating, they shifted, both consciously and unconsciously, into recognizing him as a spiritual authority. These both fuelled and reaffirmed readers' growing discontent with institutional Christianity, even as it enacted sweeping reforms to remain relevant in the 1960s and 1970s. Muggeridge lambasted what he saw as the hypocritical and secularizing tendencies of the churches, even as he encouraged his readers to draw closer to Christ. Likewise, fans' emotional practices drew them closer to Muggeridge just as they drifted away from the churches they felt were inauthentic expressions of honest faith. Their desire to maintain genuine faith actually served to weaken the churches' hold on them.

# Recalibrating Religious Authority

Thank you for being an apostle – an apostle for those who believe and yet fear the boundaries set about us if immediately we accept a denominational cloak.

E. French to Malcolm Muggeridge, 2 March 1977

The previous chapter described the kind of relationships Muggeridge's readers formed with him as they read his books, wrote him letters, and, in many cases, received a personal reply. It argued that they saw Muggeridge as a friend and kindred spirit whose religious life ran parallel to their own. This personal connection enabled Muggeridge to hold considerable influence over their lives of faith, as they admitted repeatedly how he crystalized their nebulous thoughts on religious issues. In this way, reading and writing were emotional practices fans used to shape their religious identity as part of their self-reflexive projects. As this chapter shows, this relationship had profound effects on readers' evolving perceptions of religious authority.

The question of who curates religious knowledge has been a perennial source of tension throughout the history of Christianity, and this was no less the case in the late twentieth century. This was an emotionally vexing issue for Muggeridge's readers; after all, the vast majority of them had grown up with a local church as a central part of their lived religion. They defended, attacked, and tried to understand how their status as Christians in a secular age related to the churches that were increasingly held in suspect. Some of these readers did, in fact, leave their churches altogether, but their rationale was much more complex and varied than simply losing their faith, becoming apathetic, or joining a different religion. Some remained committed Christians even as they shifted away from conventional sites and sources of religious authority. In this way, Muggeridge's readers reveal what the "declining scope of religious authority" looked like in practice for ordinary Christians.[1]

Yet, it would not be entirely accurate to categorize them as "believing without belonging," as Grace Davie aptly described the continued presence of religious faith and influence outside of church structures.[2] Muggeridge's readers may have grown detached from their churches, but they did not practise their faith in isolation. We see in these letters earnest attempts to seek out alternative forms of religious belonging through the mutually reinforcing practices of reading and writing. Taken together, Muggeridge was transformed into a surrogate cleric situated at the nexus of a spontaneous and unorganized textual community.

Muggeridge's conversion during the 1960s, and his spiritual evolution in the 1970s, was largely defined by this very issue of religious authority. As we have seen, he was a gadfly who directed substantial criticisms against religious bodies like the Church of England because he believed such structures hindered, rather than fostered, spiritual authenticity. On this count, he was giving voice to much broader trends in Christianity throughout Western Europe, North America, Australia, and New Zealand. Just as Muggeridge's readers felt he had crystalized their religious sentiments, they also saw him as one who gave breath to their institutional discontent. A small number of fans wrote letters with angry refutations and criticisms of Muggeridge's anti-institutional sentiment. But the majority were of those who agreed the churches were failing them. This included current and former church members alike. Muggeridge was not just a friend and kindred spirit whose religious life ran parallel to their own; he was their spiritual guru who, in many cases, replaced the churches they left or no longer trusted.

## MUGGERIDGE AND ANTI-INSTITUTIONALISM IN RELIGION AND SOCIETY

While the chief focus here is to understand religious change through the letter-writing practices of Muggeridge's fans, it is important to recognize the reputation Muggeridge developed that made him so attractive to these readers. Though the late 1960s witnessed the realization of revolutionary changes in religion, society, and culture, Muggeridge had anticipated many of the chief characteristics of this period decades earlier. His contempt for authority was consistent throughout

his career and this was not lost on his readers by the time anti-institutionalism and popular individualism became more culturally preva-
lent in the 1960s and 1970s. One of his first major successes, *The
Thirties* (1940), written just after the "Phony War," was a morose and
satiric reflection on the failures of a decade that came to a close without any real meaning or clear sense of direction. Muggeridge aimed
his barbed attack squarely at the establishment and its principal
actors. When the book entered a new edition in 1971, Muggeridge
maintained the same attitude. The new preface affirmed he was
"unable to take completely seriously, and therefore believe in the
validity or permanence of, any form of authority. Crowns and mitres
have seemed to be made of tinsel, [and] ceremonial robes to have
been hastily procured in a theatrical costumier's."[3] Whether political
or theological, institutions were defunct – but, significantly, not the
ideals they promoted.

Muggeridge's anti-institutionalism was less a new idea formed in
communion with the zeitgeist of the sixties than it was a continuation
of long-held convictions. His 1955 article "The Royal Soap Opera" saw
the monarchy as at best a distraction and at worst disastrous for the
nation's unity. He questioned why it was that so much attention was
paid to an institution that was, at least constitutionally, powerless. If
the monarchy was good for anything, it was to function as a symbol
for unity. But how could they do even that when, like trifled celebri-
ties, there appeared to show little of substance in their day-to-day
activities? It was a controversial piece because support and adulation
for the monarchy was quite high in the 1950s. The impressive pomp
and circumstance of Queen Elizabeth's televised coronation cere-
mony in 1953 ushered in a new dimension of fame for the royal family, but Muggeridge only saw, as he put it, "crowns made of tinsel." In
the end, the foray did more to damage Muggeridge professionally
than it did to convince any readers in 1955. He received hundreds of
angry letters that he had over-stepped his bounds. The BBC evidently
agreed, because they temporarily banned him from appearing on television as punishment.[4] Yet, Muggeridge never issued an apology and
continued to promote the same ideas after his ban ended.

These two brief examples are instructive when considered in anticipation of the cultural environment a decade later. Muggeridge's intellectual and cultural influence was not essential for the creation of the
revolutions of the sixties, but neither was he an anomalous curmud-
geon. The growing acceptance of the iconoclastic opinions that Mug-

geridge had presented for most of his career should be understood as affirming the broader trends that shaped not only British society but all Western societies. Muggeridge was also known for his vitriolic condemnations of permissiveness, but that does not make him any less part of the coalescence of activities that comprised the cultural revolution of the 1960s and 1970s. Those decades were not culturally monolithic, and Muggeridge's position vis-à-vis institutional authority was very much in step with the times. Those instincts remained consistent over decades; what changed was that the reading public (and the Christian reading public in particular) became more receptive to arguments Muggeridge had been making for decades.[5] In a way, Muggeridge was ahead of the times. His consistent position on the church raised his cultural and religious capital, and cemented his reputation as an authentic person.

This is important because Muggeridge lambasted the theological updates and adaptations churches made in the 1960s and 1970s, despite the fact that he belonged to none of them. Indeed, his anti-institutional satire of the clergy and the churches actually became more frequent and more pointed.[6] Even as an agnostic, Muggeridge had never denied original sin, and his overtly pessimistic view of the world shaped his criticism of the churches' attempts to focus more exclusively on social goods.[7] Muggeridge's theological vision constantly emphasized the stark contrast between divine transcendence and depraved humanity. He returned repeatedly to Christian authors who rejected storing up treasures on earth: Augustine of Hippo, Blaise Pascal, Søren Kierkegaard, Fyodor Dostoevsky, Leo Tolstoy, and Simone Weil.[8] Each of these authors emphasized the weakness of humanity and the utter pointlessness of attempting to establish a paradise on earth. As Muggeridge put it on one occasion, "There are various things that human beings can do; but there is one thing they can't do, and that is progress."[9] The robust attempts of religious thinkers to demythologize Christianity in an attempt to make it more useful – or at least more palatable – to modern society was one of the main trends that Muggeridge sought to subvert.

Receptiveness among to Muggeridge's fans to his anti-institutional arguments developed concomitantly with a rapid decline of religious authority.[10] Scholars regularly point to a chorus of familiar statistics tracing decline in every quantifiable religious category: church membership, Sunday attendance, baptisms, confirmations, marriages, and funerals. Clive Field has shown that public attitudes towards the institutional church and clergy mirrored these trends.[11] It perhaps comes as no surprise that just as the public was losing trust and confidence in the church and clergy, they perceived them as less important and influential in society. Especially by the late 1960s onwards, the church and clergy were increasingly seen as out of touch and, at worst, irredeemably corrupt. Other scholarship has shown this trend to be consistent throughout Western societies irrespective of Christian denomination.[12] Decreasing religious authority and growing discontent with the clergy were two interrelated expressions of the declining support for traditional institutions that characterized the cultural revolution of the 1960s and 1970s.

Nevertheless, Mark Chaves and Field are right that we should be careful not to equate Christianity's declining social significance and a growing distrust of the clergy with wholesale religious decline. There are a number of good reasons for this. First, scholars have faced recurring methodological problems with quantifying postwar religious belief. Religion has normally been measured by three criteria: behaving (attending church, becoming baptized, becoming confirmed, etc.), belonging (being a member of a particular church or church body), and believing (the actual content and shape of religious belief). A great deal of data is available that shows decline in terms of behaving and belonging. However, the most information-rich surveys that allow scholars to trace religious change did not include any questions on religious belief until the 1980s.[13] Giving up church membership or not regularly attending religious services certainly meant that someone was separating their religious lives from the institutional church. Yet it is entirely plausible for someone to leave their church while still maintaining religious beliefs. Inversely, someone might attend services and remain members of a church *without* actually believing what their church taught. They might stay involved for familial, political, social, cultural, or any number of personal reasons.

Moreover, while questionnaires tell us a great deal, they reveal little about the emotional intensity of respondents, or variations among individual interpretations of meaning. Nor do they always show how religious beliefs change over time. People with disparate religious experiences might very well have recorded identical answers on surveys. For example, Ben Clements' recent study made use of surveys that defined affiliation as Anglican, Catholic, Other Christian, or No Affiliation. There is a *great deal* of religious diversity within any one of these categories, and Muggeridge's fan mail reflects that. The

Church of England alone was a broad church that prided itself in its ecumenism, let alone categories so imprecise as "Other Christian" or "No Affiliation." Moreover, some of Muggeridge's fans wrote several letters over a period of several months or even years that reveal evolving religious perspectives and, most importantly for the present discussion, their attitudes towards religious authority.

Many began to feel they could better express their Christian piety by living out anti-institutional points of view. Geoff Troughton has demonstrated that New Zealand Christians formed a distinction between the "the real Jesus" and the church. These were a group of Christians who, on a social survey, would fall under the category of "No Affiliation." Troughton found that Jesus was simultaneously worshiped and used discursively as an iconoclastic symbol of institutional Christianity. The religion of Christ was understood as distinct and separate from what was wryly called "Churchianity." It formed an anti-institutional Christian piety that defined authentic belief by its disassociation with organized Christianity.[14] The same kind of thought pattern was present in groups like the Jesus People Movement and was commonly expressed in fan mail to Muggeridge.[15]

Muggeridge's readers reflected these broader trends in their rejection of the clergy and ecclesiastical structures as religious authorities. His fan mail fleshes out qualitatively what Chaves, Field, and Clements have demonstrated quantitatively, that secularization is most accurately understood as the declining scope of religious authority. An important addendum to this argument, however, is that while most of these ordinary readers lost respect for institutional and clerical authority, they in turn looked to Muggeridge for religious guidance. In this way, religious authority did not just decline; it also *shifted*[16] as popular individualism increasingly defined group behaviour in the 1960s and 1970s.[17] They followed Muggeridge closely in their belief that authentic Christianity meant taking a leap of faith without relying on inherited structures to guide spiritual formation.

## READING MUGGERIDGE AND INSTITUTIONAL MALAISE

Readers who wrote about religious authority fit into three general camps. The smallest group included those who remained in the church, and who strongly defended traditional modes of religious authority. The second group included those who remained members of an institutional church, but who nevertheless harboured criticisms for their pastor, or held crippling doubts about their church's authenticity. Readers who can be placed into these first two categories often self-identified with a particular church body, with the Church of England/Anglican and Roman Catholic being the most common. The last and largest group of readers were those who had stopped going to church altogether because they no longer believed it could nourish their faith. As one might expect, it was characteristic for readers in this category to self-identify generally as "Christian," rather than to think of their identity in denominational terms. They tended to mention specific church bodies only as reference to what they had left. For readers of each of these categories, Muggeridge was recognized as a religious guide. The second and third groups wrote to vent their frustrations and uncertainties about their church. They very often did not feel comfortable voicing such sentiments within an institutional setting, so writing a private letter to a popular religious writer was one way to do that. These readers, though coming from diverse theological perspectives, all could agree that Muggeridge was someone with whom they could share their thoughts, complaints, and questions. Even if the first group wrote to Muggeridge with intentions of proving him wrong, the very act of taking him seriously was an acknowledgement of his influence.

Letters criticizing Muggeridge's anti-institutional positions, while united in a common enemy, in fact reflect the sort of ideological fissures that characterized churches in Western societies during the 1960s and 1970s. Adrian Hastings observed that much theological development of those years "gives the impression of a sheer surge of feeling that in the modern world God, religion, the transcendent, any reliability in the gospels, anything which had formed part of the old 'supernaturalist' system, had suddenly become absurd."[18] John Robinson's *Honest to God* is perhaps the most famous example of this, where in less than 150 pages, he synthesized in widely accessible prose the demythologized Christianity of Paul Tillich, Dietrich Bonhoeffer, and Rudolf Bultmann.[19] Robinson was convinced that if the church was going to survive, it required a radical updating of its language to become more relevant. That meant integrating the life of the church into the idiom of modernity while adapting its ethical and moral precepts to accommodate social change.[20] Indeed, during the sixties and seventies churches revised their positions on a myriad of social issues, ranging from censorship and gambling to homosexuality, divorce, extramarital sex, and reproductive rights.[21]

The negotiations on individual behaviour included a fundamental restructuring of the relationships between the clergy and laity. Christian churches recognized the Second Vatican Council, or Vatican II, as the leading example of this general trend: It championed a more active role for the laity in the life of the church, supported the authority of personal conscience in matters of the faith, allowed a hierarchy of essential teachings, and ushered in a more ecumenical environment.[22] Yet, while there was considerable optimism in the benefits of these changes, they also exacerbated long-standing divisions within church denominations. The direction churches would take in the future – whether they would become increasingly open, or whether they would resist change – was a matter of heated debate in the upper ranks of churches. Divisions and theological debate became defined less and less by denominational identity, and increasingly more by liberal, conservative, moderate, and radical factions within churches.[23] These tensions were felt most intensely in the local parish, where clergy, let alone members, did not always know how to respond to ongoing debates that were fundamentally reshaping the religious character of their church and how it related to others.[24]

Muggeridge's readers reflected these tensions as they struggled with how to understand the source of the church's authority and, consequently, the reasons to obey it. Even readers who wrote to defend their churches reveal sharp disagreement on why it was meet and right so to do. In fact, readers who defended the church's traditional structures promoted two distinct arguments that were not entirely compatible. The first group defended the institutional church on grounds that it was essential to Christianity. This argument was most commonly promoted by High Church Anglican and Roman Catholic readers, who believed ecclesiastical authority depended on apostolic succession beginning with the Apostle Peter. This reflected a much more conservative vision of the church's future direction in society, and they often resisted the spirit of ecumenism in the wake of Vatican II. For these readers, criticizing the institutional church was tantamount to criticizing Christianity itself. Ecumenism by some was an expression of Christian love and forgiveness, but for many traditionally minded churchgoers, it signalled doctrinal weakness and spineless compromise.[25]

From this position, authentic faith existed inside the traditional structures of the church. W. Rogers, a High Church Anglican, articulated a logical conclusion of this premise when she flat-out told Muggeridge, "I do not think that ultimately one can be a full member of Christ out of contact with the Church."[26] Readers like these took for granted that hypocrites or unsavoury figures would claim a position within their ranks, but they were confident they posed no serious damage to the church. They were hopeful, as S. Macartney was, that church leaders like John Robinson were "just a phase" in a history that had weathered the guile of heretics for two thousand years.[27] The church, properly understood, was incorruptible because it was distinct from the composition of those who happened to be within its physical gates. They could take confidence that the "wheat and tares grow together until harvest."[28] Because the institution was understood as inseparable from the practise of Christianity, these readers took it as a tenet of the faith to remain within the fold, regardless of any apparent "failures"[29] or "weaknesses."[30]

The second, and much more common, argument that defenders of institutional churches made was one of expediency. For this group of critics there were not any dogmatic reasons to remain faithful to a particular church body. In fact, many of these readers conceded that Muggeridge's satire on institutional Christianity was partially justified. The Australian-born A. Tate was "quite sure that there are people like yourself who are strong enough in themselves – both intellectually and in the will – to be committed to loving and serving Christ without the support of an institution."[31] But as she saw it, "Only rare spirits can stand alone." Her experience was different. She, her husband, and their three children had converted to Roman Catholicism "after several years of quite harrowing soul-searching." Since her family had struggled spiritually, she felt Muggeridge's criticisms of the church ended up "unwittingly defeating the very cause" he promoted. She continued, "I am equally sure that the ordinary man NEEDS the props and imposed disciplines of the institution."[32] Her fear was that readers would listen to Muggeridge's "quasi-authoritative voice" and then justify leaving the church to pursue their spiritual life independent of any church. It might work for Muggeridge, but not everyone had his "particular eccentricity."[33]

D.L.B. Howell was likewise critical of Muggeridge's anti-institutional position. His experience as a medical missionary in the Katanga Province of the Democratic Republic of Congo for the past twenty-seven years had been formative in this regard. His views were not dog-matic, but rather were based on what seemed to function the best. He had worked closely with the Ba-Luba people, who organized their churches along tribal relations. According to Howell, "they found brothers and sisters in every village, whereas previously all contacts with those who were neither blood nor tribal relatives were danger-ous on the account of the treachery of witchcraft."[34] In the end, How-ell was using the example of the Ba-Luba to criticize Muggeridge's anti-institutionalism. As Howell saw it, the church was becoming increasingly incompatible with the current environment of Western societies. At the same time, the single biggest problem was the "reck-less spirit of independence" that produced "broken homes [and] cal-lous separations."[35] Atomized Christianity eschewed institutional religion, but it seemed to offer no solution to the need of building Christian community. Howell argued that religion would break down without the support offered by congregations to individual Christians.

Diverse understandings of the nature of the church and the source of its authority have important implications. Muggeridge's readers who were also professing Christians were much more likely to remain within an institutional church body if they believed that authentic Christianity did not depend upon those structures. However, believ-ers who thought the institutional church was not essential to Chris-tianity, but merely expedient to its practice, were more ready to grant that membership and attendance were only required if you were weak in your faith.

That was L. Furniss' experience. She was a sixty-nine-year-old from Buckinghamshire who had struggled with religion for much of her life. She had broken her wrist recently, so her six-page fan letter to Muggeridge is in places difficult to decipher. What becomes clear is that she knew nothing about her biological past apart from the fact that her birth mother in Ireland abandoned her. Even though she had a home growing up, she felt as though she "had no *real* relations at all root-wise, & still have no *record* of being on this earth."[36] In her attempt to develop a sense a community, she began to dabble in reli-gion. However, throughout her upbringing her father (who was an atheist and lawyer by profession) would strongly dissuade her from becoming religious. This was an ongoing source of tension between them throughout her upbringing, and it continued for some time after. Her father died in 1959. She wrote to Muggeridge over two decades later, but the memory of her father still caused her some pain.

One day she had rebelled against her father's wishes and joined the nearest church that was "within walking distance," which happened to be the Church of England. She began taking confirmation classes because she "needed to belong to a church – to belong somewhere."[37] In her letter, Furniss did not assert that every Christian must be a member of a church, nor even that it was theologically mandated. Her argument was that her particular circumstances made it necessary, even if it meant estrangement from the man who adopted her. Her interaction with the church was not one in which she humbly submitted to the church because of apostolic succession. She joined a church because she felt she needed it; the fact that she happened to be Anglican was more a matter of geographic convenience than principle. Beneath her conflicting emotions was a theological position that understood religious authority not as something ontologically present in the structures of the church. On the surface – and recorded in statistics – readers like Furniss and Tate would have defended the institutional church on the grounds of their own personal experience. Yet, however passionate, arguments such as these allude to why churches declined in the 1960s and after: people increasingly believed that the church structures, even if they were important, were not strictly necessary for Christianity to exist.

Even ministers doubted the footing of their own position. The Methodist minister S. Arthurs' letter to Muggeridge expressed several conflicting emotions. His interaction with the church from his youth was overwhelmingly positive. He had been raised in a working-class home with a father who was a "rationalist" and faithful reader of *The Freethinker*. While his mother had a "luminous Christian Faith," she did not attend church herself, nor did she insist her son attend, either. Both parents agreed that he should be free to form his own views. At an early age, he began attending Sunday school at the local Methodist church, largely because it was what his friends did. What began as an environment for social interaction grew into religious faith. As he described it, "the Church became a wider experience (and warmer) of family life … I discovered the Church, before I discovered Christ."[38] He experienced a great deal of tolerance for his questions and uncertainties. At the time he had not cared much about the "dogmas about [God] or methods of Church Government," and he never "came within a mile of the 'great and wise' who run the Church at 'the top.' I only met the rank and file."[39]

His experience in the church with the ordinary Christians changed once he became a minister. All of a sudden it began to feel so superficial: "One can wax enthusiastic about a Sale of Work, one can discuss the Church building, one can get heated about liturgy, one can advocate change, or protest at it," but he thought spiritual authenticity was nowhere in sight. The problem was exacerbated by the great difficulty he had connecting with his parishioners on an emotional level. How could he shepherd his flock on theological matters when he could not establish a close personal relationship with them? "Spiritual fellowship ... is largely overlaid with associated trivia [and] spiritual talk is most often carried on indirectly in surface concern over exteriors such as the Building, or the Establishment." They seemed to think that those who spoke about religious matters were "either professionals, or specially saintly, or hypocrites."[40] It was only in settings outside of the church – on deathbeds or in times of intense crises – that people opened up and shared their spirituality. These observations and experiences, together with reading Muggeridge, made Arthurs question if he really had discovered the church at all.

Most readers who harboured some of these same doubts and criticisms about the life of the institutional church did not have the inclination to go on defending it. Some thought the church and its clergy were embarrassingly corrupt. N. Frost was a Roman Catholic convert of about forty years. Once she read *Something Beautiful for God*, she felt an uncomfortable cognitive dissonance between the character of Mother Teresa and the state of her church. "It is a dreadful but true fact that the Church, which teaches Christianity, is the very means of turning people away from it ... there are many things which simply appall me ... Unfortunately, the field in which the 'pearl' is hidden is a very dirty field. There are stones, lumps, weeds, rabbit-holes, and cow muck everywhere."[41] M. Biersmith of Stony Brook, New York, would have had a lot to talk about with Frost. He had read *Chronicles of Wasted Time* and confessed to Muggeridge that "It is so hard to be a Catholic nowadays; one succeeds in doing it almost in spite of the Church."[42] The supplement of private devotions and frequent readings of G.K. Chesterton and Hilaire Belloc seemed to do the trick, in addition to attending services weekly. I. Taylor of Edinburgh agreed – the clergymen were too often corrupt, or obsessing only to "demonstrate their own cleverness."[43] N. Green of Suffolk extended to the Church of England what Frost and Taylor had said of Roman Catholicism: the problem stemmed from "bad leadership" and was continued by pastors who thought of their high calling as little more than a day job for a paycheck.[44]

One fan from Ridgegate, just south of London, felt that church was becoming detached from the experiences and problems of its parishioners. They were much too materialistic, only exploiting members ("predominantly middle-class mostly female and elderly") to keep a steady stream of income flowing into its coffers.[45] The result was a church that had become "cold, physically and spiritually."[46] Like Parliament, it had turned into a "ramshackle institution" that was in dire need of a change to the "whole structure of the Established Church" if they wanted to survive.[47] This was why J. Stewart of Edinburgh appreciated *Jesus Rediscovered* so much. The book was released while he was participating in the General Assembly of the Scottish Presbyterian Church. He felt "it is the kind of book to call us back from our tiresome irrelevancies to the things that really matter."[48] Like S. Arthurs, Stewart was not content with the superficial topics that seemed to preoccupy his church. Unlike Arthurs, however, Stewart did not elaborate on what precisely constituted irrelevancy and what mattered (his fan letter was less than two hundred words), but his letter nonetheless points to the common sentiment that the institutional church was in need of reform.

The type of reform needed was another story. Churches were willing to, and certainly did, adapt by accommodating to cultural and social change. But these reactions caused divisions and dissent, especially among more conservative members. They felt the church was changing too much and too quickly. N. Frost, who we met previously, strongly criticized the corruption of the clergy after comparing their attempts at reform to the work of Mother Teresa, but the church was also failing because "the constant changing of everything in the name of Ecumenism makes one dizzy."[49] M. Hayes was an Anglican from Middlesex and felt similar emotions: "I am completely bewildered by the constant changes taking place so quickly in the church ... Oh for a leader with the courage to thunder against the sick world and not lower the standards of the church by trying to get with it."[50]

Hayes and Frost both expressed frustration with changes inside their churches in general terms, and they almost certainly had worship practices in mind. Indeed, of all the changes that resulted from Vatican II, its "flagship programme" was liturgical reform.[51] The central purpose of *Sacrosanctum Concilium* was to enable the Church and the laity to "keep up to date with the changing conditions of this modern world."[52] Yet, these changes, begun in Advent of 1964, resulted in some of the faithful feeling increasingly detached from their churches.[53] Meredith McGuire notes how "Religious ritual is like a chain of ... embodied practices, each link having the potential to activate deep emotions and a sense of social connectedness, as well as spiritual meanings."[54] That's why ordinary Catholics in the Diocese of Westminster saw the gradual loss of the Latin as a direct affront to their English identity and an insult to those who had fought and died to preserve it.[55] For them, worship was not just a trivial matter of personal preference, but a fundamental part of who they were. Stephen Bullivant has recently concluded that "it is difficult to imagine a scenario in which the Council's reforms are *not* causally related to the very significant decline in Mass-going among British and American Catholics – and ultimately, to the high and growing levels of Catholic disaffiliation."[56]

This tension was felt acutely among Muggeridge's readers. T. John expressed alarm at the liturgical experimentation in her local parish. She was a Roman Catholic who had read several of Muggeridge's books and enjoyed watching his interviews on William Buckley's *Firing Line* at her home in Greenwich Village. At first, she was determined to refute his criticisms of institutional Christianity. She confessed having written several drafts full of carefully crafted arguments supported by numerous scriptural proof-texts. But she eventually realized she was being dishonest with herself. Really, she agreed almost entirely with Muggeridge's criticisms – she just felt compelled to defend the institution she associated with. She had to admit, "There is a sort of madness going on in the institutional churches today."[57] She still regularly attended services in order to experience congregational fellowship and to celebrate the Eucharist, but she was growing "very annoyed at the changes being made in the liturgy." Particularly irksome to her were attempts to make liturgical language more gender-neutral. Such movements in her view were patronizing because they assumed women were too stupid to know they were included in the older phraseology. Most upsetting of all was that there seemed to be no end in sight. She expected worship to become "more bland, homogenized, 'modernized', and overall meaningless year by year. These changes are jarring on the ear and a distraction to prayer."[58] In short, for these readers and countless others in the Anglophone world, liturgical innovation "eroded any erstwhile sense of permanence" in their churches.[59]

But for Christian conservatives it was not just a worship problem; it was a doctrine problem. C. Bartley was a medical doctor in London. He was a committed member of John Stott's church, All Souls, Langham Place, which was the heart of the evangelical movement in the Church of England.[60] Bartley's evangelicalism is confirmed by the fact that his fan letter reflects every corner of the David Bebbington's quadrilateral.[61] In only about 300 words, he used Scripture as a proof-text four times (Biblicism), emphasized that his church preached "Jesus Christ and Him crucified" (Crucicentrism), called for Muggeridge to accept Jesus as his saviour (Conversionism), and mentioned his involvement in religious organizations like Inter-Varsity Fellowship and the Keswick Convention (Activism). As he saw it, the Church of England was in need of a revival.[62] He estimated that "perhaps not more than five per cent of the whole Establishment" was truly sincere in its confession. The problem, as he diagnosed it, was that the vast majority of churches were not "in accordance with Biblical promises and true Church of England doctrine as defined in the Book of Common Prayer, and the Thirty-Nine Articles."[63]

T. Kern was also an Anglican evangelical who thought of things in the same way as C. Bartley. He saw All Souls as an exemplary church, but he recognized it was highly unusual for its doctrinal commitments. "The crux of the matter," he asserted, was that "the clergy themselves although assenting to the 39 articles of the church seemingly without shame neither practice, preach nor uphold them. It is [no] small wonder that the power of conviction and direction have gone out of the churches and that they are in the main empty."[64] In short, he thought the churches were the cause of their own demise.

The churches faced something of a catch-22. The same object of criticism for some was a point of pride for others, and preference for any course of action inevitably alienated one or several groups. Evangelicals like Kern and Bartley were upset that their churches were loosening their doctrinal focus. But there were others with equal stakes in their churches' futures who felt quite differently. Church of England ministers J.R. Percey and C.J.H. Mill, and C.E. Pocknee all wrote to Muggeridge defending clerical freedoms not to believe every jot or tittle of the Thirty-Nine Articles.[65] They each explained that it was perfectly acceptable to support, or as they each put it, give "assent," to them. Percey described much of his church's teachings as "symbols" that have a great deal of meaning, but need not be taken literally. Indeed, he saw such attitudes as an expression of Christian humility – "only the small minded can define exactly" the meaning of the creeds and confessions of the church. He continued, "I glory in the comprehensiveness of the C of E. We are wide enough to realise that the whole truth needs the whole Church to interpret it."[66]

There were clearly some fundamental divides within Christian churches.[67] With so many different positions represented, some people felt entirely uncertain about what to do next. Another Church of England minister, H. Waddams, illustrates how ideological tensions between clergy and congregation members were at the heart of the religious crisis of those years. He read *Jesus Rediscovered* and struck up a correspondence with Muggeridge to confess his internal conflict:

> What you write about the feebleness of Christianity and the
> Churches finds an equal echo within myself. I am almost wholly
> in agreement with your scathing criticisms of the structures of
> the Churches as they are, and of the posturings of many of its
> more prominent members. But whereas you can safely indulge
> these feelings of yours from the outside, I find myself inside,
> entangled in the spider's web of millions of strands which hold
> me prisoner.[68]

Waddams was sure that *some* kind of structure was necessary to promote and preserve Christianity, but he had no idea what it would look like. Would it require a radical updating of the church's language? Should worship reflect better the broader cultural trends? Should the churches double down on doctrinal purity? Or was the problem that the church had become too materialistic? Waddams was not sure. Muggeridge, he admitted, was excellent at pointing out errors – those he recognized. But could Muggeridge help him to devise some strategy of how to positively promote the church?

> I am really asking for help myself, caught as I am in the Estab-
> lishment and [part of] the establishment, unable to see a way
> forward. I have gradually become convinced that God is kicking
> the Churches to pieces anyway, and I am happy to hasten this
> process.[69]

Waddams may have admitted that it was a good idea for another structure to rise up for the spreading and preservation of Christianity and, perhaps controversially, even to help the disintegration of the

Church of England. However, as he admits, he was too immersed in its machinery to do much of anything about it.

Many of Muggeridge's Christian readers did not feel these internal conflicts because they no longer associated with any church. Fans who no longer attended or remained members of any church had three general reasons for not going. Some readers were not raised in a religious home and, after they converted to Christianity, had not yet found a church they liked, or perhaps did not feel the need to join one.[70] Others left their churches because of innovations in doctrine or worship practices.[71]

The third and most common reason for readers to leave institutional religion was that they did not feel it supported authentic Christianity. As we have seen, what constituted "authentic" was not always clear in the 1960s and 1970s. Authenticity signals trust fostered in human relationships, though how that trust developed is highly individualized. It made no difference if Muggeridge's readers were conservative, liberal, moderate, or radical: Christians of all perspectives found reasons to leave their churches. What links them is their common practice of interpreting the Bible and Christian tradition without the hermeneutics of organized religion. Whether they made this shift willingly or with painful regret, they found Muggeridge an inspiration.

Indeed, it was these readers who most closely aligned with Muggeridge's own approach to Christianity. They reflect a resurgence of popular religion that was at once dogmatic in its insistence for hyper-individualized religious experience, all the while remaining tolerant of the shape one's religious beliefs took. Very few of these readers offered Muggeridge any criticism at all, which is a clear departure from those who defended institutional Christianity, or even those who remained in the church while harbouring some criticism towards it. Like the New Zealand Christians analyzed by Geoff Troughton, who saw disassociation from a church as an expression of Christian piety, many of Muggeridge's readers likewise distinguished between "Christianity and Churchianity."[72] "Churchianity" was rigid, overly dogmatic, stuffy, and inhibited authentic spiritual expression. These readers were not shedding their Christianity; rather, they left their churches because they felt they could more faithfully express their faith independently of them. The Australian A. Smith summed this up succinctly when he wrote, "I am a Christian like yourself – I was an Anglican before I was converted."[73]

This kind of sentiment that true and authentic Christianity was inhibited by church structures was common throughout the Anglophone world. E. Kelly was a thirty-six-year-old sales representative in the printing industry living in Kent, just southeast of London. He did not belong to any church, and was in the middle of a dispute with a local curate. The spiritual isolation he felt inspired him to channel Samuel Taylor Coleridge: "'Water, water, everywhere, nor any drop to drink,' fantastic amounts of religious syrup available on all sides, and yet hardly a drop of it runs in accord with one of the more simple statements of Jesus: 'Blessed are the Meek.'"[74] He had a wife and two children, but he felt his only spiritual companions were books: those by Kierkegaard, Pascal, Bunyan, and now Muggeridge. When he read *Jesus Rediscovered*, he found it "strange to find myself reading a book which seems to say many of the things I think but which, with me, are only vague thoughts which do not find expression in words." It was the same sensation he had when reading the works of Kierkegaard, who dramatically shaped his religious outlook.

> It was as though the veil had been drawn aside and all that I had heard before concerning Christianity was so much rubbish ... Before this time I was of the opinion that clergyman while occupying no great place in my life must, at least, know what they were talking about and yet now I can see straight through them. Never again will I be able to listen to a clergyman as though he speaks with authority. Before I read Kierkegaard I seemed to have an unconscious secularity, in that if I did not know the great secrets of life at whom I could turn for guidance and comfort if need be, but now I find that I really am alone.[75]

For Kelly, Muggeridge stood alongside Kierkegaard as the two authorities who gave him "guidance and comfort."[76]

J. Henderson of Saginaw, Michigan, did not quite have the feelings of isolation that E. Kelly did, but he shared the critical view of institutional Christianity after reading *Jesus: The Man Who Lives*. His emphasis differed from Kelly's in that he aimed his criticisms less at ministers and more at the historical baggage the church had accumulated over the past two thousand years. Muggeridge's journalistic exposé of the Synoptic Gospels gave him a vision of the "real" Jesus that the churches were incapable of delivering: "You have such a gift for cutting out the fat, the 'goo,' the confusing tradition ... all the sediment and sentiment of centuries upon the realities of Jesus, the will of God, and man, His creation." Henderson compared Muggeridge to C.S. Lewis in how much he had shaped his spiritual life, but he felt Muggeridge was in some ways better because he didn't have such an "over-reliance upon the church ... the institution and its rites and ordinances."[77] The church might work for luminaries like Lewis, but for Henderson, disassociation allowed for a greater practise of Christian freedom. The comparison with C.S. Lewis is telling, too. Henderson's letter only points to a broader consensus that Lewis was associated with rigid dogmatism in a way Muggeridge was not. Stephanie Derrick has recently established that it was the perceived dogmatism that hampered Lewis's reputation among his British readers.[78] Muggeridge's rough and tumble personality as one who had lived a hedonistic lifestyle only to realize it and then dramatically and independently pursue spiritual meaning on his own terms appealed a great deal to the eclectic religious character of his readers.

Spirituality for many during the 1960s and 1970s was about independence and self-discovery.[79] The idea of deferring to a clergyman for spiritual guidance or becoming indoctrinated through catechesis was repulsive, even childish, to some of Muggeridge's readers. J. Buffield almost echoed Immanuel Kant's definition of enlightenment as the process of emerging from one's own self-incurred immaturity:

> I think it is merely pre-adolescent to expect to pay one's admission fee (speaking metaphorically) at a sort of spiritual box-office, go in and expect to find all the secrets about the source of life, the precise reasons why we are here, the where we have come from, the whither we pass to, all flashed on to the screen.[80]

At almost sixty years old, Buffield had had enough of that. He reminisced that as a young boy,

> The old world had still many years to go; all the years of my schooling up to almost eighteen it was daily prayers, Church, instruction, religious study and the Bible all the way. It was after years of adulthood that I began to understand one has to interpret all the teaching according to one's own understanding; the resulting vision or knowledge then becomes one's own.[81]

For Buffield he was much more content spiritually to pursue his own devotional practices – which included reading Muggeridge's spiritual books.

E. Russell felt similar emotions to Buffield. She had been reading an article in the *Sunday Post* by Muggeridge entitled, "The Crucifixion," which was later reprinted in *Jesus Rediscovered*. The article seemed to crystalize her thoughts and give meaning to actions she had taken.

> I have simply *had* to give up going to church, because I just couldn't find God there. And when I came out, I was so depressed & unhappy. It took ages for me to fight my way through this fog of Pauline Doctrine. You may know the sort of thing – what Paul thought Jesus meant when he said … or what he ought to have meant when he said … this plus the minister's own interpretation – so worried and depressed me that I couldn't find the Heavenly Father so simply exemplified by Christ's teaching. It is a great relief to find that a man with a clever penetrating mind like yours has had similar feelings.[82]

C. Mylne likewise felt that institutional churches were incapable of directing the people to God. That activity was best left to yourself. He had long respected Muggeridge for promoting this view, but after he read *Something Beautiful for God*, he was inspired to write a letter. Muggeridge did not join the Roman Catholic Church for over a decade after meeting Mother Teresa, but their interaction made him sympathetic to, and even romanticize, corporate worship and a sense of belonging within a religious community. Muggeridge pined:

> What is more difficult to convey is the longing one feels to belong to the Church; the positive envy of those the bell calls to Mass. How often I have watched them, particularly in France – those extraordinary old women in black with their lined faces, clutching their prayer books; the children in their Sunday best, the muted fathers and bustling mothers with wisps of black veil about their heads, all making their way to Church on a Sunday morning. What joy to be one of their number! To kneel with them, advance to the altar with them, there, side by side, swallowing the Body of Christ. Then the plainsong, the flickering candles, the solemn familiar words, the acrid incense. Of all the purposes which draw

people together – excitement, cupidity, curiosity, lechery, hatred –
this alone, worship, makes them seem like a loving family; abolishing the conflicts and divisions of class and race and wealth and
talent, as they fall on their knees before a Father in heaven and his
incarnate Son; confess their sins, renew their hopes, find the
strength to snatch another mortal day from the splendid prospect
opened before them of eternity, their immortal dwelling-place.[83]

Upon reading these sentiments written by Muggeridge – this symbol
of spiritual independence and iconoclasm towards religious institutions – Mylne wrote to make sure he stayed on the straight and narrow path of anti-Churchianity:

There is absolutely no need whatsoever to be envious of those
who go to church. On the contrary, "going to church" reduces the
Spirit of the living Christ to the level of a spectator sport for most
people, though obviously not for such as dear Mother Teresa.
    Indeed, it is rather touching to read of her adoration of the
church but things are really in exactly the opposite perspective.
The church should be following Mother Teresa. The Mother Tere-
sas of this world are the true church and the hierarchy is worse
than useless – it is deadening ...
    So it is that we leave churchianity altogether ... *All* priestcraft,
whether spiritual or political, must eventually go. To hand over
the responsibility for your own spiritual welfare to a priest is as
much a folly as to hand over your material welfare to a politician.
In either case, you sell the birthright of your own integrity for a
mess of most unreliable pottage.[84]

Mylne thought it was something of a poetic coincidence that, even
though he was British, he wrote his letter of spiritual independence
on the Fourth of July.
    Each of these three groups of fans illustrates the crisis of the insti-
tutional churches. Those who shared with Muggeridge their criticisms of the church – whether they remained members of not –
demonstrate the growing resentment towards conventional religious
authority. Even those who wrote to Muggeridge with the intent of
defending the church reveal how fractured the churches were. There
was no shared vision of what the church was or why it was worth pre-

serving. Some defended it on theological grounds, but most did so on the grounds of personal experience. Yet, within that argument was the concession that not every Christian needed to be a member of a church. Muggeridge was a prime example of someone who could thrive spiritually without the tutelage of a religious institution. The assumption that the church was not necessary for everyone to have a healthy spiritual life, combined with the anti-institutional fervour of the 1960s and 1970s, produced a climate unfavourable to conventional sources of religious authority.

## MUGGERIDGE AS A SPIRITUAL GUIDE

It is true that the public perception of the church and clergy worsened considerably in these years. Statistical surveys and countless anecdotal evidence prove that the scope of conventional religious authority declined during those years. However, it would be a hasty generalization to suggest that this trend necessarily indicates declining religious belief. Muggeridge's readers confirm Grace Davie's conclusion that while "Europeans have ceased to participate in religious institutions," they did not necessarily shirk their "deep-seated religious inclinations."[85]

It is nevertheless important to recognize that although people were growing distrustful of religious institutions in droves, they also found alternative religious authorities to take their place. This was true for Christians of all three categories discussed above – defenders of institutional religion, critics who remained in their churches, and the checked-out who left. Muggeridge could serve as a religious authority among many, or in some cases as the central source of spiritual guidance. After the Australian E. Harrington and her friends found themselves returning repeatedly to *Something Beautiful for God* in their book club, she casually remarked, "So you see all these miles away you are carrying out an apostolate you were not aware of."[86]

Through readers imbibing his books, writing him letters, and even receiving replies, Muggeridge became, essentially, a surrogate cleric. He was never ordained, did not conduct worship services, and never administered any sacraments, but his books and correspondence performed many of the functions parishioners might expect from a minister. He provided spiritual counsel, served as a confessor, gave guidance in times of crises, and helped people grapple with questions of meaning and purpose. Readers who saw Muggeridge as a kindred spirit whose spiritual development paralleled their own began to look to him as an authority for directing their religious lives.

Muggeridge even took on a prophetic quality for many readers. K. Parnell and S. O'Brien read his books as if they were Biblical literature.[87] J. Johnson of South Carolina "reached a firm conclusion that your body dwells here on earth, but your mind is among the heavens viewing the true meaning of Christianity."[88] Johnson's minister at the local Southern Baptist Church simply did not compare. The Armenian-American H. Gregory could not help but think of John the Baptist when he read Muggeridge. Not only did Gregory feel Muggeridge was calling the world to repentance, in his native tongue the word for "Baptist" (մկրտիչ/mkrtich') was onomatopoetic with Muggeridge.[89] If he was not a prophet, then Muggeridge's readers at least insisted on placing him on par with other theological giants. E. Kelly linked Muggeridge with Søren Kierkegaard.[90] Where D. Murphy saw Leo Tolstoy, J. Kett saw Dietrich Bonhoeffer.[91] K. Williams thought of Saint Francis, and J. Lisle was reminded of C.S. Lewis.[92] These attitudes do not appear to have been determined by age, social class, education, national origin, or sex. People from a wide range of social settings looked to Muggeridge as a spiritual guide. Like the letters analyzed by Clarence Karr in his groundbreaking study on fan mail, "It was the shared experiences, shared concerns, shared values, and shared hopes which linked them."[93] From the evidence of the fan letters, the common denominator that defined these shared experiences was mutual detachment from, or dissatisfaction for, institutional Christianity.

Much like with the relationship between parishioners and ministers, readers often felt the impulse to write in times of personal crisis, or when they were trying to make sense of tragedy that had befallen them.[94] Many of these readers were explicit that priests and institutional Christianity did not help them, or that they had no desire to see if they would. J. Willey was a young woman from Warwick who wrote a letter to Muggeridge after six months of grieving the death of her infant son:

> I was utterly confident that he was being cared for and that my love and the love of God would see him through. He was born shortly after 28 weeks and weighed 2 lb. I was overjoyed to hear him cry and, when he was in the incubator, to see his tiny chest moving as he breathed. A couple hours later, when a nurse came to tell me that he was struggling and it would take a miracle to

save him, I was still completely unafraid, because I *knew* God
would give us that miracle and that my baby boy would grow and
laugh and play in the sunshine. But he died.[95]

She had met with a priest for guidance but, according to her, "his philosophy appeared to be that life is like a piece of machinery – we are
fed in at one end and come out at the other, with no divine interfer-
ence." She would not accept that explanation, but she began to feel
guilty anyway because her confidence in a loving God had been broken: "This worries me deeply as I can see it like a worm eating slowly
away at my soul. I know that I must come to an understanding, as well
as an acceptance, of what has happened, and I see no way. As a Christian, can you, please, help me?"[96] We do not know how, or if, he managed to help her, but the margins of the letter include a time stamp
that a response had been sent.

Letters like these speak to Muggeridge's bona fide status as a surrogate cleric. Fans often made prefatory remarks, such as "I have nobody
I feel I can turn to"[97] or "of all living people I know or know of, you
are the one person who can answer my question, or so it seems."[98] But
the plethora of rich examples are all so embedded in the raw emotions of personal experience that it is difficult to find representative
examples: a daughter who asked Muggeridge to help her struggling
father cope with an advanced case of aplastic anemia,[99] a man who
was in an acute crisis of faith,[100] a woman whose husband had just
died of brain hemorrhage,[101] an ex-convict with four children who
was wrestling with alcoholism and guilt for having multiple extramarital affairs,[102] an underemployed college graduate who was facing
eviction with nowhere to turn.[103] Young or old, rich or poor, highly
educated or not, male or female – people of all sorts of social settings
and circumstances found in Muggeridge someone who provided
guidance and solace.

Sometimes this occurred once Muggeridge and a fan began to write
back and forth, but most of the time it occurred through reading.
Reading can be deeply formative, but we are not always privy to the
internal struggles that people have as they wrestle with challenging
ideas. The unfortunate reality for the history of reading is that most
ordinary readers never think to record their innermost thoughts on
paper. If by chance they do, it is seldom preserved in the archive. That
is why examples like Londoner G. Althaus and a Canadian named
Enid are so rich.

Althaus had read Bishop John Robinson's *Honest to God* and Enid had worked her way through Ernest Renan's *Life of Jesus*. Their letters reveal how two ordinary Christians worked through crises of faith and doubt that began and ended with reading. Just as Althaus picked up Bishop Robinson's book, he also happened across an article called, "I Believe," which Muggeridge would later republish in *Jesus Rediscovered* as an impressionistic piece that perhaps he was becoming Christian after decades as a sceptic. Althaus had to admit, "Recently, I've been through a very rough time & in any case, I am a weak man, with a struggling weak faith. Then along came the book by the Bishop of Woolwich, which affected & shattered me deeply ... you see, your article appeared before the Bishop's book, & I put it aside. Then came the book 'Honest to God,' which I found very distressing & then happened to find your article again & re-read it. I must say, it has renewed my faith & helped me enormously."[104] Althaus did not elaborate on the intricacies of theological analysis or expound upon the revelation he had after re-reading, but he did not really have to. What seemed to have helped him was not the erudite expression of theological acumen. Even though he had a "weak faith," it was faith nonetheless, and he could take confidence in the fact that a kindred spirit had doubts, too.

When Enid read *Jesus: The Man Who Lives* at her home in Victoria, British Columbia, she felt the impulse to buy three more copies: another for herself, one for her son-in-law, and one for a friend. She was excited because the book, in dramatic fashion, fundamentally transformed religious convictions she had held for fifty years. There were two defining moments in her spiritual life: the first was reading Ernest Renan's *Vie de Jésus* (*Life of Jesus*) when she was pursuing a master's degree in French. The book shaped her so deeply, as she remembered it, because it provided fresh contrast to the fundamentalist Christian Student's Union she had joined at the time. Additionally, she felt reading it in the original language made it more meaningful. The second was reading Muggeridge. By the time Muggeridge had written *Jesus: The Man Who Lives*, he had arrived at a more creedal understanding of Christianity, though he nevertheless stayed clear of any institutional religion. Muggeridge in fact used *Vie de Jésus* as his foil in *Jesus: The Man Who Lives*, his central criticism being that Renan's Jesus was humanized at the expense of his divinity. For Muggeridge, *Vie de Jésus* was just a Gallicized version of D.F. Strauss' *Das Leben Jesu* that "amounted to a first rough draft of *Jesus Christ Super-*

*star.*[105] Muggeridge placed miracles, the resurrection, and transcendence at the centre of the book. Enid's engagement with such a voracious rejection of a book that had so centrally shaped her youth was jarring: "But – Renan? Oh, Malcolm, do I need to read him all over again, because I think you judge him harshly?"[106] Renan was influential, but Muggeridge was a higher, and more current, authority.

> You must be right – you've read him more recently, and I must admit that Renan reconciled me to the point of view that Jesus was a wonderful human being, rather than, as you say, "part of the Christian godhead." But, when you say Renan's Jesus was a rough draft of Jesus Christ Superstar (that I loathe!) you make me realize that to me, as a young student, Renan's Jesus *was in effect* the … equivalent of Jesus Christ Superstar! Odd, isn't it, and Renan, though dead, innocently spurred me on to the agnosticism that has plagued me ever since, though Renan (like Voltaire) denied being an atheist.
>
> And now I can't afford to be an agnostic any longer, so I will finish your book, dear Malcolm, and hope it will cure this ache in my heart for all the dear ones I have lost, I hope not forever.[107]

Other intellectuals who saw Muggeridge as a spiritual guide followed a similar path as Enid. Readers remembered their lives as if they were following the narrative structure of a voyage and return.[108] Their general account was as follows: they had a religious upbringing that was shaken by a negative interaction with religious institutions. Along the way, they read literature critical of Christianity, which spurred a crisis of faith and subsequent departure from the church. Then, after coming into contact with Muggeridge's books, the reader reconsidered the reasons they had left Christianity in the first place, and ultimately reconverted.

This was Enid's experience and it was how H.P. Breuer described his life. He was born in Germany before becoming a naturalized American citizen when he was nineteen. He was raised Roman Catholic, but had left the church during Vatican II. He entered into a "rationalist phase" during his college years after becoming interested in the life and work of Samuel Butler.[109] He went on to earn his PhD in English from Stanford University, where he produced an annotated critical edition of *Brehon* for his dissertation. He had a distinguished career that included stints at a number of universities, grants from the National Endowment for the Humanities, and several publications. At the time of his letter to Muggeridge, he was teaching in the English and Comparative Literature department at the University of Delaware.

A few years into his time there, he came across *Jesus: The Man Who Lives* in a bookstore over winter break. As a Butler scholar, Breuer would have been familiar with *The Earnest Atheist*, which Muggeridge had written while in a "rationalist phase" of his own. Breuer had never thought about Muggeridge as a religious thinker, so Muggeridge's journalistic expose of the Synoptic Gospels piqued his interest. Reading that book was a turning point in his life: "I bought it, and Christmas was quite different that year. I read your evaluation of Pascal, of Simone Weil; that led to reading them, your autobiography, and your essays on rediscovering Christ, on Mother Teresa."[110] These books had put him, as he described it, "back on to a wiser path." At the time of his letter, he was reading *Jesus: The Man Who Lives* for the third time,

with as much, even more, excitement as before; and I think you ought to know that. You have not provided just another book among the all too many, but one very much needed, one which has met, I believe not just in me, a great hunger: in dry moments I have read snatches from it to be inspirited, and so it has been for me a light that shines luminously in the general darkness of our confused time. Your retelling of an ancient story is so bracing because you tell it boldly, bluntly, and eloquently, without the evasions and qualifications with which others seek to make it "acceptable" to the sophisticated; and without yet another set of Germanic abstract arguments, but rather with the wisdom garnered from reflecting on a long career in the hurly-burly of the world. Stressing as you do so clearly, in counterpoint to the modern illusions to which we have all fallen victim, the blessed paradox at the heart of Christianity, you have helped me – rather faint of heart and all too skeptical – to see again the powerful alternative it is to all the predictable dead ends of modern thinking. How curious that what is considered the great enemy of human development and dignity turns out to be the only true justification and defense of either.[111]

Is it possible that readers like Enid and Breuer were able to look to Muggeridge as a spiritual authority only because they had experienced a formative upbringing in Christianity? Perhaps experiencing a "reconversion" in their forties (Breuer) and seventies (Enid) speaks less to Muggeridge's influence and more to the lasting impressions of their youth. That is possible, especially given the paucity of evidence available from a single fan letter. Then again, maybe Muggeridge was just as influential as these readers attest, with or without a formative religious upbringing. We have cases of readers without any religious background who looked to Muggeridge as a guru to guide them on a path of enlightenment.

G. Jones was a Canadian university student who struck up a correspondence with Muggeridge during his first year. He was not raised in a religious household and at the time of his first letter was a self-avowed agnostic. Like many first-semester freshmen away from home for the first time, college was a time of discovery and new experiences. During those first few months, he became uncertain about who he was and what his values were. Muggeridge had piqued his interest in a TV interview, and he found himself agreeing with many of the things Muggeridge said. Jones wanted to learn more, so over the next six months he systematically worked his way through Muggeridge's books, and looked for his television appearances whenever he could. His first letter was less a typical fan letter full of fawning praise, and more a request for prolonged guidance:

> I wonder then if it might be possible to somehow carry on some form of correspondence with you and by some chance to meet you should you ever find yourself within some reasonable distance of Toronto. Perhaps sub-consciously I have a desire to become some kind of disciple ... I have a number of specific questions and problems to ask, but, I thought I should first of all establish some communication with you.[112]

If his desire to make Muggeridge his spiritual counsellor was subconscious, he evidently had reached a point of self-realization. Muggeridge sent out a reply a couple of weeks later.[113] We do not have the carbon copy, but Muggeridge did jot down a few brief notes in the margin of Jones' letter that he would be happy to correspond and meet with him the next time he was in Canada.

These were not empty words. Two weeks after Muggeridge had sent his reply, Jones wrote back. In that short time, he had finished *Jesus Rediscovered* and blazed through both *Tread Softly for You Tread on My*

*Jokes* and *Muggeridge through the Microphone*. What he really wanted was some advice on what he should do with his life. He thought he might become a journalist, like Muggeridge, and asked for some help on deciding a major. But it is clear that Muggeridge's influence went much deeper than steering him towards a career choice. Imitation is a form of flattery, and Jones was imitating more than Muggeridge's profession: his entire worldview was undergoing a reconstitution.

> The most remarkable thing about reading you has been that you have challenged the validity of many institutions which I have always felt to be relatively invulnerable: the U.N., heart transplants, psychology, education (paradoxically I ask for advice on just this subject), liberalism, the franchise, birth control, and the notion of creating heaven on earth. But to my amazement I find myself in very great agreement with you. I don't mean to say that I am a different person but I have come to examine and criticize myself with the result that a large part of my philosophy of life has completely reversed itself. As I sit here, I can't help but think of the many questions to ask the SAGE but I am sure that you must be occupied with other correspondence.[114]

Muggeridge sent a short reply two weeks later, including a pointed suggestion that Jones should study history.[115] It should not be underestimated the effect of writing personal replies. Much of the criticism directed at institutions during the 1960s and 1970s had to do with a yearning for experiences that were more "authentic." Developing a personal connection with a well-known critic, and then receiving thoughtful replies, meant a great deal to people like Jones.

It meant even more to meet in person. At some point between February and June of 1970 (when Jones wrote his third letter), Muggeridge had followed through on his promise to meet him if he were in the Toronto area. By then he had read *Jesus Rediscovered* two more times and had begun to self-identify as a Christian. Significantly, he did not attend church – Muggeridge gave him all the spiritual guidance he needed: "I find that I am very often trying to apply, what are now, your 'teachings' to almost everything I do and think. If I am ever lucky enough to meet you again, I can't think of anything I would want to discuss more than religion and life."[116] Reading some books, exchanging a few letters, and meeting on at least one occasion in the course of six months had dramatically reshaped his self-identity.

It thus appears that age, religious upbringing, education, and sex were not significant factors in readers who saw Muggeridge as a spiritual guide. Neither does class appear to have played much of a significant role. J. Adams and R. Kendrick were in very different financial circumstances, but they both sent letters to Muggeridge seeking his guidance. Between the two of them, they had read almost every book he had published. Indeed, from what can be gleaned from their letters their love of Muggeridge was the only thing they had in common. Adams was a middle-aged woman who had recently divorced her husband of eighteen years. They had seven children together and the husband's lack of care was at the root of her abject poverty and the central cause for their separation: "hardship & struggling, not just myself, but the children, not being able to feed them, or cloth them, not being warm in winter, & shoes to wear, having to beg free school dinners, etc., as the one I married, had no interest in any of us, except for personal pleasure, he never provided food or clothing for them, never spoke to them, he never provided anything, as we were never able to buy anything, or go anywhere, all we had, was what friends gave us."[117] She was not begging for money. The description of her situation served as context to the central point of her letter: to explain how Muggeridge's books had helped her and to solicit spiritual advice. She had tried out Baptist churches, the Church of England, Methodism, and Roman Catholicism, but nothing seemed to work.

> I am still searching, I cannot find peace, or that I belong … I cannot find it in any of the ordered denominational Churches, they seem to be set against each other, by their set rules, you can go for years, and not learn anything, you just go, and sing the same hymns, say the same prayers, and read the same lessons year after year. What I am looking for is a way of life, which is FREE, and not dominated, and ruled over.[118]

Muggeridge was her spiritual role model and, since he had no association with institutional religion, she thought he could help. She went on to ask him to write back with a description of what he did for spiritual devotion. The only record we have of his reply was marginalia noting, "Finished 7.9.73."[119] Given what we know about Muggeridge's habits of responding to his fan mail, there is good reason to think that he probably honoured her request.

R. Kendrick also wrote to Muggeridge asking for spiritual guidance. But his search for meaning and belonging was not born out of
the hardships of poverty and marital abandonment; his emerged from
a sense of emptiness after achieving his career goals and enjoying the
wealth that followed. He was a thirty-one-year-old solicitor, married
to another lawyer, and had no kids. As a "dink," he had no financial
problems, and wrote his letter while vacationing on a Rhine River
cruise: "Approximately 18 months ago, I became a partner in my
firm – effectively the highest pinnacle that I can reach in private practice – and having for so many years, striven to reach that goal, I now
find that I am asking myself – where next!"[120]

For the greater part of the last decade, he was entirely preoccupied
with achieving his goals that when he finally reached them, he experienced a sensation of being a stranger unto himself. He could not
shake the feeling there was some greater purpose for him to dedicate
his energies to, rather than just representing "criminals in their
defense, husbands and wives in dispute, businessmen taking money
from other businessmen, etc."[121] *Things Past* and *Chronicles of Wasted
Time* made him believe Muggeridge could help, so he requested that
they meet and talk in person. The two-hour drive from Shefford to
Park Cottage at Robertsbridge seemed like it would be worth the trip.

## CONCLUSION

By all quantifiable measures, the scope of religious authority declined
rapidly during the 1960s and 1970s. Muggeridge's readers were
emblematic of the "increase in subjective spiritualties" that characterized the theological shift of churches not only in England[122] but also
throughout the Anglophone world. Yet, Muggeridge's readers were
not anti-authoritarian; they were anti-institutional. His fan mail
shows how conservatives, moderates, liberals, and radicals alike
responded once that trust was lost. As their trust in conventional
Christianity declined, Muggeridge's readers began to recognize him
as a surrogate cleric. Even those who wrote to defend their churches
did so without any unified ecclesiological vision. In those instances
they showed just how pervasive the crisis of religious authority was, in
that even those most committed failed to articulate why churches
remained essential to authentic Christianity. Moreover, the attempts
churches made to interact more effectively with the growing pluralism in society backfired by deepening internal divisions. Radical the-

ology that envisioned an obsolescence of spiritual authority succeeded only in moving some "ordinary" Christians to look elsewhere
for religious guidance. In this setting, some remained within their
churches as faithful, but disgruntled members. The incongruence
between the doctrinal prescriptions of churches and the actual beliefs
and practices of their members is a regular feature in the history of
Christianity, but this became especially pronounced in the 1960s and
1970s.[123] Muggeridge's readers reveal how, often in emotionally
fraught ways, they created new communities of spiritual belonging
on their own terms even as they rejected their churches. They reflect
just how "contested, shifting, and malleable" was the lived religion of
Muggeridge's fans as they used the practices of reading and writing
for spiritual self-fashioning.[124] To this end, Muggeridge's readers used
their letters to seek spiritual guidance, to confess their sins and fears,
to offer prayers, and more. In that process, readers placed him in a
position to fundamentally shape their religious lives, even to the
point of directing how they understood the future of the churches
and the destiny of the religion they practised.

3

# Reading Religious Decline

There was an old man: Malcolm Muggeridge
Who seemed to belong to anotheridge
  The age he was in
  Was all sorrow & sin
And he blasted & damned it to buggeridge
T. Putfield to Malcolm Muggeridge, circa December 1980

"Nobody would deny," lamented the Anglican layman D. Cooper, "that the majority of our countrymen are to a large extent ignorant of and indifferent to the Christian message, whether proclaimed by the Church of England or any other branch of Christ's Church."[1] Cooper had been a communicant member for twenty-five years, served as a lay reader at his local Hatfield parish, and led an active life in church functions within his community. But his 1966 letter admitted in no uncertain terms that he felt like he was part of a remnant. Clearly, believing that Christianity was in a state of irreversible decline had profound implications for how people imagined themselves. The psychological shift contributed to what Hugh McLeod has described as "a rupture as profound as that brought about by the Reformation."[2] Not only were social and cultural norms transforming at an alarming rate, there was a sense that society was entering a new era inimical to faith. Cooper was not alone in his concern. As this chapter shows, the changing state of affairs had a deep emotional resonance for Muggeridge's readers. Their letters reveal how ordinary people throughout the Anglophone world felt an acute dissonance between an ongoing commitment to Christianity and their internalization of the "alternative paradigm" that not only took secular society for granted, but also encouraged participation in a set of normative practices, beliefs, and behaviours. This worldview, in addition to normalizing "a whole new set of metanarratives for thinking about the modern world,"[3] also included distinct emotional styles for feeling about it. In this context, their reflexive projects were animated by a navigation of feeling.[4] The recrafting of self-identity simultaneously required recalibrated emotives, with which readers translated internal feelings amidst newly recognized cultural and social norms. Yet, Muggeridge was also a counterpoint to the very narrative of decline that facilitated their distress. He offered an alternative path for expressing honest faith in a secular age. As fans read his books and poured their innermost thoughts into personal letters, they sought emotional refuge from their fear that they were witnessing the death of Christianity, as they knew it.

Where readers saw Christendom's decline, the sexual revolution – invented by Christian clergy, promoted on the media, and then legitimated by real social reforms[5] – was the usual suspect. I. Miller was a twenty-five-year-old Londoner who had been a teenager in the 1960s. After reading the first volume of Muggeridge's autobiography, *Chronicles of Wasted Time*, he wrote a letter relating his concern that "modern apostasy," caused by "unrestricted sexual adventures," was increasing at an alarming rate.[6] Miller was not alone in seeing a direct connection between morality and secularization. Fans wrote often of their plight of living in a "morally sick society,"[7] whose "sex-crazed and greedy"[8] character reflected a "moral degradation"[9] that was unlikely to reverse itself. No doubt a focus on sex was in part inspired by Muggeridge's own life story, the promiscuity of which he had repented, and then denounced in his lectures and writings. Much more than this, Muggeridge had for years argued there existed a close and inseparable connection between secularization and the sexual revolution, which he believed had begun as early as 1965.[10] By the time Miller wrote his 1973 letter, the idea of a sexual revolution was a matter of fact:

> The tragedy of modern life is that moral standards are being discarded and nothing is being put in their place. The absence of any authoritative moral standard is the primary cause of so many young lives being shipwrecked. We cannot realise our true selves, I believe, apart from moral standards. Moral ideas are not invented like a political theory, by man. They are the foundation stones of the world God has made. This is a moral universe. Moral laws

belong to the nature of things ... Without such a standard man is like a rudderless ship with the engines running: He has drive without direction.[11]

Miller's letter exposes a painful realization felt by many of Muggeridge's readers: "modern life," as they understood it, was antithetical to moral Christianity. As he put it, more and more people considered "that in modern society with its great tensions and stresses, purity is an unrealistic ideal." The media was to blame for inundating people with sexual lechery, to be sure, and this made Miller feel increasingly out of touch with the culture he inhabited.

Miller was venting. His letter may have expressed frustrations about the trend of society, but he did not struggle with how he was to act within it. His lament was driven by a sense of powerlessness to make any kind of meaningful resistance against the tide of secular society. While moral redirections in previous decades or centuries had typically elicited calls for conservative resistance or evangelical revival, in the 1960s and 1970s it met with a resigned acceptance that it was Christianity itself that needed to modernize its moral precepts.[12] This narrative that sexual revolution was the normal state of modern society was powerful and convincing. More than just a British phenomenon, it was present throughout the Anglophone world and had profound implications on the choices ordinary people made. Indeed, many of Muggeridge's readers wrote to document the kind of internal struggle they experienced while being pulled towards both accepting and resisting the "new morality." For readers like Miller, this kind of transformation made him feel as though he were living without hope. For Muggeridge's fans, reading and writing provided the emotional context in which they worked through these conflicting goals.

One such person was N. Stone-Macdonald, a young woman who was living in relatively isolated Kamloops, British Columbia, a small city of roughly 50,000 people at the time of her 1974 letter. She had internalized the narrative of sexual liberation from the media and her network of friends. Reading Muggeridge intervened amidst emotional crisis:

Dear Mr. Muggeridge –
    I want to thank you for the help and encouragement that you, throughout your book, *Jesus Rediscovered*, have been to me.
    For a number of years there has been great pressure on me – and most women – to leave my husband, break up our home

and fulfil myself. During this time I often saw your book on the newsstand and would pick it up, look at it, and then put it back. I knew it had in it that which would require me to do something difficult and I wasn't ready to do the hard thing. I asked my husband for a copy as a Christmas gift and I read it December 26th. I am very glad I did. I am no longer torn apart by the media, Women's Liberation or the urgings of my liberal friends. I know where I am going now and I can see my way clearly. Thank you.[13]

Thus, even though Muggeridge's readers had internalized the sexual revolution as a normal part of modern life, they actively resisted or lamented it, as both Miller and Stone-Macdonald show. Their belief that it was permanent caused considerable distress or even apathetic resignation. T. Simpson was a seventy-year-old man from a London suburb who described himself as a "lazy old chap" who had suffered a stroke, was diagnosed with sclerosis, and endured ulcers in both his legs and feet ("Collecting these things seems to be my hobby!"). On top of it all, he had been hit in the face with bomb shrapnel during the Battle of Britain, which forced him to hold up his eyelids with one hand as he penned a letter with the other:

Well, Malcolm, what do you think of our poor old world today? All honesty, kindness, courtesy, morality, love of God and neighbour, willingness to work and earn our daily bread, etc. seems to be slowly dying out, and being replaced by greed, violence, lawbreaking, sexual filth for entertainment, and getting money by any means seems to be growing.[14]

Significantly, Simpson's age and health prevented him from leaving his home in Stanmore, Middlesex. His understanding of these issues was not shaped by large-scale personal interaction with greedy, violent people who were obsessed with sex. On the contrary, his opinions about the state of the "poor old world" were informed primarily by his reading practices, which, by his own admission, included the Bible and Muggeridge.

L. Ransond felt similarly as he wrote to express his discontent about the society he inhabited. In his letter it seemed that only quoting Jimmy Porter from *Look Back in Anger* could capture his feeling that there really were "'no great causes anymore' ... All that is left to defend is the indefensible."[15] As a newlywed living in Fordingbridge, a small town in Hampshire, he feared for his future children:

> I envy people of your generation who have been able to bring up their children in an atmosphere which contained at least a degree of moral stability. Sometimes one dreads the prospect of having children at all, but I suppose that is cowardly. However, it is difficult to reject the new attitudes without appearing to be a crank and I fear that it will be made more and more difficult as time goes by. If I had a daughter I wouldn't want her to wear "sexy" clothes and make-up at the age of twelve, but when other kids have these things it must be hard to deny them to one's own without making them feel left out or different ... We are told there is more freedom today, but it seems to me that the pressures to make us conform are as great as ever. All that has changed is the pattern that we are expected to conform to.[16]

Ransond's letter is instructive because it reveals the kind of internal struggle one father felt as he reflected on the present he inhabited and the future he imagined. He conflates secularism, materialism, and permissiveness with modern existence itself, and for that reason complained of the pressure to "conform" to "patterns" with which he fundamentally disagreed. His desire to avoid the ripples of cultural revolution was held in uncomfortable tension with not wishing social isolation for his potential children – to "feel left out or different." While scholars like Steve Bruce and Tony Glendinning continue to emphasize socio-structural changes to explain parental neglect in passing on religious identity to their children,[17] Ransond offers another possible explanation. He remained resolutely committed to Christianity – that much is obvious in his letter – but after internalizing narratives of decline, he began to question the feasibility of transferring Christian principles to his children. It was not that he became secularized and therefore grew apathetic; instead, he seems to have accepted it was a lost cause.

Readers followed Muggeridge in their tendency to conflate religious decline with seemingly every other version of declinism that animated the cultural politics of postwar Britain. A common theme was their interpretation of the kind of technocratic society promoted by C.P. Snow in *The Two Cultures* as evidence of a religious crisis, just as Muggeridge had in "England, Whose England?" This is what led the twenty-four-year-old Roman Catholic J. Heywood to be "horrified at the way the mass media machine is being used to influence the minds of my generation."[18] Technology giveth and technology taketh away, and Muggeridge's readers thought it took more than it gave. According to F. Goodwin, Christianity was declining mostly because of the BBC, with "it's too great output of violence, sex, blasphemy, and so-called satire."[19] All of this amounted to several readers echoing Thomas Carlyle to conclude that "swift technological development has outstripped our rate of spiritual growth."[20]

It was for that reason that some readers could thank Muggeridge for his rejection of the scientific culture promoted by Snow. One such example was P. Harris. He was a twenty-five year old from Brierley, a town in the West Midlands with only a few thousand inhabitants. He had been following Muggeridge since he converted to Christianity and saw him as "a wise and fatherly figure." He looked to Muggeridge as one who would "put to *silence* and shame those amongst us who advocate the 'blessings' of the 20th century science and technology – the so-called 'age of enlightenment' – with its space labs, computers, 'higher criticism' vacuum-packed potatoes ... and propaganda – all boasting of intellectualism."[21] It was primarily a scientific culture that "polluted the mental and moral atmosphere in which our society somehow manages to continue."[22] The only solution Harris thought would work would be a return to spiritual vitality, which he believed Muggeridge's books could accomplish. K. Wyndham also thought science and technology were outpacing society's spiritual development, but she could not put much hope in the churches because they were "bogged down in outworn dogma & have all but lost real contact with the people."[23] Christianity needed to break free from the churches if it wanted to survive secularization.

We have seen that readers were shaped by Muggeridge's presentation of declinism throughout his works. But what kind of effect did the acceptance of decline have? As one point of comparison, all of these themes (affluence, neophilia, sexual liberation, technology, the churches themselves) have been explored thoroughly in current historiography. We can thus say that, for the most part, Muggeridge's readers – and likely most thinking people by extension – were generally aware of all the categories scholars today point to as characterizing or shaping the religious dynamics of the 1960s and 1970s. The important difference, however, is their interpretation of those categories.

The language may come across as somewhat histrionic, but there is little reason to think it was exaggerated in their own minds. What reason would they have for admitting such emotional turmoil in a private letter, if it were not genuine? Practising a hermeneutics of suspicion can be useful to any historical interpretation, but it would not be accurate to conclude that these letters were little more than facile attempts to seek attention from a minor celebrity. A handful of melodramatic letters might be written off as anomalies. Hundreds suggest a plot. Together they indicate the reality of an authentic social phenomenon during the 1960s and 1970s that cannot be explained solely by class, sex, or even religious denomination. The threat of religious decline created real anxieties, produced actual fears, and inspired reaction in the form of letter writing to one they felt understood what they were experiencing.

Some of fans were feverish in their concern of what religious decline meant for them personally, or what it would mean for the future of the world. This went beyond agreeing with Muggeridge's haphazard definitions of decline – religious or otherwise – that appeared throughout his works. L. Smith of Edmonton believed that "perhaps never before in the world's history has the conflict been so strong between good and evil, with the evil forces organized as never before, and threatening the very existence of man, and perhaps the earth itself."[24] Smith did not elaborate on what these forces were, but he was at least sure they were making things worse than they had ever been. T. Stroud of Kent not only knew that "Western Civilization is in decline," but that the rate of decline was speeding up "not yearly, but almost daily." "The signs of decline are so obvious," he continued, "I am amazed that most people fail to recognise them, let alone argue that they don't exist!"[25] Unlike Smith, Stroud did take a stab at what was causing decline. He cited pollution and environmental damage, modern art (especially Tachisme and Action painting), surrealism in philosophy, affluence, vandalism, sexuality, and even pop music. To him this all spelled the imminent "breakdown of law and order, and governments – any government – leaving only the forces of organised labour and organised crime to fight it out for dominance."[26] Others entering into this line of thinking conflated religious decline with a laundry list of events and circumstances: a few poor wheat harvests in Russia, the 1970s energy crisis, Cuban immigration into the United States, the creation of the state of Israel, and the possibility of nuclear attack as anticipating the end of the world.[27]

These were disconcerting issues, and Muggeridge's fan letters reveal how ordinary people coped with religious change. Beyond grief and hysteria, readers expressed sentiments of ambivalence, victimization, forlorn isolation, and pessimism that together might be described as a kind of *sehnsucht*, an intense feeling of detachment and unfulfilled idealism.[28] Readers historicized their own present moment by assuming that the "modern world" consisted of various essential attributes that included, and was explained by, the teleology of religious decline.[29] It was as if they accepted a future history with themselves written out of it.[30] Their acceptance that to be modern was to be secular created a sense that they did not belong to the world they inhabited. This was how C. Fink felt. He was a Catholic priest whose internal crisis began once he entered seminary:

> I saw scripture demythologized ... morality relativized, and dogma made meaningful to modern man; this last a particularly bitter pill to swallow as, not finding the new theology very meaningful to myself, I was forced to conclude that I was not a modern man. I still haven't figured out quite what I am.[31]

It was not until he came across Muggeridge's books that he had a turning point: He first read *Jesus Rediscovered*, but then moved on to read *A Third Testament*, *Jesus: The Man Who Lives*, *Something Beautiful for God*, and *Chronicles of Wasted Time*. "Just knowing that you remain to walk the same earth as me makes my pilgrimage a lot more bearable and a little less lonely."[32]

This idea that the logic of history was one of unfolding secularity inspired B. Heffner to conclude, for example, that Christians had only very recently become "strangers in a strange land."[33] Likewise M. Commell, a Sussex native living in a town with only a couple thousand people, sympathized with Muggeridge when she said, "I know what you mean when you say you feel like a visitor here. I feel the same way now."[34] This feeling of displacement could provoke quite pessimistic outlooks: J. Casella was still young by all accounts, but he admitted, "I am now thirty years old, and for the last ten years, I have felt increasingly alone in this tottering, meaningless world that we have created."[35] *Sehnsucht* applied to Christianity was distinctly external in the sense that the shared experience of these readers was caused, nebulously, by forces outside of themselves that had prevented an alternative reality – in this case, one in which one's personal faith did not exist in a state of inexorable decline. Readers concerned with living in a secular society were not just dealing with typical bouts of depression that people go through from time to time: the salient point here is that their feelings of incompleteness and displacement were intrinsically linked to their belief that they were witnessing the end of Christianity. In short, internalizing the secularization story caused them to grieve the death of religion as they knew it.

*Sehnsucht* helps to explain the experience of R.J. Russell, a young high school teacher in a Sydney suburb who wrote to Muggeridge in 1976. She had been re-reading a chapter of *Jesus Rediscovered* in preceding days and expressed how it made her feel more and more "unworldly." This posed a significant challenge as she faced her students, who, in her mind, appeared to display resolute secularism. Attempts to share her faith with them on occasion forced the conclusion of just "how unspiritual they are," a realization that instilled in her a deep sense of pessimism for the future. "I sometimes see myself, at only 32, as one of the last group of tourists through this life who was still able to capture, before the evening gloom of materialism, pleasure, and sensuality, a glimpse of the edifice unseen."[36] Her letter expressed a forlorn sense that the opportunity for spiritual renewal was long passed, and that the only option was to accept that modern society was at the twilight of faith. "Those under my charge at school, as 'the evening' closes in, listen to my descriptions of what [faith] is like, why it is important, but THEY CANNOT SEE IT!! And often, myself enclosed by the darkness, I fight to recall the serenity [of faith]."[37]

But did the reality of cultural change merit such despair? Undoubtedly Australia was undergoing religious change just as Britain was when Russell wrote her 1976 letter. David Hilliard has shown that despite some regional variances, religious decline accelerated throughout Australia after 1965, and especially after 1970.[38] Indeed, the 1971 census even added the option, "if no religion, write none," in recognition of a growing population who did not associate with Christianity. Yet the same year as Russell's letter, pollsters recorded just over 8 per cent of respondents in the "none" category, while self-identifying Christians still approached 80 per cent.[39] By any standard Russell still inhabited a Christian society. A trend is not an explanation, but assuming an "end of the story," so to speak, had profound effects upon how she understood her place within society and culture.

Yet, at the same time, readers reported serious uncertainties about what, exactly, they were witnessing. Reading Muggeridge provided the framework they needed to make sense of the ongoing changes in and around their churches. This was the case with M. Vaughn of Edinburgh. Like many fans, she wrote only a short letter (it was less than a hundred words), so she does not divulge much detail about herself (we know only her religious denomination, return address, and date of letter) other than acknowledging Muggeridge's profound influence. She wrote to tell Muggeridge that "many of us 'feel in our bones' that things are wrong" and that "this is a terrible time for the Church, & much prayer is needed."[40] Vaughn's 1966 letter was written just as numbers measuring Scottish religiosity were only beginning to decline steeply. Despite these figures being within only a few percentage points of what they had been sixty years previously,[41] Vaughn nevertheless accepted inexorable decline as a foregone conclusion. Then again, she probably did not have access to, or cared to look for actual statistics measuring the religiosity of her country. Her conclusions were shaped primarily by reading Muggeridge. In her short letter she budgeted space to say that before reading about his views on the state of institutional Christianity she did not know "how to put [her] feelings into words"; it was only thanks to him "for explaining things so clearly" that she understood what was amiss in the church.[42]

E. Poxon provides another example of how reading Muggeridge crystallized otherwise scattered thoughts into a coherent narrative of decline. She was the wife of a butcher in the industrial city of Walsall, not too far from Birmingham. Her letter was sent in 1970 after seven years of wrestling with how to understand the religious change happening around her. She felt that her church "grew visibly smaller after 'Honest to God'" and she was equally perplexed that financially it was "in the red."[43] Her experience was quite similar, then, to the subjects of Ian Jones' study on generational change in Birmingham.[44] A reference by Poxon to 1963 and the publication of *Honest to God* corresponds to both Callum Brown's and Arthur Marwick's dating for the onset of rapid cultural and religious transformation, as well as Hugh McLeod's emphasis on Bishop Robinson's text for shaping this period.[45] At the same time, Poxon did not have the benefit of historical perspective, sophisticated theory, or creative methodology. Just like Vaughn, it was only after reading Muggeridge that financial woes and a drop in church attendance were cast into a narrative of decline:

It wasn't until I read the book "Jesus Rediscovered" by Malcolm Muggeridge that I saw what I knew in print. I could feel the various pressures within my Church, and throughout society as a whole, but couldn't place them. If I could write, I would say exactly what he says. I don't think a day goes by that I don't come across a problem, find what he says about it in one or other of his books – in his own "dry" way.[46]

Poxon and Vaughn are examples of readers who may have had a nebulous feeling that religious culture was changing, witnessed declining attendance and membership in their churches, or perhaps encountered first hand in their day-to-day experience an increased ambivalence towards Christianity. Those feelings were widespread among Christians who remained active members of their churches amidst religious change. But anecdotal evidence does not prove macroscopic changes in society. A trend reaffirmed by personal experience is not an explanation. What Muggeridge did for readers such as these was to offer them a broader narrative of decline into which they voluntarily situated their personal experiences. This act could prove profound in shaping their religious identity within a society they now accepted as secular. His influence was not just in helping them articulate their observations – it was giving them the categories through which to select and attribute meaning to past experiences.

What makes Muggeridge particularly important for this history is the degree to which readers used his life and work as a means to placate their fear. Muggeridge was a living counterargument to religious decline. His public conversion inspired hope in his readers that even if the churches continued to decline and even die, it was not a death sentence on the future of Christianity. In the words of one Oxford fan and his wife, Muggeridge was a "light amidst the encroaching gloom."[47] This could ease the concerns of Christians who experienced a sense of not belonging to the time or place they inhabited. For many readers, Muggeridge's conversion "reaffirmed"[48] or helped them to "gain ... reassurance"[49] that maybe decline was not inevitable and that Christianity might still be an important force in society. It gave some relief to the middle-aged Canadian J. Savin, who said, "Your writings, your thoughts reinforced my belief that Christianity is not only still relevant but more important to our society than ever."[50]

As we have seen, readers made a sharp distinction between Christianity and "Churchianity." M. Horley's lament was typical: "Can you image what it is like to be a Catholic today? In this appalling world – & this appalling world of no values, no morals, no adequate justice – & I turn to the Church & the Church isn't there."[51] She still attended mass, primarily to continue receiving the Eucharist, but she felt disillusioned by its politics. The foreboding she expressed was consistent with the attitudes of others, that Christianity as they knew it was in a period of irreversible decline, and that this problem was caused both by the culture around them and the leadership within their churches. In spite of this, Horley's letter was in fact written with a spirit of optimism because Muggeridge's public conversion and continued defence of Christian faith (if not its structures) provided the hope her local church did not: "How refreshing, how miraculous, it is to find today someone – & someone as well-known & intelligent as yourself – bearing public witness to Jesus."[52]

This was a common sentiment among Muggeridge's readers, that the world was becoming more secular and that their churches were either too inept to do anything about it or, worse, that they were complicit in Christianity's decline. M. Vaughn, who we met earlier, lamented, "One of the deepest sorrows, to us Catholics, is that it is our own Priests who are betraying us."[53] Similarly, J. Halcomb consoled herself by thinking "the Church of England and Christianity are not the same thing." Because the church had compromised with the "affluent society" they inhabited, it was "no wonder" the church "was like a sinking ship."[54]

Yet, crucial to this dynamic was readers' use of Muggeridge's life and writings to placate their anxieties. B. Fitzpatrick was an Australian farmer who experienced the same feelings of displacement as C. Fink. Yet, in his case, Christianity made him feel, not as though he were living in the wrong time period, but as though his mind was out of sync with "the world." He explained:

the reason for this letter is to thank you for either saving my sanity, or for the assurance that it is quite normal to be insane …
Thanks to you, I can now see my experience for what it was, and it gives me great comfort to know that there are others too, who have known what I have known. If, as you say, one of your friends considers you a little mad for your view of the world and

your beliefs, then I too am a little mad, and could wish for no finer company.[55]

L. Lang-Sims thought of the same thing after she read *Christ and the Media*. "Thank you ... for helping to reassure me that I am not mad when I feel as if I were living in a criminal lunatic asylum, being one of the very few who, although doubtless criminal, have resisted becoming a lunatic."[56] She went to describe how she felt "out of step" with modern society and even her church, which she believed to be partly responsible for its own decline. "Here in Canterbury I wage continuous battle at the Cathedral – where straightforward commer- cialisation joins forces with a weird phenomenon known as 'secular Christianity' and the two surge forward together destroying every- thing in their path – holiness, worship, beauty, order, even the most elementary normality and reverence."[57] She believed that Christianity and its institutions would continue to decline as they became trivial- ized by the media and desire for profit. Nonetheless, it gave her some comfort to know she was not the only one who thought modern life was a "mind-blasting nightmare."[58] Likewise, I. Taylor of Edinburgh thought, "The Light of the World has chosen you to shine at an increasingly dark period in our history."[59] In R. Overall's mind, Mug- geridge was like Ezekiel: "Your voice has become that of a prophet in our age," offering "sanity" in a period of "confusion and despair."[60] It was Muggeridge, he wrote, who gave to the remnant "guidance and encouragement in these difficult times of disillusionment" by being a living counterpoint to the "chaotic age" in which they lived.[61] Mug- geridge did not only inspire authentic faith outside of institutional Christianity; he was living evidence secularization was not the death of religion.

## CONCLUSION

Just as religious decline was a topic that vexed clergy, the highbrow media, sociologists, and student organizations alike, religious decline was also felt deeply by ordinary people as they struggled to make sense of their religious identity in an age they accepted as secular. In the first case, this chapter has emphasized the emotional turmoil felt by Muggeridge's readers. This was particularly true for the British con- text, but the geographic and social diversity of Muggeridge's fans sug- gests a much more transnational scope to the argument that "secular-

isation exists as a belief fed by the power of narratives."[62] This narrative was not always coherent in the minds of Muggeridge's readers,
and they situated the fears and anxieties they felt into the framework
he provided. As well, it has been shown that Muggeridge's readers felt
betrayed by, became disillusioned with, and grew cynical of institutional Christianity amidst this struggle. The loss of confidence led
them to either redefine what the church meant to them (often emphasizing for themselves the church's invisible nature), or leave the
church altogether. Thus, ironically, the most robust attempts of the
churches to meet the challenge of religious decline (by revising doctrinal positions and updating worship practices) alienated otherwise
sympathetic believers. In this way, these believers enacted the narratives they accepted, and, in the process, inadvertently decreased the
social significance of the religious institutions they had once supported. Finally, the unexpected conversion of Muggeridge in this context was a counterpoint to narratives of decline, and was like a sooth-
ing balm upon open wounds. He was living proof that the end of
Christendom was not the death of Christian faith. Thus, crucially, the
decision to leave the church was not always entangled with losing the
faith, whatever resulting attendance and membership statistics might
otherwise suggest. On the contrary, Muggeridge's readers remained
sincere, if emotionally wrought, believers who actively sought alternative modes of spiritual belonging as they came to terms with religious change.

Together these letters suggest a number of important characteristics
of the popular reception of the secularization story. First, the specter
of Christianity's inexorable decline created a sense of intense emotional and spiritual insecurity that was felt regardless of class, age, gender, geographic region, or denominational persuasion. While many
welcomed the liberation offered by secular culture as a positive development, Muggeridge's readers grieved the death of Christianity as
they knew it. But they did not always have a clear sense of why or how
this was happening. Unlike sophisticated renderings of decline by
sociologists like Bryan Wilson,[63] their insecurity reflects highly anecdotal and theoretically imprecise understandings of decline.[64] Oftentimes fans admitted it was Muggeridge's writings that crystallized
their otherwise scattered observations, thoughts, and feelings into a
coherent framework. In this way, reading Muggeridge was crucial for
fans who discerned their place within the evolving relationship
between Christianity and culture. Second, this popular response

reveals a vexed relationship with institutional Christianity that varied from lamenting the challenges churches faced to criticizing their inability to foster authentic belief. In either case, fans were frustrated with their churches' engagement with the social conditions they inhabited. Just as Christian clergy in the mid-1960s promulgated narratives that were enacted by those who internalized them, Muggeridge's popularized arguments about secularization similarly inspired what is a third key lesson of these letters. Losing confidence in their churches led otherwise sympathetic Christians to stop attending their churches altogether, which confirms the argument that secularization could function as a self-fulfilling prophecy.[65] Yet a readiness to forsake their churches did not mean a willingness to give up their faith.[66] For readers such as these, Muggeridge took on special significance. He inspired the creation of alternative, and informal, expressions of spiritual authenticity that sidestepped conventional religion. Simultaneously anti-institutional and professing Christian, he modelled honest faith in a secular age.

# 4

# Reading for Social Engagement

Considered apart from reading, the world of the text remains a transcendence in immanence ... It is only in reading that the dynamism of configuration completes its course. And it is beyond reading, in effective action, instructed by the words handed down, that the configuration of the text is transformed into refiguration.

Paul Ricœur, *Time and Narrative*, vol. 3, 159

We have seen how readers interacted with Muggeridge's writings as they wrestled with issues of faith and doubt, redefined their relationship with institutional Christianity, engaged with permissiveness in society, and even how they understood the future of the religion they practised. Yet reading and letter writing were much more than tools to reconfigure thought, self-identity, and their perception of society or a minor celebrity. Reading inspired Muggeridge's fans to transform the world around them. Their earnest desire for activism was embedded within the larger social and cultural context of the rise of the welfare state, the decreasing visibility of Christian voluntarism, and the rediscovery of poverty. Muggeridge was a vocal participant in the larger conversation about these issues, especially by the late 1960s and early 1970s when he promoted Mother Teresa of Calcutta. His articles, interviews, a documentary, and a book on her life and work placed a decidedly religious slant on the rediscovery of poverty and the proper Christian response. He offered readers a distinct philosophical alternative to prevailing social attitudes towards welfare and poverty in the 1960s and 1970s. Nancy Ammerman has observed that communities of faith have a central role in shaping how societal "practices of charity" and cultures of "community volunteering" develop.[1] Reading and writing situated Muggeridge's fans within a textual community defined by shared religious experiences across felt distances through-out the Anglophone world. They were inspired to donate money, vol-unteer their time and energy, and even dramatically change their careers to something that felt more meaningful. Muggeridge's fan mail illustrates how emotional practices of reading and writing fos-tered spiritually motivated social activism in domestic and interna-tional contexts. In the process, readers formed social bonds with Muggeridge, with others through the organizations they joined, and with the people they sought to help as a result. Their actions were dri-ven certainly by compassion for an "other," but they were also, and per-haps chiefly, motivated by a reflexive process of understanding themselves amidst the ongoing interplay between religion and social action in society.[2]

## THE WELFARE STATE AND CHRISTIAN VOLUNTARISM IN POSTWAR BRITAIN

The 1942 Social Insurance and Allied Services report marked a crucial turning point in the history of welfare in Britain. More commonly known as the Beveridge Report, it envisioned a path towards recon-struction after the war that, in contrast to Nazi Germany's "Warfare State," promoted a welfare state that would target five evils of modern society: want, disease, ignorance, squalor, and idleness. The election of the Labour Party in 1945 reflected the popularity of these suggestions. Indeed, in 1948 pollsters found that nine out of ten people in Britain thought that charity was no longer necessary in Britain.[3] Thus, parlia-ment went on to systematically pass and implement a series of acts in the following years that included, most importantly, the National Insurance Act (1946), which began the National Health Service in 1948, and the National Assistance Act (1948), which formally abol-ished the Poor Law. These marked nothing less than "cradle to the grave" social services for people of all classes.

One unforeseen implication of these acts was to shift gradually the responsibility of providing social services from private religious and philanthropic organizations to the bureaucratic structures of the state. Before the Beveridge Report and 1945 Labour victory, governmental welfare largely worked in cooperation with religious charities. The rhetoric of a "Christian civilization" had provided ample motivation to assist the impoverished and needy, and its institutions had provided the infrastructure to accomplish it. Frank Prochaska reminds us it was Victorian Christians who built schools and hospitals, trained personnel, and administered services. Christians who inherited this vast philanthropic network, however, transferred control to the state in the climate of postwar Britain. It was not forced, but welcomed as more efficient, effective, and, indeed, godly. The Church of England provided theological justification in 1948: "The State is under the moral law of God, and is intended by Him to be an instrument for human welfare."[4] Linda Woodhead has marked this moment as the "sacralization of political ideals" among Christians and church leaders alike.[5] State-organized welfare was hardly a replacement for Christian voluntarism in the eyes of Christians; it was simply a more effective expression of God's command to love thy neighbour. This attitude, widely held by Christians and clergy, explains why the institutional church supported so many social reforms. Relaxing laws on abortion, homosexuality, and divorce while modernizing theological language and practice were part of the same cultural shift as transferring the responsibility of welfare to the state. The priority was to accomplish the greatest possible human flourishing in the immanent frame, whether in the form of state-run welfare, or in the form of loosening doctrinal and social strictures. The conclusion was that the machinery of the state provided the best tools to achieve Christian ends.

Nevertheless, early on, leading figures – no less eminent than William Beveridge himself – feared the expansion of the welfare state would diminish and replace the long-standing tradition of voluntarism in British society. His 1948 *Voluntary Action: A Report on Methods of Social Advance*, which was published as an extension of his recommendations for a postwar welfare state, argued as much. In his view, state-controlled welfare would have the double effect of reducing the need for volunteers and eliminating their purpose by doing their job for them. Beveridge believed a robust and well-funded system of government welfare was necessary, but he hoped it would not come at the expense of free association with others. Such voluntarism was essential to the health of democracy. He argued:

The making of a good society depends not on the State but on the citizens, acting individual or in free association with one another, acting on motives of various kinds – some selfish, others unselfish, some narrow and material, others inspired by love of man and love of God. The happiness or unhappiness of the society in which we live depends upon ourselves as citizens, not only the instruments of political power, which we call the State.[6]

Beveridge's fears came true. Church-run charities largely did become redundant. And since the philanthropic arms of churches served as their public face, historians have noted they "became increasingly invisible in the welfare era."[7] When church charities were visible, they became increasingly disparaged. Part of this was due to the mushrooming anti-institutionalism during the 1960s and 1970s. But also important was the growing professionalization of society. The "white heat" of industry promoted by Harold Wilson and the concomitant scientific culture championed by C.P. Snow had little patience for amateurs. Of course, it was because charities depended on amateurish volunteers that they were able to keep costs so low. The welfare state, by contrast, was designed to be run by technocratic professionals with higher standards of practice. Philanthropy and charity in this context were recast with negative connotations as being both patronizing and inefficient.

At the heart of these changes was a philosophical transformation of how poverty was understood in British society. Poverty, once seen as a problem designated chiefly as religious and ethical in character, became in the modern era a political issue reserved for the interests of the state. The fundamental shift in social thought was one in which poverty was seen less as an inevitable condition of sinners in a fallen world, and more as an unfortunate price of economic growth and industrial development. In the former case, poverty took on an almost metaphysical quality that made it part of the natural order. In the latter view, it was possible, if terribly difficult, to eradicate it, if only the state applied the right policies. These policies, like those recommended by the Beverage Report, worked to integrate the impoverished into the economic community by finding ways of encouraging self-sustaining work – whether through education, health services, or state insurance. Amateurish charity efforts, according to critics, "serve[d] only to reinforce the social and psychological attitudes which generate poverty."[8] Of course, if poverty was an inevitable and natural part of human existence, then alleviating its symptoms was an act of compassion. After all, no amount of charity would ever eliminate it. Yet, if social programming could eliminate poverty and squalor, then doing little more than assuaging symptoms was unhelpful or even cruel, for allowing them to persist.

For over two decades following the publication of the Beveridge Report, Britain's welfare state was "optimistic, progressivist and utopian."[9] During the 1950s and 1960s, the general climate was that scientists knew better, and that the government could be trusted to create a better, healthier society. In 1951, Benjamin Rowntree and George Lavers published *Poverty and the Welfare State*, in which they concluded triumphantly that there was minimal poverty in urban settings and that this reflected the condition of England in general.[10] Confidence was high that the state really could stamp out want, disease, ignorance, squalor, and idleness.

This assumption was increasingly challenged during the mid-1960s, and became deeply problematic by the 1970s. Brian Abel-Smith and Peter Townsend's 1965 study *The Poor and the Poorest* inaugurated a "rediscovery of poverty" by drawing attention to those not eligible for social assistance as well as the shortcomings of those programs accessible to the impoverished.[11] It invited a reconsideration on both the political left and right of how to define and understand poverty, as well as whether or not the welfare state was at all sufficiently capable of solving it.[12] *The Poor and the Poorest* was crucial for deflating the optimism of the professionalized technocratic state regarding its ability to quell social evils like economic inequality. Indeed, some scholars have suggested that this loss of confidence in government experts was a partial cause of Harold Wilson losing power in 1970.[13] Confidence eroded even further as the welfare state came under financial strain due to the 1973 oil crisis, rising unemployment, and stalling economic growth.[14]

Muggeridge had been a long-time critic of the welfare state and its philosophical underpinnings well before the "rediscovery of poverty" and the economic crises of the 1970s. He expressed distaste – even fear – of the welfare state both privately and publicly ever since he had lived in Moscow during 1932 and 1933 as an investigative journalist for the *Manchester Guardian*. His criticisms were primarily of two kinds. In the first place, he thought that any expansion of the state threatened personal freedom.[15] It was the second criticism that is perhaps more salient for the present purposes. He believed the problem with the welfare state was that it fundamentally compromised the motives for helping others at all. During his short tenure as editor of *Punch*, Muggeridge published a barbed attack in an editorial entitled, "The Importance of Being Beveridge." There he asserted, "The basic fallacy ... in the whole Beveridge concept of welfare" was that "it leaves out of the account charity" and turns helping others into "no more than yet another manifestation of the demanding ego."[16] Ironically, Muggeridge here expressed agreement with Beveridge just as he attacked him, but his critique resulted from the recognition of the welfare state's unintended consequences on voluntarism in British society.

Muggeridge thus did not share the popular social attitudes towards poverty and charity that characterized British society in the first decades of the postwar settlement. As his national fame grew to a global scale, those same positions disseminated through his writings to transnational contexts in which welfare systems had developed differently. The views he championed had more in common with the classic view of poverty as a natural and inescapable reality of the human condition that no amount of charity could fully eradicate. For him eradication was not the point of charity, a view he held even before his conversion to Christianity. His 1955 *Punch* editorial that lambasted Beveridge described charity as a vital expression of human solidarity. Once he converted to Christianity in the 1960s he continued to assert this view, but recast in religious terms. Then, just as attitudes regarding charity and the welfare state transformed within the context of a "rediscovery of poverty" and economic crises of the early 1970s, Muggeridge's ideas were viewed with new eyes. Muggeridge must have been aware of the developments in the social climate, because after 1968 he began to promote his vision of poverty, charity, and social engagement in earnest through a series of books, articles, and interviews. In 1972, for example, Muggeridge's BBC program *The Question Why* (which ran from 1968 to 1972) dedicated an entire episode to the very subject. One of the headlining guests was none other than Peter Townsend himself. He was one of eight experts who appeared on the program, but his spot on the seating chart placed him in a prominent front and centre position.[17] Muggeridge's opening statement was prepared beforehand and read verbatim to establish the framework for discussion, which was to interrogate the irony of why poverty appeared to increase in the midst of vast technological developments. Muggeridge put his ideological position on full display when he complained, "the exaltation of poverty as such which so uplifted Christians like St Francis makes little appeal nowadays. At the same time, it has to be admitted that abolishing poverty, in the sense of assuring for one and all the basic necessities in the way of food, warmth and shelter, does not necessarily make for contented, fulfilled citizens."[18] Muggeridge was not just reacting to the "rediscovery of poverty," he was actively using his position as a prominent media figure to shape it.

Nothing Muggeridge did shaped the conversation about poverty and charity as much as his work exploring the life and work of Mother Teresa of Calcutta. Muggeridge first interviewed her on the BBC's *Meeting Point* in June of 1968. The massive and unexpected success of the interview prompted a repeat broadcast within a month. The success was enough for the BBC to commission Muggeridge to produce a documentary the following spring about Mother Teresa's organization, the Missionaries of Charity, which was broadcast at the end of 1969. The grassroots response to just the interview appearances and documentary resulted in over £20,000 in donations, many of which were sent to Muggeridge's personal residence. Muggeridge later adapted the documentary into a book of the same name, *Something Beautiful for God*. The text included the transcript of the documentary with added commentary that challenged the idea that the state ought to be the sole authority for promoting social welfare. Muggeridge defended amateurish forms of voluntarism as emblematic of Christian love:

> Mother Teresa was almost laconic when I asked her whether she did not think that the destitution she was trying to cope with in Calcutta required a government agency disposing of vastly greater resources of money and manpower than her Sisters of the Missionaries of Charity did or could. The more government agencies did the better, she said; what she and the Sisters had to offer was something else – Christian love. Criticism of Mother Teresa is often directed at the insignificant scale of the work she and the Sisters undertake by comparison with the need. It is even suggested that, by seeming to achieve more than she does, or can, she may actually lull the authorities into a complacency the situation by no means warrants, or at any rate provide them with an excuse for inaction. Again, her necessarily limited medical resources and the old-fashioned methods allegedly used, are pointed to as

detracting from her usefulness. It is perfectly true, of course, that, statistically speaking, what she achieves is little, or even negligible. But then Christianity is not a statistical view of life.[19]

Controversially, Muggeridge thought there was something noble – even beautiful – about poverty and suffering. He therein rejected the assumption that poverty and crime were necessarily entwined, seeing them instead as embodying the human condition. He continued that poverty and hardship

> are not the breakdown of a machine, but part of the everlasting drama of our relationship with our creator. Far from being an unjustifiable violation, an outrage, they exemplify and enhance our human condition. If ever it were to be possible – as some arrogant contemporary minds are crazy enough to believe – to end suffering, and ultimately death, from our mortal lives, they would not thereby be enhanced, but rather demeaned, to the point that they would become too insignificant, too banal, to be worth living at all.[20]

On a rhetorical level, these arguments benefited from a sort of Chestertonian-style of paradox that invites contemplation without settling on practical solutions. On a theological level, Muggeridge had much in common with the Roman Catholic doctrine that poverty and suffering were redemptive, though this was a solid decade before he formally joined the fold. This perhaps helps to explain one of the reasons why so many Roman Catholics read and appreciated his journalism. It was not just that he was providing good press for what many considered a living saint; Muggeridge was therein also promoting Roman Catholic social theory. Theology is important here, but it alone does not explain why his journalism resonated so deeply. Its widespread receptiveness – popular among many who did not accept Catholic social theory – was more likely due to the concomitant dwindling of confidence in the welfare state that had already led to a rediscovery of poverty and a reconsideration of charity.

It is a woolly business attempting to estimate just how influential *Something Beautiful for God* actually was. The short answer is *very*, both in terms of raw sales and actual impact. Obtaining sales figures for books is notoriously difficult, but Muggeridge did keep some scant figures that give us a snapshot of how the book sold. This is mainly because he designated that all royalties would go directly to the Missionaries of Charity. As a result, he received regular updates reporting how many books sold as well as how much money they earned. During its first three years on the market, reports indicate that the book sold just under 200,000 copies and was translated into Swedish, Italian, Polish, German, and Korean.[21] It is likely Richard Ingrams's note that *Something Beautiful for God* was reprinted over twenty times is a low estimate[22] – the German edition alone went through eleven printings between 1972 and 1984.[23] A closer estimate is that the text went through about forty editions between its publication and Muggeridge's death.[24] Yet these statistics fall short of communicating the true distribution of *Something Beautiful for God* because they do not tell us how often the book was gifted, shared, or discussed. As will be discussed below, it was quite common for the same copy to be distributed among friends or an entire reading group. And that does not take into account how many times library copies were checked out from a library. We do not have records of book sales in the years following 1974, but we do have a 1986 letter from the treasurer of the Missionaries of Charity, Patrick John. He indicated that in terms of pounds and pence, the book raked in £109,252 in royalties between 1971 and 1985.[25]

These figures do not count the money from other financial awards that came, at least in part, because of Muggeridge's work. Muggeridge was instrumental in Mother Teresa being the first recipient of the Templeton Prize in 1973. Not long before the submission period was over, the vice-president of the organization, W.G. Forker, sent a letter to Muggeridge about the state of Mother Teresa's application:

Dear Mr. Muggeridge,
    Mother Theresa [*sic*] of Calcutta is one of a number of people who have been nominated for the Templeton Foundation Prize for Progress in Religion. Unfortunately, the nomination is very scantily written and I think it does not do her justice.
    Knowing of your interest in the life and work of Mother Theresa, I wonder, would it be possible for you to make a detailed nomination? If my recollection is accurate, I think you recently published a book on this …
    Time is not actually on our side, as I would require this by the end of this month in order to have it processed for the various judges.[26]

Whether this points to unfair bias on the organization's part to justify Mother Teresa winning the prize is a matter of debate. Whatever the actual intentions, Muggeridge did reply one week later:

> Dear Mr. Forker,
>
> I am submitting a copy of *Something Beautiful for God*, and also the 1971 report of the International Association of Co-Workers of Mother Teresa. From these the scope and value of her International mission can be readily assessed.[27]

Muggeridge may have been in a hurry to leave on a month-long lecture tour in Canada when Forker sent the request, but simply submitting a book already widely accessible in print with a twenty-page annual report as application is unconventional to say the least. After all, Forker was already aware of *Something Beautiful for God*. Nevertheless, the fact that it succeeded in winning a £34,000 prize for Mother Teresa's organization points to how influential the book was.

Additionally, Muggeridge was an active proponent of Mother Teresa's selection for the Nobel Peace Prize in 1979. He began the campaign for her to win in the early 1970s, even submitting an application for her on his own accord in 1975. He sent letters to heads of state, religious leaders, and other dignitaries in his attempt to muster up support for her. He contacted American diplomats like Sargent Shriver, British politicians Harold Wilson and Philip Noel-Baker, former Nobel Prize winner Lester B. Pearson, the prime minister of India Indira Gandhi, the governor of West Bengal A.L. Dias, the president of Zambia Kenneth Kaunda, and Pope Paul VI.[28] He even tried his luck a second time and sent August Schou, the director of the Nobel Institute, *Something Beautiful for God* as part of the application. It is uncertain how instrumental he was in Mother Teresa winning the Nobel Prize – nothing as precise as his letter to the Templeton Foundation exists – but he was undoubtedly an active proponent years before it was awarded. And after she failed to win in 1975, he was part of the campaign to resubmit her name for the award in following years.[29] Since Muggeridge was the first major journalist to introduce Mother Teresa to Western societies, there is good reason to believe he was not only instrumental, but also essential to that process.

Muggeridge's influence was not just financial or honorary. There is good evidence that his work contributed to an increase in the ranks of Mother Teresa's organization. Whenever a fan wrote to Muggeridge asking how they could volunteer their time or where they should send a cheque, he or his secretary directed them to the International Association of Co-Workers of Mother Teresa, an organization begun by Ann Blaikie in 1969 to support the work of Mother Teresa. The annual report of the Co-Workers includes worldwide statistics for the Missionaries of Charity from the previous year. The annual reports include reports of professed nuns, novitiates, and postulants. Numbers in every category rose between 1970 and 1973.[30] As will be discussed in more detail below, some of Muggeridge's letter writers directly cited reading *Something Beautiful for God* as their reason for giving money to or joining the Missionaries of Charity. Indeed, at least some of the increase was because the Co-Workers used Muggeridge's book and documentary as their primary marketing materials.[31]

The reception of Muggeridge's journalism on Mother Teresa – and by extension his alternative understanding of poverty and charity – was overwhelmingly positive in the press. A close reading of critical reviews of *Something Beautiful for God*, however, does reflect the ongoing tensions surrounding poverty and charity in the context of the welfare state. Indeed, some of these reviews anticipate the most famous of Mother Teresa's (and Muggeridge's) critics, Christopher Hitchens. Hitchens' investigative journalism lies outside the chronological scope of this study, but it is nevertheless important to be aware that some of his chief criticisms were expressed in less forceful terms by contemporary reviewers of *Something Beautiful for God*. His 1994 documentary *Hell's Angel*, later published as *The Missionary Position: Mother Teresa in Theory and Practice*, was a biting critique of her methods and activities. His arguments were not entirely original, but he was the one who made them most effectively. An important objective of his overall argument was to show that Mother Teresa's understanding of poverty was cruel because it meant people under her care were given improper treatment. He believed that promoting suffering as something beautiful, even redemptive, was "evil."[32] Their lot was one of "austerity, rigidity, harshness, and confusion," as they were allowed to die in conditions well within the financial resources of Mother Teresa's organization to improve.[33] Hitchens admitted that his own anti-theism informed his criticism, but it would be incorrect to assume that the reception of Muggeridge's journalism on Mother Teresa was cut along religious lines. The ideological tension is more complex than that. Some of Muggeridge's most noteworthy critics on this matter were religious leaders and committed Christians. This is true whether we are talking about the press or his fan mail. Conversely, as will be shown in the next chapter, some of Muggeridge's agnostic readers were inspired by *Something Beautiful for God* and expressed their desire to donate their time or money to helping Mother Teresa's organization. The immediate reception of Muggeridge's journalism was shaped by several factors, including the context of rising religious pluralism in society, the rediscovery of poverty, and the concomitant crises of the welfare state after 1965.

Some reviewers objected that Muggeridge seemed to disparage those who pursued charity through the mechanism of the state. One reviewer argued:

> many modern social reformers and revolutionaries who also claim
> to derive their thirst for social justice from evangelical principles
> can be judged with equal reason to be authentic followers of
> Christ. Muggeridge would have little sympathy with the Helder
> Camaras, Dorothy Days, Berrigans or Camilo Torres of this world.
> Indeed, he would use the example of Mother Teresa to berate their
> ilk. Therein lies his blindness and folly.[34]

But it was not just a question of motivation. It was also one of efficiency. The Anglican Bishop of Southwark, Mervyn Stockwood, had lived through the postwar settlement twenty years prior when his church had assented to the formation of the welfare state. His 1971 review of *Something Beautiful for God* criticized the work chiefly because Muggeridge appeared

> to dismiss with contempt the people who try to remove the causes
> of suffering. By all means let us salute Mother Teresa and her
> devoted companions who tend the lepers, but let us be equally
> generous in saluting the devoted doctors and research workers
> who quietly and often anonymously give their lives and their
> skills for the elimination of leprosy ... to engage in cancer
> research in the hope of eliminating disease can be as beautiful.[35]

But it was not just Muggeridge's disregard for scientific professionals making medical advancements that irritated some reviewers. It was also his insistence that trust in government-directed welfare was misplaced. "Many would disagree with the methods," said one reviewer, "that, seemingly needlessly, she will accept no government grants of any kind, relying solely on voluntary contributions." He continued, "In the brutish inequalities and injustices of poverty, begging can never be anything but further degrading both for the recipient and the giver."[36] The methods confirmed the "acceptance of the most degrading poverty."[37] These few reviews were the minority opinion, but they remain important examples to show that Muggeridge's journalism on Mother Teresa was not universally praised prior to Hitchens's investigative journalism in 1994. There remained significant tensions that reveal the moral, emotional, and religious struggle people navigated while reading Muggeridge's books, in particular *Something Beautiful for God*.

## MUGGERIDGE'S READERS, POVERTY, AND SOCIAL ENGAGEMENT

Book sales, royalties earned, prizes won, and raw statistics of Mother Teresa's organization provide evidence that Muggeridge's journalism, and *Something Beautiful for God* in particular, was widespread and noteworthy. And the reviews in the press, with a few important exceptions, confirm that people felt its influence was largely positive. But what about Muggeridge's ordinary readers? Statistics tell us nothing about how the book was actually read by all those who purchased, borrowed, or were given the book. How did it influence his reader's actions? Did they agree with his presentation of poverty? Or did they find it highly romanticized and ultimately unacceptable? If we would take Muggeridge's words at face value, we might be led to assume that the response of his fans was universally positive. That, at least, was the impression he gave in *Something Beautiful for God* where he discussed fan letters he had received length. He summarized:

> I myself received many letters enclosing cheques and money
> orders ranging between a few shillings and hundreds of pounds.
> They came from young and old, rich and poor, educated and une-
> ducated; all sorts and conditions of people. All of them said
> approximately the same thing – this woman spoke to me as no
> one ever has, and I feel I must help her.[38]

Closer inspection shows that his fan mail formed something of a parallel with his reception in the press. It was overwhelmingly positive, but not a few letter writers expressed sincere reservations about what

Muggeridge was advocating for in nuanced ways. Taken together, Muggeridge's readers who, in their fan mail, discussed the issue of poverty and social activism were of roughly two types. First were those who engaged with the text on a purely intellectual or emotional level. It helped them to reconceptualize how they thought about poverty, suffering, and the role of God's Providence in the developing world. The second and much larger category were those whose reading prompted social activism, whose letters exhibited and constituted "observable action."[39] Together these letters provide a lens through which to observe changing attitudes towards poverty, the emotional responses of readers, and even how reading could directly inspire attempts to enact social change.

Take Dr C. Vossen, for example. He was a linguist who had read *Something Beautiful for God* with pleasure. He felt he could agree with most of what Muggeridge said, except for his disparaging comments about secular social reformers like Beatrice Webb. Vossen held her in high esteem because, in his view, she, like Mother Teresa, "gave up comfort and pleasures to help the poor."[40] Muggeridge's reply to Vossen explained his opinion: "I consider Beatrice Webb was a prig … Her virtue was of the abstract variety." Muggeridge believed the difference was that charity was motivated by Christian devotion whereas social services were devoid of compassion because they operated through the machinations of the state and not by impulse of feeling or faith. "The Christian does good for a person," he continued, "the social worker for an idea."[41] The false dichotomy Muggeridge formed here reflects his ideological position generally, but the statement is perhaps partially explained by the fact that Beatrice Webb was Kitty Muggeridge's aunt, and that Malcolm and Beatrice Webb had a falling out after his return from Moscow and subsequent disillusionment with Soviet communism. She remained committed to the political system, while Muggeridge went on for the rest of his career denouncing it as evil and ineffective. Whatever the case, Vossen's criticisms reveal significant tensions layered between otherwise glowing praise for Muggeridge's work.

The same could not be said for S. Haddock. She was an eighty-six-year-old journalist who had written a column for the *Methodist Recorder* for forty years. She listened to *Something Beautiful for God* on tape three times before typing out her short letter in July of 1973. She concluded that Mother Teresa was "a very mistaken saint. The very

Church to which she was born, to which she is obedient without question, is one of the major causes of poverty whose victims she serves."[42] We do not have the reply that Muggeridge must have sent, but we do have Haddock's second letter of 10 August. Whatever Muggeridge said, it did not have much effect:

> I agree with every word you say about reverence for life, but I just cannot see how you can believe that the Roman Catholic Church teaches that reverence. In my opinion, it teaches the exact opposite. Human beings, poor mentally, poor physically and financially, are taught by that Church that they can produce huge families, so poor miserable weaklings are born who should never have been conceived. Do you seriously call that reverence for life?[43]

Haddock's views reflected those of a large percentage of the population, but among Muggeridge's readers, she was in the minority. Even though cries of "no popery" were a thing of the nineteenth century, there remained prominent criticism of Roman Catholicism throughout the Anglophone world, as Haddock's letter instantiates. What characterized these views of Roman Catholicism was less the fear that the pope was a bogeyman ready to undermine Britain's constitutional structures and more the suspicion that Roman Catholic visions of social justice were depressingly outdated for modern ethical common sense.

The examples of Vossen and Haddock are important because they offer a sense of why some readers were critical of Muggeridge's vision of poverty and welfare. For the most part, however, Muggeridge's fan mail shows striking changes in readers' understanding of, and motivations for, supporting the welfare state. C. Lake explained that her first career as a shorthand typist had left her deeply unfulfilled. She then trained for social work "as a non-Christian" out of "a little love of humankind," and worked for the local governmental authority in Wolverhampton.[44] For a while thereafter she "groped and dithered" with religious questions, when she eventually joined the local Anglican church. Even though she did not accept everything it taught, she felt joining a church – any church – was an important expression of her newfound faith. Converting to Christianity led her to redefine her motivations for social work, and even to reformulate her perception of the welfare state:

As a Christian, I see my paid social work as having been inspired by Christians who lived to follow the example of Christ by caring for the poor, and crippled, and aged people. Humanists were not responsible for starting these services, although I get "Trade Union rates" and "equal pay" for my part in them. It pleased me to think that the Saints have made it easier for ordinary unsaintly people to do good in a practical way. The dangers of an increasingly "non-Christian" welfare state are very obvious, and perhaps you have a vocation to expose them. But don't be too hard on us.[45]

She did not expand on what she felt those "very obvious" dangers were, but her letter is nonetheless revealing for how reading about Mother Teresa reshaped how she understood her own vocation.

Some fans wrote with no other purpose than to share with Muggeridge the emotional feeling that arose when reading his books. M. Therese was a Roman Catholic nun who was so "struck with compassion and admiration" at the "suffering [and] honest openness" that it "made me want to do such a thing as writing to you the thoughts that welled up in me."[46] For W. Haines of Berkshire, reading Muggeridge helped him reformulate the way that he perceived poverty. After reading *Something Beautiful for God*, he began to think that that God was "present in the slums, in the broken body, [and] in the children."[47] Seeing Mother Teresa dedicate her life to impoverished conditions caused some readers to experience mixed emotions of admiration and guilt. M. Alperen wrote that, "I just finished reading your 'Something Beautiful for God' and cried and yet feel full of joy and a deep sense of loss, that I – with all my striving cannot reach that state of selflessness that Mother Theresa [*sic*] has."[48] Many readers expressed similar sentiments, whereby they felt intense emotions after reading Muggeridge's books, but did not feel they were worthy or able to act on those emotions. In the words of W. Haines, he confessed, "I lack the vocation (or will or love) for the Poor! I see it theoretically but I fear it – fear to fail."[49]

One of the most common responses was when readers wrote to signal their *wish* to engage in social activism. It is possible that some of them did, too, though we have no way of knowing if they followed through and volunteered their time. What can be said about such letters is that they were clear instances of emotional sympathy and intellectual assent. They thus have more in common with readers like L.M. Wallace, who changed his perception of poverty, or M. Therese, who wrote only to express the emotions she felt after reading. M. Bracey of London, for instance, wrote to say, "I have some spare time & would like to offer my services to the Mother Teresa Organizations."[50] There was F. Loral who wanted "very much to work for her in India or elsewhere,"[51] or an anonymous fan who could "think of nothing that I could do for *her*, but if there is the smallest thing I am completely at her service."[52] They are all very short letters that say just about the same thing in a rather vague way, but they nonetheless demonstrate attempts to mobilize, name, communicate, and regulate emotions through letter writing.

P. Lowes' letter reflects something of a similar sentiment, but with a little more detail. He was a divorced fifty-six year old who had worked in non-profits for his entire career. At the time of his letter, he was stationed in Geneva as a coordinator for the International Drinking Water Supply and Sanitation Decade (1981–90), an initiative begun by the United Nations. Lowes had travelled to many developing countries with the overarching goal of supporting access to clean water and sanitation. When he wrote his letter the program was in its early stages, but his authority was built on a long career of successful leadership in other philanthropic initiatives. Before moving to Geneva for his current post, Lowes had been a resident representative for the United Nations Development Programme in Rabat, Morocco.[53] By the program's end, it would help some 1.3 billion people gain access to clean water.[54] Yet his twenty-five years in nonprofit and philanthropic work for the United Nations had somehow left him unfulfilled: "I feel I have received so much in life and I would like to find the inner strength and discipline and faith to live in a better, more spiritually based manner."[55] At the time of writing, Lowes was not a practising Christian, though he had been raised Anglican while growing up in England. Throughout his life, he had felt he was always "in a search for God," though any sort of intellectual paths towards Christianity fell on rocky ground. What inspired him to seek spiritual meaning were those who expressed Christianity through their actions.[56]

A teaching or nursing nun in the malarial lowlands of Malawi or a Father among the Moslem Berber tribesmen of the High Atlas or a simple priest in a USA slum move me much more ... than does the conspicuous consumption of intellectual resources, which abound around me. Mother Theresa's [*sic*] example lived out right there in the guts of the "developing" world when my work is in so called development, puts any secular efforts like mine to shame and I would like to learn from it.[57]

Reading *Something Beautiful for God* created in him a sense of guilt that despite all his efforts, he was not doing enough – or at least that he was not doing his work for the right reasons. He went on to explain his fervent desire to do something, but he had no idea what that would be or even what it would look like. He wrote his letter in the hope Muggeridge would give him some direction on what to do next.

What was it about reading Muggeridge's books that caused such a desire to make dramatic changes in one's life? The sort of longing for more meaning expressed by Lowes was common. A great number of readers wrote of how Muggeridge's books forced them to redefine themselves and their interaction with the world around them. K. Thompson had just been promoted to the board of a large manufacturing company in Ireland when he felt guilty about how much of his life revolved around money. He read Muggeridge and even thought of joining a relief organization or charity, but decided against it when he realized that would only be "pandering to [his] ego."[58] He finally decided that a more humble act would be to quit his job and begin training for the ministry in the Irish Methodist Church. In his telling of his story, it was reading Muggeridge that sparked his decision to make a dramatic change in his life. Likewise, K. Hutchison of Wellington, New Zealand, worked for the government until he read Muggeridge, which led him to quit and begin training as a nurse.[59] A young woman named Michaela from San Diego was moved to become a Carmelite nun after reading Muggeridge and corresponding with him.[60] E. Ball from Essex read *Something Beautiful for God* and was inspired to visit homeless families on London on her own, without being connected to any philanthropic organization. She later decided to join the Co-Workers so that she could continue, "serving the poorest of the poor, the sick and any in great need."[61] R. Clayden of London wrote to Muggeridge telling him of how, two years earlier, after she read his work on Mother Teresa she joined her organization.[62]

What is interesting about these instances is their almost impulsive character. It was not common for readers to finish one of Muggeridge's books and then mull over the decision in their mind of what they should do. Some readers seemed to drop everything to donate time and energy to philanthropic work. That sort of behaviour perhaps lends itself to the genre of fan mail. Sometimes it seems the decision to act was so sudden that there was little preparation at all. M. McBride was a student at the University of Surrey who was inspired to contact the Missionaries of Charity and volunteer to live in India for two months during the summer holiday. It does not appear she thought through what this decision would actually mean for her, so she wrote to Muggeridge for advice:

> I have never been in a hot climate before and have no idea about the practicalities – and even less about Calcutta itself. Could you help me? ... I'd be grateful if you could tell me what to take with me in the way of clothes and money. Mother Theresa's [sic] secretary wrote saying that I could work with them but that there were probably no vacant places to sleep actually in the home but that there were cheap hostels nearby. Do you have any addresses of any places I could look for accommodation, or is it better to find somewhere to stay when I get off the plane? ... I speak English and a little French only, can you advise me of any language or any cultural customs to be aware of?[63]

McBride's eyebrow-raising request might be written off as youthful, albeit naïve, idealism, but her attitude was shared by others in different social settings. S. Brackfield lived about twenty miles away from the University of Surrey when he sent his letter a few years before McBride. Having just finished reading *Something Beautiful for God*, he decided quite suddenly that he had to help Mother Teresa: "I have felt a calling to help the poor of the third world in any small way that I can. Your book has acted as a final catalyst to put these thoughts into action. As a result, I have made arrangements to take a month leave of absence ... to be able to go to Calcutta and be of help to the Mission of Charity in any one of their numerous projects to relieve the suffering and enhance human dignity."[64] He had rediscovered poverty through Muggeridge's work and felt emotionally compelled to act. "I think that the comfort that we are accustomed to in the West tends to blind us from the harsh realities of life in the third world and forget our common duty to the poor and uncared for."[65]

The problem was that due to the circumstances of his job he had to take his leave of absence from the middle of February until the middle of March. His letter of 5 February thus allowed very little time to make preparations. He had sent a request to the Missionaries of Charity in Calcutta to organize his time with them, but he had made the decision so quickly that he feared there would not be enough time for them to respond by the time he was ready to leave. While he waited, he wrote to Muggeridge to share his plans and also to ask him about "the severity of the conditions and the type of work that I may be asked to do."[66] Like McBride, Brackfield made a commitment before learning the details of what he was signing up for.

Most readers did not have the flexibility of student life or the benefit of taking a leave of absence to fly to another country where they could volunteer for weeks or months at a time. A more common practice was to donate money as an expression of their desire to enact social change. Some donations were as small as a single pound while others were gifts in the hundreds or even thousands. Not every reader knew how to make sure their donation made it to Mother Teresa's organization, so they just opted to send it to Muggeridge instead, trusting that he would take care of it. This was probably due to the fact that in book version of *Something Beautiful for God*, Muggeridge discussed how after the documentary many people sent him donations to pass on to Mother Teresa. Discussing fan letters as much as he did in that book probably motivated some of his readers to follow through and donate money.

Some fans trusted Muggeridge enough to send a cheque made out to him personally – or even a wad of cash with a note requesting that he kindly pass on the funds to the Missionaries of Charity. Is it possible Muggeridge pocketed some of this money? From what evidence exists in the letters themselves we have reason to believe he did not. One example is from K. Surin, a student at the University of Birmingham who was studying theology. He was one who mailed a cheque made out to Muggeridge. The carbon copy of Muggeridge's reply instructed Surin to include "for Mother Teresa" on the cheque so that the organization could then send him a receipt of donation.[67] Another is M. Millenbach. She had given Muggeridge a cheque after reading *Something Beautiful for God*, which he ended up losing. When the cheque did not clear, Millenbach cancelled it and then mailed another to him to pass on to the Missionaries of Charity.[68] In his reply Muggeridge said, "Thank you for your letter and I am delighted that the business of the cheque has been cleared up. I have sent it off at once to the co-workers. Actually – again divine intervention: Mother Teresa will get double the amount because I was so conscience stricken at losing your cheque that I sent $100 myself for the co-workers."[69]

Some readers, instead of sending their own money, organized charities or other types of events to raise money that they then mailed to Muggeridge to pass on to Mother Teresa. C. Hall, J. Butters, and B. Lowndes were three middle-school students from Stoke-on-Trent who organized raffles on two different occasions. In February of 1973, they sold a Harry Secombe record, and a few months later sold off one of their dolls. Altogether, they managed to bring in five and a half pounds, which they sent on to Muggeridge with their personalized pastel-decorated letters.[70] M. Blake read *Something Beautiful for God* and then found a group of friends to go carolling during Christmas of 1972, from which they raised £14.[71] More often than not, the donations from Muggeridge's fans were small. Few had the money or desire to send large donations. But donation size really is not the point here. What matters is their stated motive, which emerged through their encounter with Muggeridge's books. Plain and simple reading was an effective catalyst for inspiring various forms of voluntarism. Their reading was in large part embedded within the larger context of the rediscovery of poverty. In the words of A. Wintle, their motive was to help "the poor and dying through Mother Teresa's work."[72]

It is an imprecise business trying to gauge just how much money readers sent to Mother Teresa because of reading *Something Beautiful for God*. In the first place, there is no way of knowing how many fans donated money without mentioning so in a letter. Even when they did note the inclusion of cash or a cheque, they often did not state the precise value. For that matter, Muggeridge's replies typically did not state the exact amount, either. The letters that included donations are scattered throughout the many thousands of letters he received, so it is difficult to collect exact figures. For whatever reason, Muggeridge's secretary did decide to keep a file of Muggeridge's correspondence to fans about donations from 1977.[73] About two dozen letters roughly evenly distributed throughout the calendar year enclosed a combined total of £2,644.53. One of these letters included a £2,000 donation from a Mr O'Donnell, who gave his life savings to Mother Teresa. This amount was unusually high. That said, many of the letters frustratingly do not indicate how much their donation was for, so even though the actual figure was higher, it is impossible to guess precisely by how much. It nevertheless leaves us with a good if incomplete picture of the grassroots donations people spontaneously gave after reading Muggeridge's books.

An important expression of social activism was the dissemination of Muggeridge's books to other readers. Readers like G.L. Kane read *Something Beautiful for God* and explained that because it was "one of the most inspiring books" he had ever read, he went out and purchased forty copies that he then distributed to friends and relatives.[74] Of course, we cannot know how any of those forty copies were read, if they were read at all, but it does tell us a great deal about Kane's reading experience. Sometimes individual dissemination meant the books would travel many thousands of miles. W.H.P. Ager lived near Hyde Park in London. After he read Muggeridge's work on Mother Teresa, he sent it to a friend who was a Roman Catholic priest in Patna, India. The book took nearly two months to arrive, but when it did, Ager reported that the priest passed it around to an untold number of people, who also read it.[75] Instances like this are good reminders that books may be read by multiple people. This is especially the case with library copies, which is precisely how M. Mart got a hold of a copy. She had never heard of *Something Beautiful for God* until her daughter had checked it out from a public library in Leeds, and then gave it to her after she was finished.[76] Sometimes the most avid of fans are not those who look for a particular book, but those who chance across a text that has a deep effect upon them.

There are several other examples of people sharing *Something Beautiful for God*, or one of Muggeridge's other books, with close friends, acquaintances, church groups, or family members. For example, M. Nichols and Sister Martinia wrote their letters to Muggeridge within months of each other.[77] Nichols was a Trappist monk in Utah and Sister Martinia was a nun in Watford, England. After they each read *Something Beautiful for God* alone, they were moved to read the book aloud to their religious communities during meal times. Both essentially created immediate textual communities within their convent or monastery as they read, yet in a way also formed one across felt distances. Even though they never knew of each other's existence, they nonetheless shared similar responses and expressed shared emotions despite their difference in sex, age, and geographic location. Both were inspired to read aloud to their religious communities because of the emotions they felt while reading, which they hoped would be shared by the various kindred spirits in their midst. Their reasons for sharing the book with someone else ran parallel to why people loved reading Muggeridge in the first place. Their desire to grow the textual community was simultaneously a desire to spread collective emotions, or, at the very least, they recognized that Muggeridge's books resonated with an already established emotional community.[78] Thus, S. Girling or Birmingham "cried after reading" *Something Beautiful for God*, and for that reason he shared his copy with "special friends" of his who he suspected might read the book in the same manner he did.[79] In the words of M. Klingber, it was a book worth sharing because he felt it "talks our language and reaches like a surgeon's scalpel deep down to where we think and live."[80]

The same impulse inspired fans around the world to translate Muggeridge's books into French, Spanish, German, Japanese, and Hungarian. In most cases, the fan sought to organize their efforts through a publisher with Muggeridge's consent. Others, like Sister M. Choquette, just went ahead, and then wrote after they had finished their work. Choquette was a nun whose primary duty was to care for the library at her convent in Sherbrooke, Canada. Her letter explained, "For almost two years now, I have your beautiful book, Mother Teresa of Calcutta, translated into French. All the sisters read it with greatest interest."[81] Her case is yet another demonstration of how book sales are a misleading indication of how much a book was read. Here was essentially a pirated translation imbibed by multiple people within a religious community. Sister Choquette's letter continued with a request for how she might get a hold of more English copies because she wanted to buy some and share them with some of her English-speaking friends. Muggeridge did not appear to mind the unauthorized translation of his work. He sent two letters afterwards: one to Sister Choquette, the other to the Distribution Department at Fontana requesting they send three copies of *Something Beautiful for God* to the convent in Sherbrooke, billed to his account.[82]

## CONCLUSION

Perhaps Beveridge was mistaken after all, at least in part. Christian voluntarism may have become "increasingly invisible" during the postwar settlement, but it did not disappear. Muggeridge's journalism, and especially the publication of *Something Beautiful for God*, entered the public at a crucial moment when the rediscovery of poverty became entangled with a loss of confidence in the power of the welfare state to eradicate want, disease, ignorance, squalor, and idleness. Amidst that conversation, Muggeridge promoted an understanding of poverty and suffering sympathetic to the Roman Catholic theology he would later accept as his own. When readers interacted with his work, they proved that the voluntary spirit that had characterized British public life for generations was not dead yet. These letters reveal snapshots in the lived history of compassion in postwar Britain, as they make clear how readers saw Muggeridge's books as an invitation to redefine their emotional appraisals of the world. They wrestled with the nature and scope of poverty just as it was being rediscovered, they expressed sympathy in letter writing, they donated money to the Missionaries of Charity, and they even volunteered their time to help those in need – sometimes travelling to different parts of the world to do it. As they shared Muggeridge's books, read them aloud, and even translated them, Muggeridge's readers made an intentional effort to enact social change. Though Muggeridge's writings were deeply shaped by his own interaction with the British welfare state and its development, the global scope of his readership meant this expression of voluntarism was not merely a British phenomenon. Together these readers formed a textual community that sought to enact social change, even if only by writing a letter to Muggeridge.

# Reading Muggeridge in Plural Societies

I have no religion but you have the power to bring me nearer to what I feel religion could be.

R. Dixon to Malcolm Muggeridge, 17 August 1970

I read and reread with tremendous absorption your Jesus Rediscovered, and was profoundly moved by it. This in spite of the fact that I hold no religious belief, which is something I cannot explain. Now I am wallowing in Muggeridge: Ancient and Modern, and the Diaries are queuing up to await their turn, jostling somewhat in impatience.

A.S. Pimeoff to Malcolm Muggeridge, 21 July 1981

Until now, we have been dealing exclusively with Muggeridge's Christian readers. Indeed, nearly 85 per cent of the letters he received were from people who belonged to some expression of Christianity. This number was likely higher, too. About 10 per cent of the letters did not include any indication the letter writers were Christians, but it is likely many of them were. However, it would be a mistake to suppose that all of Muggeridge's readers were Christians. The religious demographics of Muggeridge's readers were shaped by the pluralism that defined the Anglophone world generally during those decades. Muggeridge received fan mail from readers who were Buddhist, Jewish, Muslim, Sikh, Bahá'í, spiritualist, Hindu, agnostic, and atheist, as well as some practising Transcendental Meditation. While these readers made up less than 5 per cent of Muggeridge's fan mail, they remain essential if we are to understand properly the full scope of Muggeridge's audience. Situating such a broad array of perspectives together enables us to consider the kind of role Muggeridge's works played in the formation of self-identity across religious and secular boundaries. In fact, as these readers made use of Muggeridge's books alongside sacred texts from Eastern religions, or as they contentedly expressed no religion at all, they reveal the extent to which institutional, religious, and secular boundaries became "porous" in the late 1960s and 1970s. They invite a consideration of their lived religion, and lived secularity, as forms of hybridity that disclose not only how they practised their self-fashioning, but also how they understood belonging.[1] What is most striking about these readers, however, is that their experience shared a great deal in common with Muggeridge's Christian readers. They also saw him as a friend and kindred spirit, even if they did not see themselves as particularly religious. They wrote to come to terms with the idea that Christianity and Western Civilization were in a period of rapid decline, and they struggled with the challenge of redefining how to understand poverty and the welfare state, and how to cope with suffering.

Just as scholars are paying closer attention to the lived experience of those who remained Christians while their churches emptied,[2] so also should we pay closer attention to how those who rejected Christianity (as well as those who were never a part of it) made use of its cultural resources in their own lived secularity. How can subtraction theories of secularization account for, say, an Anglican-turned-Hindu who still read Christian literature to slake her spiritual longings?[3] What about a lifelong atheist who picked up *Jesus Rediscovered* hoping to find solace in the midst of personal crisis?[4] Few would doubt Clive Field's realistic reminder that "statistics reveal [Christianity] to have been in long-term decline,"[5] but such measures of religiosity do not account for the ongoing interplay between Christianity and its detractors. Here, again, the typical categories of "believing," "behaving," and "belonging" miss the mark. These readers made use of Christian cultural resources in the crafting of their own identity. In this way, they fused together multiple practices, beliefs, and attitudes that comprised their hybrid spirituality – or lack thereof. Lived secularity, like lived religion, is defined by the actual experiences of people as they carry out their self-reflexive projects. The religious crisis of the 1960s and 1970s was also for many an identity crisis. Muggeridge's readers who rejected Christianity carved out their identity in a rapidly changing religious landscape. A cultural focus on the personal experiences of these religiously plural readers reveals the manifold and ever-changing character of spiritual and secular formation practised by those discontented with Christian civilization. Even as they rejected Christianity, they nonetheless made meaningful use of its resources in the life and work of Muggeridge.

## SELF-DISCOVERY AND SPIRITUAL AUTHORITY

North America, Western Europe, and Australasia each have religiously diverse communities with long histories,[6] but minority religions were all so small that these regions remained overwhelmingly Christian well into the 1950s and early 1960s. The late 1960s and 1970s, however, marked a watershed moment when the rapid decline of Christianity's social significance became especially pronounced in the context of increasing religious pluralism.[7] A growing number of immigrants and the subsequent internal growth of those communities transformed Britain – and by extension the Anglophone world – into a more ethnically and religiously diverse society.[8] The British Nationality Act of 1948, spurred by economic insecurity, provided pathways for Commonwealth citizens to migrate to the United Kingdom. One important consequence of the Act was a small but important shift in Britain's social and religious makeup.[9] Many of these migrants did not practise Christianity. Muslims, for example, became the largest religious minority by the 1960s, with Hindus and Sikhs likewise growing significantly in size.[10] This demographic shift picked up especially in the 1970s and played a crucial role in destabilizing the idea of a monolithic British (i.e., English) national character. It became increasingly difficult to talk about an "essential" national character when immigration, individualism, and the concomitant "death of Protestant England" opened up possibilities for creative self-fashioning never before experienced on such a large social scale. Britain's overseas political expansion had developed in close alliance with a shared Christian (i.e., Protestant) character, and so the demise of empire was tethered to the decline of Christianity's social significance. Britishness became less a prescribed cultural ideal that one inherited or aspired towards, and more a descriptive phenomenon of all the people who participated in a shared political process. During and after the 1960s, British identity became, according to Peter Mandler, "a bricolage of traits, habits, [and] preferences"[11] that was more globally oriented in its scope. Alister Chapman has explored how this cultural shift became positively "toxic" to the language of Christian nationhood, which was increasingly seen as both atavistic and exclusionary.[12] As a response, the church establishment, the schools, and the media changed their tone to accommodate new audiences. The Church of England began to emphasize more pointedly the need to show "kindness towards those outside the bounds of traditional Christian morality and belief," a rhetorical shift consistent with the doctrinal reforms made during those same years.[13] It was more willing to welcome dialogue with other faith traditions (and earn a few pounds) by selling redundant sanctuaries to other religious communities, as John Maiden has recently showed in his case study of the Church of England in Bedford.[14] Similarly, multifaith education began in the 1970s as a direct response to the ethnic and religious diversity that had grew rapidly from the 1960s.[15] Moreover, between 1960 and 1979, the BBC changed its religious broadcasting quite dramatically by departing from predominately Christian programing to include more discussions of religious diversity.[16] By the time Muggeridge converted to Christianity, both the character of Britain as a multicultural and religiously diverse society was widely recognized at all levels of society.[17]

Additionally, rising affluence and new media provided people the ability to access alternative belief systems and practices. Indeed, Muggeridge's television career facilitated this just as he converted to Christianity. He was often found with furrowed brow, discussing some hot-button religious issue with a panel of religiously diverse leaders on BBC programs he ran such as *The Question Why*. For those Chapman analyzed in Derby, their reaction to diversity in this setting was to work in concert for the benefit of society as a whole. Conventional religion could thus remain an important social force because of, and not despite, increased religious diversity. The general trend of institutional Christianity to accommodate, rather than resist, changes in society is another example that runs parallel to the development of multiculturalism in Derby.

Yet, the same diversity that transformed the religious culture of Derby also led to a greater willingness among people to become eclectic in their religious beliefs – often at the expense of Christianity. The cultural scripts of the 1960s and 1970s encouraged the exploration of subcultures broadcast on the new media, which enabled greater freedom for people to develop their reflexive selves without the guiding hand of the churches.[18] For some readers, the form of religious expression was less important than the Bunyanesque journey of self-discovery through which one realized it. One non-observant Jewish reader put it this way: "The truth is that the search for meaning in life could be futile and that there is no meaning, that the real and only truth is our searching; that we seek a meaning that meets our requirements."[19] The Celestial City was the sense of meaning and fulfillment that could be experienced in the self-fashioning of identity. Anti-institutionalism worked hand in glove with the desire for freedom and self-determination beginning in the late 1960s.[20] Readers could agree on their right to self-determination; what they could not quite figure out was where and how it could be found. The burden of each individual was to find something authentic, and, as Anthony Giddens notes, that is made possible through the trust fostered in human relationships.[21] That's where Muggeridge came in. Just like his Christian readers, these other readers saw him as one who had overcome the anxieties of the modern world and obtained self-mastery.

This dynamic was present in Australian reader M. Ginsberg.[22] She had faced quite a number of heart-wrenching hardships throughout her life. She had lost her home and was forced to flee South Africa for "political reasons," which led to financial insecurity and the need to rebuild her social network in a different country. The stress of this situation led to her first husband suffering a "prolonged mental breakdown [and] committing suicide." She also learned shortly thereafter that her two-year-old son had brain damage, and, though he survived, the constant worry that his health would deteriorate wore her down physically and emotionally. She remarried, but then her second husband died of a heart attack in his forties. She eventually found another man with whom she had a relationship for five years, but then "suddenly he rejected me & has remarried" someone else. The course of her past made her admit, "I am disillusioned & unable to reconstruct my life." Everything changed when she found Muggeridge's *Jesus Rediscovered*: "Quite at random one day I picked up your book in paperback. I hadn't gone out to buy a book & I don't know how or why I should have done this. How astonished I was to find the message it conveyed." She found herself "reading and re-reading" it as the meeting point of a "soul who has made progress along the spiritual path." But the text did not drive her to Christianity. Even though her mother was a "devout" member of the Church of England and her grandfather had even been a rector, she had long "rejected the trappings & emptiness of the Church." Instead, she identified the text, and Muggeridge's spirituality, as important influences on her path towards Eastern religion. "I never rejected Christ because his words & life are truth," she continued, but "so also are the words of Krishna & Ramakrishna & Yoganadra."[23] She read *Jesus Rediscovered* alongside the Bhagavad Gita in order to live more in accordance with the "Divine Will."[24] It was through these mutually reinforcing emotional practices of reading, writing, and intertextual weaving that Ginsberg fashioned her own religious identity. Thinking back on her life made her interpret through an oft-quoted passage from the Bhagavad Gita:

Restless man's mind is,
So strongly shaken
In the grip of the senses:
Gross and grown hard
With stubborn desire
For what is worldly.
How shall he tame it?
Truly I think
The wind is no wilder.[25]

All of the twists, turns, struggles, and uncertainties in her life finally made sense because, as she saw it, "your book to me has been a light in the darkness. I pray that I might cling to the light."[26]

Many readers were like Ginsberg in following the path towards an alternative spirituality to Christianity, with Muggeridge as their trusty companion. This way of thinking animated the lived religion of E. Corfe of Wiltshire, who was inspired to share her newfound faith with Muggeridge once she had read *Jesus: The Man Who Lives*. She had recently decided to become a follower of the Indian guru Meher Baba, who she believed was only the most recent "historical manifestations" of God's love, a line of avatars that also included Krishna, the Buddha, Jesus Christ, and Mohammad.[27] There was also T. Halbert of London. She had been a Christian for many years before coming to the realization that "all religions – such as Buddhism, the Jewish Faith, Islam, etc. – taught the same spiritual truths. Then I came across the Bahá'í World faith … and found the answer to the predicament of religious thought today."[28] The answer, in her mind, was to empty religion of divisive doctrines to preserve its spiritual authenticity. Joining the Bahá'í faith was just one way of doing that. Muggeridge's anti-institutional Christianity reflected just the kind of unencumbered spirituality that she was looking for. The spiritual hybridity reflected in Ginsberg, Corfe, and Halbert instantiated the ongoing reconstitution of religious character in the Anglophone world generally, while also reflecting widespread assumptions about the future of Christianity in it. The attitudes represented here played a fundamental role in weakening the degree to which young people were enculturated to a tightly knit, doctrinally defined Christian nation.[29]

Rejecting one's Christian upbringing and experiencing the multiculturalism that resulted from immigration, affluence, and the media inaugurated a flurry of creativity in the arts and philosophy. For many it was a liberating experience to find oneself in a culture no longer defined by Christian institutions. Not least of all were those professing "no religion," whose numbers rose significantly in all Western societies after 1960.[30] Callum Brown's project of writing a history of "no religion" as the "growth of a positive ideology" calls for recognition that "a person's drift from a religion within a religious society … was also an act or journey of adventurous rejection – involving neglect of family values (frequently involving revolt against parents), dismissal of school compulsion, and a counter-cultural revolt."[31] For readers like Halbert and Corfe, the "journey of adventurous rejection" felt like blissful freedom from the chains of oppressive religion. Yet, this was not the case with everyone. This was especially true among those atheists and agnostics who had written a fan letter to Muggeridge, and who expressed difficulty in crafting their identity after leaving the religion of their youth. H. Wilman of Potters Bar, Hertfordshire, is typical.[32] He had rejected Christianity once he concluded that religion was just an expression of humanity's need to imbue meaning and order on those things outside its control. Prayer, he concluded, was a highly effective therapeutic technique, but this was only because it stimulated the necessary bio-chemical responses in the brain to cope with trauma. Wilman's crisis of faith had lasted eight years – his questioning of the "fundamentals of religious belief" that he had learned in his youth had led to an "open mind" that was liberated by evidence, reason, and logic – all those things that he found wanting in his Christian upbringing.[33] The other side of enlightenment, however, was "a terrifying feeling of vacuousness, pointlessness, of there being no rhyme or reason, direction or purpose, to my life or

those of my fellow men. The fabric of my life had been built upon
sand – quicksand."[34] The hopeful liberation and optimistic anticipa-
tions of new beginnings was certainly a prominent aspect of those
decades, but Wilman is a reminder that Christianity's detractors also
experienced trauma in the religious crisis of the 1960s and 1970s.
Charles Taylor has defined a "Secular Age" as one in which Christianity is only one option among many, but that sometimes resulted in a
crippling number of choices available with which to define oneself.
Oftentimes Christianity was people's chief frame of reference, so that
they drew liberally from its resources even as they rejected its teachings as untenable.

But why Muggeridge of all people? His alliance with moral activists
like Mary Whitehouse and his involvement in the Nationwide Festival of Light, together with his recurrent lambasting of permissiveness
in society, might give the impression that he was strict about his theology, too. Moral strictness often derives from theological conservatism, but the two did not go hand in hand for Muggeridge. His
conversion to Christianity did not include an immediate jump to
orthodoxy. Indeed, *Jesus Rediscovered*, itself a chronicle of Muggeridge's spiritual development during the 1960s, included his initial
skepticism about standard-fare teachings of Christian orthodoxy, such
as the Virgin Birth, the divinity of Christ, and a literal death and resurrection. He admitted the irony of his current state of mind: "I find
myself praising a position I cannot uphold, enchanted by a religion I
cannot believe, putting all my hope in a faith I do not have."[35] It was
by only accepting an allegorical interpretation of Christianity's central tenets that he was able to come to terms with this dilemma. This
early stance against conventional Christianity was animated, at least
in part, by its doctrinal specificity. It is not a coincidence that Muggeridge's criticisms of institutional Christianity during the 1960s and
after was directed primarily at its evolving positions on morality. The
idea of debating esoteric points of theology was foreign to him. It was
not until the mid-1970s (around the time he published *Jesus: The Man
Who Lives*) that he arrived at a more creedal version of Christian theology. Yet, even then, doctrinal difference was not altogether important to him. In 1977, while delivering his lectures, which would
become *Christ and the Media*, Muggeridge said there really was not
any substantial difference between "Roman Catholics or Anglicans or
Jehovah's Witnesses." As he saw it, "All the different categories we have

devised just don't apply. There is but one category: our common fellowship in Christ."[36]

What drove Muggeridge's conclusion was the fundamental conviction that everyone must ultimately find out for themselves the content of their religious life. Not only was this at the heart of his anti-institutionalism, it was the basic attitude shaped his theology. Authentic faith could not be taught – it had to be experienced. Despite Muggeridge's ongoing project of defining himself apart from trends of modern society, he had a great deal in common with it. It is not that Muggeridge, after accepting Christian orthodoxy, ultimately was disingenuous in his confession in doctrines like Jesus' divinity or the Virgin Birth. Rather, Muggeridge's own personal experience taught him that one had to arrive at such convictions on one's own. He sensed, and was a participant in, the hyper-individualism that animated postwar religious culture. The popular individualism that characterized the 1970s had "multiple political and cultural valences" – but there were religious valences, too.[37] Even though Muggeridge was a gadfly who denounced everything from the pill to Monty Python, the basic attitude of popular individualism was still a prominent feature in Muggeridge's theology.

Nonetheless, practising popular individualism does not mean people practise their religion or secularity in isolation. Most of Muggeridge's religiously plural readers spent their letters emphasizing how they saw him as a fellow traveller on a journey of self-discovery, wherever it might lead. T.L. Williams thought that he and Muggeridge were in harmony when he confirmed that he believed authentic spirituality was "not something that can be taught or preached."[38] Williams had left Christianity, but he still saw Jesus as someone worth emulating. For the most part, Muggeridge's non-Christian readers came from a similar background as Williams. The majority were raised in a religious household, but then joined another religion or left Christianity altogether. Seldom were his readers born into a religion other than Christianity. R. Poole of London is a good example of this. His seven-page letter described how in his youth he looked to find meaning and purpose by joining various causes – at one point even travelling to South America to fight in political liberation movements. The turning point was reading *Jesus Rediscovered*, which "filled me with strength and resolve and soon freed me from the wells of man-made ideas in which I had become deeply entangled."[39] As he reflected on Muggeridge's role in his spiritual journey, he confessed that it was "easy to believe that my hand was guided along the book shelf, because from the first instant of reading I felt myself filled with a joy that I had unknowingly longed for all my life but never experienced."[40] Ultimately, however, Muggeridge was just one important step among many on his personal journey to spiritual enlightenment. What he found inspiring was that Muggeridge had found spiritual meaning in his life after so many years without it. Hitchens once suggested that Muggeridge should be understood as a "divine discontent,"[41] an apt description for someone who, at least between the 1960s and 1982, was on a constant mission for deeper spirituality outside of an institutional framework. Poole thought of his own life as running parallel to Muggeridge's, though his journey ended with a home in the Bahá'í Faith. His letter included not only a narrative of how he found it, but something of a rough apologetic of his new religion, even hoping that Muggeridge might spread its message.[42] The emphasis in the Bahá'í Faith on the equality of humanity and fundamental unity of religion throughout the world generated in Poole a freedom to seek out spiritual inspiration wherever it could be found. This perhaps explains why he told Muggeridge, "I feel so drawn towards you, perhaps as one person whose life has taken the form of an unfettered search for Truth."[43]

Muggeridge's response to Poole reveals much about his position on the various ways that someone could arrive at a sense of spiritual meaning. He wrote, "Thank you so much for your very interesting letter. I am not personally familiar with the Persian cult you write about so I don't believe I would be able to help much in propagating it. However, after reading your letter and the enclosure, I feel that now I know a little and feel sure that your own devotion is not misplaced."[44] Muggeridge wrote this response in 1977, several years after he had embraced the traditional tenets of Christianity. From someone who wrote and spoke on so many occasions of berating the cultural revolutions of the 1960s and 1970s, his response to this Bahá'í convert was not just a matter of being polite. It aligned with his principle that every person's spiritual formation was different and that doctrinal rectitude, while important, was not the priority.

The same year that Poole sent his letter, Muggeridge received a note from I.S. Stoby of St Helier on the island of Jersey. Her letter complained of her daughter, who had left the Christian faith and was experimenting with various aspects of Eastern religions (though she does not specify which). Stoby hoped that since Muggeridge was a convert to Christianity himself, he might be able to provide some advice on how to convince her daughter to return to Christianity and, by extension, their church.[45] Muggeridge's response was not what she asked for and, in fact, does more to confirm the daughter's choices than the mother's wishes.

> I am so sorry to hear of your troubles. A lot of young people today, in a way to their credit, find contemporary life intolerable and because of the poor leadership often of the Christian Churches, turn to these eastern cults. I have lived some years in India myself and I think I can assure you that your daughter is not likely to come to any serious harm and may even be helped in sorting herself out. I can imagine how painful it must be for you but good may come of it.[46]

Muggeridge's response reflected his attitude that, though Christianity was his confession, each person must ultimately arrive at their own conclusions about the content of their faith as they carried out their reflexive projects. This perhaps explains why people of such religiously plural backgrounds saw Muggeridge as an authentic figure whose self-mastery they could emulate.

Yet it was in times of crisis without anywhere else to turn that drew people to Muggeridge's spiritual confidence. A poignant example is J.W. Atkins, a Sheffield bartender:

> Dear Mr. Muggeridge,
> I am writing this letter at 7:00AM after having identified the bodies of two friends who were killed in a car crash earlier this morning. I am obviously very shocked – and you may ask why a letter to you. I am NOT a Christian – I have never believed in "life after death" as I totally question the validity of Christian beliefs based on assumptions over 2000 years ago. I desperately want to believe in "something" – something to follow after my own death. I believe you were a non-Christian for most of your life and then suddenly changed your beliefs. I would like to know why – what motivated you to change your mind (I fully realize your reasons wouldn't be mine) but I guess I need an "intellectual shoulder" to lean on at this moment. I admire you very much – the reason for writing to you and I would value a reply.[47]

We do not have a copy of Muggeridge's reply, but Atkin's second letter, dated four months later, thanked Muggeridge for sending him a
copy of *Jesus Rediscovered*.[48] It would appear that in those four months,
Atkins transitioned from atheism to some form of agnosticism. He
did not know if there was a God, but he admitted to praying for therapeutic reasons when he felt like it. He had since lost his job and was
trying to pay his bills by working two part-time jobs, adding on hours
as a janitor at a local factory. Ultimately, *Jesus Rediscovered* was not convincing to him because he felt Christianity did not make the world
any better. His lot included dead friends and financial hardship. He
continued that "Religion to me doesn't seem to represent reality, a
mere belief in something just doesn't seem to answer our problems
let alone provide the answer for them ... We are surrounded by a society which doesn't care."[49]

Atkins was typical of Muggeridge's atheist and agnostic readers,
who tended to write because of some intense struggle in their lives.
The difficult circumstances he was then facing – as he seems to
admit – were what drove him to contact Muggeridge for a spiritual
take on his problems. He was looking for answers, and even enter-
tained religious sources, but that did not mean he was seeking
to become religious himself. *Jesus Rediscovered*, and Malcolm Muggeridge by extension, functioned as intellectual and cultural resources
through which he wrestled with the struggles of his own life. It is a
clear example, not of growing secularization, but of how someone
who defined himself outside of Christianity participated in a continual process of reconstituting his own identity in the crucible of personal crisis. Ammerman has noted that those on the "margins of
organized religion" and the "spiritually disengaged" often lost their
faith not because of some typical "secularization story," but because of
"a failure to connect the vicissitudes of an individual life with the spiritual resources of a faith tradition."[50] Community is important for the
religious and irreligious alike. Brown points to the variety of organizations that atheists and agnostics joined to form a sense of belonging
throughout their lives.[51] We see here a similar move among these
readers, though for them it was Muggeridge himself rather than a
freethinking society. Regardless of their religious or irreligious background, they used reading and writing to establish community as they
worked through their spiritual questionings.

This was precisely what R. Hunter did as she embarked on a multi-
year search for spiritual meaning. She had read a number of Mug-

geridge's writings while studying at the University of Aberdeen, which led her to attend a public lecture he delivered at Marischal College in 1968. She wrote him a letter mostly because she had not been able to pluck up the courage to ask him a question during the Q&A session. It was easier to express herself in writing rather than face the pressures of a live audience. She struggled with finding meaning in her life and thought it rather perplexing that Muggeridge displayed such confidence in his beliefs:

> My question would have been how can you be so sure that there is in fact a god? I try to practise Christian ethics in my daily life simply because I think they speak of utter truth and beauty and know that had I known Christ I should have loved him dearly and would have undoubtedly been a "follower" of Him. I was interested in the talk of modern knowledge being capable of driving us mad. I am aware of this increasingly and times, more and more frequently, just because I have no faith whatsoever, [and] feel utterly suicidal ...
>
> Can you possibly help me in this? I have talked to so many theologians but [they] just seem to be talking into a dark vacuum. I cannot accept the modern church at all and if I were ever to believe that Christ were the son of god I doubt I could worship him through a church medium.[52]

She continued to describe her doubts that Jesus could really be anything more than "one of the greatest men the world has ever had in it." In her youth, she had been a "fervent" believer, but once she lost the feelings of "peace and serenity" that had accompanied her faith, it seemed like she had become something of a fraudulent Christian:

> If I am sure there is no god – while yet longing with my whole being to believe in Him, and therefore life taking on a completely futile, meaningless and hopeless form. Why cannot I commit suicide? I see this objectively. The very beauty all around me, which I love so much, becomes almost unbearable because it, too, seems without point. The only fact which has stopped me committing suicide has been the knowledge of my parents love for me and their need of me ... but even this sometimes seems to become less sharp in its "staying power" and I am so afraid. Could it not be that Man's need for a God is so

great that he has simply created God in his own image to satisfy this great need?[53]

Muggeridge was moved enough by Hunter's letter that he wrote her twice within the next two weeks. We do not have the first letter he sent, but we do have the second and it is worth quoting in full.

> Dear [R.],
>     I read your letter over again when I got back here and was more than ever impressed with it.
>     I am getting my bookshop to send you the Simone Weil book I referred to in my other note because I think she was so exactly in your case.
>     There is never any occasion to despair, I promise you. I can give you this assurance with the utmost confidence from forty years, away, as it were.
>     Behind our lives and behind the universe itself there is a principle of unity, a God, expressive of love not hate or indifference, creativity not destruction, light not darkness. It is possible to establish contact with this God through the living person of Christ. This is what the Christian religion is about.
>     These may seem just empty words to you, but they are not. They're the only truth there is.
>     Please write again if you feel like it.[54]

Why does Muggeridge's letter here seem to take on such a different tone than what he sent to Stoby and Poole? The answer lies in what his fans were looking for. Poole had found confidence in the Bahá'í Faith and so did not write to Muggeridge for any actual spiritual guidance. His letter told of the influence *Jesus Rediscovered* already had on his spiritual journey. His sought to articulate the similarity between Muggeridge's spiritual development and his own, drawing the same kind of life-story parallels that hundreds of Christians had (explored in chapter 1). Muggeridge's reply thereby met Poole where he was, responding with tolerance rather than taking the correspondence as an opportunity to convince him to return to his Christian roots. Stoby's letter requested the very thing that Muggeridge found unacceptable within institutional Christianity: she wanted Muggeridge to instruct her daughter on why she ought to return to the church of her youth. But Muggeridge's theology was consistent in that the content of one's faith could not be taught. That is why he was confident "some good may come" out of Stoby's daughter experimenting with various Eastern religions. But what about Hunter? Here he tells her Christianity is "the only truth there is." Was Muggeridge talking out of both sides of his mouth? What makes Hunter different from either Stoby or Poole is that she was actively seeking out his advice, whereas Poole and Stoby were not. In this case, Hunter invited Muggeridge to be an active participant in the self-fashioning of her religious identity. The fact that she claimed to be depressed and suicidal added a sense of urgency to the message Muggeridge wanted to her to have. That is why he sent two letters in such a short time. The layered and complex responses that Muggeridge wrote reveals in another context how deeply attached Muggeridge was to his fans. It was not the vainglorious conceit of a public figure who was in desperate need of validation. These letters were the result of a genuine concern for the people whose lives his books changed.

It would be over a year before Muggeridge received another letter from Hunter. She sent her next reply in August of 1969, though Muggeridge was travelling at the time, so he did not receive it until September. Between her first and second letter she had experienced several momentous changes in her life. She took a break from school, married a physics lecturer who happened to share her agnosticism, and moved to London where they purchased a flat in Forest Hill.[55] She still struggled with questions of meaning and purpose, but she appeared to have been slowly working through her troubles by alternative methods than what Muggeridge had advised. She was thankful that Muggeridge had sent her Weil's classic, *Waiting on God*, and had even read it, but it did not do what Muggeridge had hoped. She affirmed,

> I am still an agnostic and seem to see no other way of being. I wonder if you know Th. Hardy's poetry; I seem able to identify well with him – an agnostic with joy and a feeling of wholeness in nature but sad because it all seems to pass …
> I had a breakdown ~ 6 weeks ago and have been in the Maudsley since but seem to be on the "mend" and should be discharged in 2 weeks' time.[56]

Whatever the exact causes of her mental breakdown, she and her husband felt it was necessary to find a quieter place to live than London, so they purchased a house near Ware, about thirty miles north of the city. Meeten (née Hunter) sent her letter mostly to thank him for the book, and expressed some optimism at the thought of enrolling in the nearest university to finish her degree. At this point, she did not want or need Muggeridge's guidance as she had while living in Aberdeen. There is sense of finality at the end of her reply: "That's all my news. In your letter of 11th June '68 you said to write if I felt like it and I do today but am sorry not to have felt like it before so that I am rather late in thanking you for your book and letter."[57] One gets the sense that she was perhaps writing out of a sense of duty than any earnest desire to continue correspondence.

Muggeridge, it would seem, was more invested in their relationship than she was. After all, he wrote more letters to her than she did to him:

Dear [R.],

I was delighted to get your letter. Actually, I received it rather belatedly because I have been away.

You have often been in my mind after the very sweet way you wrote to me from Aberdeen and I have wondered how you were getting along.

Yes, I love Thomas Hardy's poetry too, but it only conveys part of the illumination one can find in life. For the whole, one has to go to a poet like Blake or Herbert.

I am so sorry about your breakdown and hope by now it's all over. Your husband sounds a most delightful man and I wish very much you would both come and see us one of these days. Please write again when you feel like it.[58]

Muggeridge signed the letter "affectionately," a complementary close he rarely used when writing to fans. But Muggeridge's emotional attachment is telling for other reasons. First is his apology at a late reply, even when it took a year for Meeten to send her second letter. It is significant that she was often on his mind given all of the fan mail that Muggeridge received each year. After all, he received roughly three letters *every day* between 1966 and his formal entry into the Catholic Church in 1982. That means Muggeridge received just about one thousand fan letters between the two Meeten sent. And that does not count the considerable business and personal correspondence he had to rifle through. But the most unusual aspect of the letter is that it was Muggeridge who initiated the idea that Meeten and her husband visit his home in Robertsbridge. As we have seen elsewhere, Muggeridge was certainly happy to oblige a visit when a letter writer requested a chat over tea, but this is a rare instance when it was Muggeridge's idea. Significantly, Muggeridge says nothing to try to convince her that she was mistaken in her agnosticism and ought to trust his advice from his previous letter. One might make the claim that his preference for William Blake and George Herbert over Thomas Hardy was a subtle form of Christian apologetics, but, then again, subtlety really was not Muggeridge's style. As far as we know, Meeten did not respond to Muggeridge's letter or accept his invitation to visit. There was nothing to indicate that in Muggeridge's date books and, as we have seen, he *did* put meetings with fans on his calendar when they wanted to visit.[59] One way to explain this correspondence is to recognize that the context in which Meeten wrote to Muggeridge was one of distress. Muggeridge was an important resource as she wrestled with faith, doubt, and meaning. Yet, by her second letter, that was ending. Like other readers – regardless of religious or irreligious background – she saw Muggeridge as a religious authority whom she could use to make sense of herself and the world around her, even if only for a brief moment.

## DECLINE AND SOCIAL ACTIVISM

Dozens of others similarly read Muggeridge's books and wrote letters. Readers who did not agree with Muggeridge's Christian faith nonetheless saw him as one whose life ran parallel to their own and, for that reason, felt they could tap him as a spiritual authority. They were likewise critical of institutional Christianity, and it often drove them to find spiritual solace in a different religious tradition altogether or none at all. And, like many of Muggeridge's Christian readers, they used reading and writing to engage with the notion that Christianity and Western civilization were in a state of decline. Take T. Foster, who was a student at the University of Victoria in 1974 when he read *Jesus Rediscovered*. His main reason for writing was that he was relieved to find that he was not the only one who thought the entire "world has gone mad."

I first started asking myself, "what the hell is going on in this world," about two years ago. Well, two years ago I started looking for that answer. I found it soon enough, in meditation. I was taught to meditate by ... Maharishi, and have been doing so (meditation) for the last year and a half ... In fact, he is doing the job that the church isn't. Well anyway, during the past year, I've been going around to different meditation groups and what I have found is a lot of good people. The people that used to be filling the churches.[60]

It was through reading Muggeridge that Foster was "introduced to the guru of gurus, Jesus Christ." No thanks to "all the crap" inside institutional Christianity that made it "so hard to find out what the teachings of Christ are." Muggeridge and Maharishi were better teachers, and it seemed obvious to him that with the current leadership, it was doubtful the "church [could] ever hope to survive."[61] A key difference between those Christian readers who internalized Muggeridge's popularized secularization thesis and Foster was that he was not at all disturbed by it. All it did was justify even more his decision to practise Transcendental Meditation. Foster's experience exhibited how religion existed in the counterculture. His thoughts were almost exactly those of the Beatle George Harrison: "it was only through India and through Hinduism and through yogis and through meditation that I learned about Christ and what Christ really meant and stood for."[62] A deeper, more spiritual experience was a way to escape the glum conventions of the church and, by consequence, the feeling they were dying.

For the most part, readers accepted as fact they were living in a period of Christianity's decline, but they fundamentally disagreed with Muggeridge's pessimism. The nineteen-year-old agnostic J. Knox was one reader who simply would not allow declinism to colonize his mind. He was a student at the University of Aberdeen and remained highly critical of the culture he inhabited. It was reading *Jesus Rediscovered* that made him see Muggeridge as a kindred spirit who also wished to "move away from the sordid, materialistic world we live in."[63] At the same time, he was not ready to wallow in glum resignation.

My youth impels me to be hopeful and to doubt your fascinating prophecy of the end of our civilization. While many of the signs exist, as you quite rightly say, you do not take account of the rate at which our present day civilization can change. Morals and beliefs have changed very quickly over the past few decades ... so there is no reason to suppose they cannot change again and this time more quickly. Besides I could not live with your morbid belief that this civilization (which I admire and even love) is going to completely destruct itself ... I live for tomorrow, I don't live my student life from day to day, I live it and work at it because I am hopeful of an exciting useful life in the years ahead and if that means I have to reform or change this civilization (or at least give a tiny helping hand to that change) then so much the better.[64]

Others were not quite as hopeful as Knox that youthful idealism and a stiff upper lip would reform civilization from within. The Australian H. Hout thought the only cure would come from without. Western civilization was dying because its Christian character "did not give the answers to the questions that the generation of today is asking, especially the young generation."[65] "Something has to change if the world is not going to blow itself up," he continued, "so why not reach out beyond our Church and see what the East has to tell us?" After all, a shift to Eastern religions had worked for Hout in his own life, so why would it not work on a grander scale? For about the last year Hout had practised Transcendental Meditation and found that "it has done me a lot of good. This kind of meditation really yields up this extra, vital energy from somewhere deep inside, and somehow I feel brighter, more energetic and inwardly more peaceful than ever." In addition to practising Transcendental Meditation, Hout informed Muggeridge: "after many years of seeking, [I] have become a dedicated follower of Meher Baba, whose teachings include all the wisdom of all the great religions of the world." Spiritual inclusiveness provided the tools for the West to "solve all problems and difficulties." Hout had to ask:

Why don't we admit that the East is far more advanced in spiritual matters and try to learn from them and eventually adopt their superior knowledge in our way of life? I believe that the future of the West can only be saved by a close relationship with the East. We have so much to give and learn! I don't agree at all with the hippy movement, but I am convinced that this movement contains the germs of the future of the whole world and they are more right than most of us think![66]

In each of these three letters, the reader wished either to escape the decline of civilization or to reverse it. All of the strategies in the reader's minds centred on avoiding excessive materialism in some way, shape, or form. On this count, they closely aligned with Muggeridge, who consistently lambasted the material excess of "modern life." One of his responses was to produce a number of documentaries that focused on poor pilgrims to Lourdes, monks with nothing but a hard floor as a bed, and, most famously, a wizened old woman with a house for the dying in India. Muggeridge's response to rising affluence was to rediscover poverty and place a spotlight on methods of care that did not depend on the machinery of the state.

When Muggeridge's non-Christian readers picked up *Something Beautiful for God*, their responses reflected the same tensions surrounding the question of the welfare state and poverty discussed in the previous chapter. Callum Brown has identified a trend that support for human rights was a sufficient cause for losing one's religion, and this bears out among Muggeridge's fans.[67] There were those who thought Muggeridge's views of poverty and the work of Mother Teresa were reprehensible alternatives to a modern welfare state that actually worked to alleviate suffering. P. Dawson was an agnostic whose personal experiences led her to see *Something Beautiful for God* as a farce.

> My main criticism on reading your book "Something Beautiful for God" was exactly this, something beautiful for God? Why not "Something beautiful for Humanity?" Why does Mother Theresa [*sic*] have to find Christ in each of her poor? Why the insistence throughout the book that everything must be done because of Christ, as if, if one does something for mere humane reasons, it is not only enough but does not work.
>
> I cannot agree, I cannot agree that an atheist & an agnostic … cannot bring joy, warmth, love and hope to the suffering, unloved and uncared for, for no other reason than love of that fellow human and human compassion.[68]

Dawson had worked in the health care industry for years and had enough personal experience with dying loved ones to see Muggeridge's view of poverty as sheer folly. Her own daughter had come close to death on several occasions as an infant and, though she survived, reflecting on this confirmed her sense that Muggeridge was entirely out of touch with reality. "It is very fine to quote the hackneyed and rather empty words about God taking care of even the smallest bird," but "has anyone actually told this to those starving children with pot bellies, stick limbs and empty expressionless eyes, where suffering has long since obliterated hope?"[69] Dawson did not need Muggeridge or Mother Teresa to rediscover poverty and suffering in the world – she already had an all too clear understanding of it. There was nothing redemptive or beautiful about it. She threw her support behind those who pursued practical measures for health care (contraceptives) with sensible motivations (for the good of humanity). On her account, the alternative was to trust a warped sense of piety that resulted in only "more of this suffering, more starving children who even in conception clutch fiercely at the flickering flame of life so uselessly."[70]

Muggeridge's arguments in *Something Beautiful for God* were jarring to Dawson chiefly because she had forged her convictions on welfare and poverty through close interactions with death and suffering. To suggest that, in the words of Muggeridge, poverty and suffering "exemplify and enhance our human condition" was offensive in light of what she had experienced firsthand.[71] Yet, having no religion did not necessarily result in a critical view of Mother Teresa and poverty. More important was each reader's personal interactions with these issues throughout their own life. This helps to explain why another agnostic, J. Baweden, wrote to Muggeridge to express her "deep appreciation of your publication, recording the dedicated life and work of Mother Teresa and her community."[72] Her letter also underscores the autobiographical nature of Muggeridge's fan mail more generally, because she felt the need to provide "personal details, which I *only* mention to emphasize the impact and sincerity of your book."[73] Baweden explained that she did not have a religious upbringing, and though she admired the fellowship of the church communities she observed, she never could imagine herself joining one for the simple reason that it would be intellectually dishonest for her to do so without knowing whether God existed. The only reason she stepped into the library at Upton Hall Convent at Wirral and checked out *Something Beautiful for God* was because of her daughter, Gail.

My only dearest daughter most happily (without influence or encouragement) always believed, asked to be Christened when she was five in a Church of England in Suffolk, and chose to become a Catholic at sixteen. There were just the two of us and she tried to help me believe, and I felt as a child when she spoke. At nineteen (although it must have always been there) she was diagnosed as being schizophrenic, and suffered a deep and continual mental depression.[74]

Baweden continued to explain how hospital staff failed to help her daughter, which led her to insist on her returning home so she could move on with her life. But since Baweden worked as a teacher full time, she had difficulty giving her daughter the attention she needed. Gail's mental condition continued to deteriorate and drove her to take her own life. Baweden's letter is full of guilt and regret that this might not have happened if only she had given her daughter more love and attention. Living through this personal hell was what made Baweden feel that "I may understand *a little* the desperate loneliness of those whom Mother Teresa and her Sisters *love*, and thus give the one and only possible form of happiness to them before they die."[75] Knowing that Mother Teresa and the Missionaries of Charity were doing their work halfway around the world somehow helped Baweden to come to terms with the loss of her daughter. She had come to accept death as an inevitable part of life that no amount of welfare or medical skill could prevent.

Given their personal histories, the contrast between Dawson and Baweden's reading of *Something Beautiful for God* is instructive. Both had daughters who suffered from serious medical conditions. Dawson's daughter went on to live, thereby putting into stark relief for her just how abhorrent Muggeridge's highly idealized vision of suffering was. In her case, the instruments of the welfare state had worked remarkably well. What is more, she had witnessed a great deal of people suffer needlessly throughout her career. Baweden, on the other hand, blamed herself for her daughter's death. Even though Baweden's daughter was in a hospital's care for a time, she implied that the welfare state – like Baweden herself – did not provide the kind of emotional care her daughter needed. Stepping into a library run by the church her daughter had joined is telling, too. She, like so many other readers, was looking for answers at a moment of crisis and it just so happened that Muggeridge's book was what she checked out.

Baweden's reading of *Something Beautiful for God* was therapeutic because it cast her suffering into a context in which it made sense. It also helped her cope with the loss to know that there were people providing the type of care she felt her daughter missed. What both of these deeply emotional letters seem to suggest is that their agnosticism did not necessarily cause them to reject Muggeridge's view of poverty and suffering, even if Dawson implied as much. Much more important were their own personal, idiosyncratic experiences, which they brought to bear on the subject matter they read. In both cases, however, reading and writing formed the textual arena in which they mobilized, named, communicated, and regulated their emotions. Though in virtual agreement religiously, the idiosyncrasies of their personal lives had the more formative impact on how they interacted with Muggeridge's texts.

## CONCLUSION

For these readers, religion was by no means a zero-sum game and their letters raise a number of implications for further consideration. It is understood that religious, cultural, and ideological pluralism in the 1960s and 1970s created an environment in which readers could forge new identities. Yet these letters show just how emotionally fraught this process was. Just like with Muggeridge's Christian fans, for these readers, reading and letter writing were emotional practices through which they could define who they were, what they stood for, and to what end they would direct their lives. This dynamic was felt as they wrestled with the role of the institutional church, the specter of decline in religion and society, and the role of poverty, charity, and the welfare state. Even if they did not believe in Christianity – in many cases remaining hostile to it – they nonetheless turned to one of its most outspoken apologists as they wrestled with personal challenges. As they did so, they felt that Muggeridge's spiritual authenticity was something to emulate or that they could depend on in time of need, even if only for a brief time. Muggeridge was their trusty companion on the path towards alternative spirituality or as they left religion altogether. That is why an atheist teenager from London could read *Jesus Rediscovered* and admit in a personal letter to Muggeridge, "your voice is strong inside me" and that he felt "seldom unconscious of it."[76] It is why an agnostic bookshop attendant from Edinburgh could confess, "For some reason which I cannot understand, I know that you will be able to help me in some way to come to some understanding about [the] question of religion."[77] And it is why another could declare, "I have no religion, but you have the power to bring me nearer to what I feel religion could be."[78] These readers give weight to the interpretation of postwar religious culture not as a simple story of Christianity's linear decline, but rather as one that was opening up to "multiple modernities," wherein secular and diverse religious perspectives could coexist in a state of "continual constitution and reconstitution."[79] This dynamic underscores the kind of spiritual eclecticism adopted in the postwar Anglophone world as ordinary people left their churches in droves. Their life stories were shaped by a kind of spiritual bricolage – a secular hybridity – in which readers synthesized beliefs and practices as they saw fit and as they needed it. These letters thus underscore the centrality of attending to the specificity and unexpected character of lived experience as we gauge the nature of religious change.

# Conclusion

On 27 November 1982, Malcolm and Kitty Muggeridge became members of the Roman Catholic Church. Richard Ingrams, one of Muggeridge's biographers, suggested, "to anyone who had followed Malcolm's career over the years, [his conversion] came as a logical conclusion."[1] Gregory Wolfe likewise described the event as though it were embedded within the internal logic of his developing faith:

> He had been an outsider and a non-participant for so long that his desire for communion finally outweighed his reluctance to join in ... Getting down on his knees with his fellow men was the final step toward communion and humility and away from loneliness and pride. At the altar rail in Our Lady, Help of Christians, he had come home. Having walked along the Emmaus Road for so long, he came to know his Lord in the breaking of bread.[2]

It would seem the consensus among Muggeridge's biographers is that his spiritual life ultimately followed the plot of the "quest." The imagery of taking a "final step" on the "Emmaus Road" and arriving "home" rhetorically suggests Muggeridge's life had an inevitable destination in Rome. It is true that throughout his career Muggeridge had worked closely with Roman Catholics – reading them, studying them, and writing for them. It is also true that he deeply admired the rich history of the Roman Catholic Church and felt a great deal of comfort from imbibing its mystical tradition. And for years his Roman Catholic fans sent him letters imploring him to join their church, especially after he published *Something Beautiful for God*. A selective reading of his fan mail might confirm the argument that his conversion was, indeed, a "logical conclusion." As we might expect, his conversion generated considerable support from Roman Catholics. In the following months, he received hundreds of letters from fans who welcomed him into their church, telling him how it was an answer to their prayers, how they knew it was going to happen all along, and so on.

But we would do well to remember that hindsight affords a certain weight of inevitability that was not necessarily felt in the everyday experiences of those we study. In the years and months leading up to it, Muggeridge's conversion was only one logical conclusion among many. Even though the content of his faith became increasingly aligned with Christian orthodoxy in the 1970s, he was consistent in remaining outside of institutional Christianity since first publicly identifying as a Christian in the mid-1960s. Yes, Roman Catholics were particularly zealous in their attempt to coax him to the fold, but so too were evangelicals, Anglicans, Baptists, Methodists, and a myriad of other Christian and non-Christian readers who wished to count Muggeridge among their own. The fact that his entry into the Roman Catholic Church came as a shock even to close friends and family members, let alone the press and general public, is a good reminder that Muggeridge's contemporaries did not see it as inevitable by any stretch of the imagination. The first biography of Muggeridge, which Ian Hunter published in 1980, said nothing that would have anticipated him joining the Catholic Church in less than two years' time. What is more is that whenever anyone asked Muggeridge why he would not join the Roman Catholic Church when he seemed to have such admiration for it, he consistently provided the same answer: he simply could not join a church that he felt was compromising with permissiveness in society.[3] His admiration for its history was held in check by knowing that "it went on crusades, it set up an inquisition, it installed scandalous Popes and countenanced monstrous iniquities ... In the mouthpiece of God on earth, belonging not just to history, but to everlasting truth, they are not to be defended."[4] Let alone to be joined. As late as 31 August 1981, Muggeridge replied to one inquisitive Roman Catholic fan named G. Porter that he was in exactly the same frame of mind as Simone Weil who, while identifying as a Christian, could not bring herself to join the church because of strong disagreement with its dogma. Muggeridge's faith drew upon Christianity's mystical traditions. Indeed, there was a certain impulsiveness to Muggeridge's conversion to Roman Catholicism that underlines just how unexpected it was. It was only mere weeks before his November 1982 reception into the church that Muggeridge began formal religious instruction under Father Bidone. Normally such a process might take several months or up to a year. Wolfe notes that it was chiefly because of the brevity of this process that so few people knew about his conversion before it was reported in the *Times*.

In statistical terms, the years following Muggeridge's conversion correlated to a general decrease in the number of letters he received from fans. In the eight years between his conversion and passing, Muggeridge received between 2,100 and 2,450 fan letters. This included the hundreds of letters that Roman Catholics sent to welcome him into the fold. If we consider the eight years before his conversion, however, Muggeridge received between 3,900 and 4,550 fan letters. Muggeridge's biographers have attributed his declining public image in the 1980s to his old age and declining productivity, but that only partially explains a 46 per cent drop in letters. In the first place, most of his best-selling books were still in print. A new edition or imprint of *Jesus Rediscovered*, *Something Beautiful for God*, and *Chronicles of Wasted Time* came out every few years, even after his joining the Roman Catholic Church. The drop in fan mail was not due to a lack of circulation of his works. Nor was it owed to a sudden reclusiveness on Muggeridge's part. He was still in good enough shape to appear on television after his conversion (interviewing, for instance, Aleksandr Solzhenitsyn on the BBC in 1983), as well as to see the publication of several more books, such as *Vintage Muggeridge* (1984), *My Life in Pictures* (1987), and *Picture Palace* (1987). Ingrams makes the additional argument that in his old age, Muggeridge was running out of things to say, and so his lack of originality played a role in his dwindling public reputation. However, that was not anything stylistically new for Muggeridge. He had a knack for returning to the same arguments, phrases, and talking points repeatedly in multiple contexts. He was a television personality, after all. His consistency made it so that people thought they knew what they could expect. That was partially why he was able to so successfully exploit print, sound, and visual media. He formed a coherent public image that traversed them all. Yet, none of those books published after November of 1982 resulted in the same kind of fan response he received during the 1960s and 1970s.

Age and energy are important, but we cannot discount the role that his conversion played in disrupting the politics of his literary reputation. For one thing, he no longer lambasted hierarchies and clerical hypocrisy, a trope that he had repeated for decades. In effect, what his conversion did was to transform him from being a symbol of anti-institutional Christianity to being one who exemplified the continued allure of the Catholic Church in a "secular age." He also began to write more so with Catholics in mind, both in the shape his writing took, and the outlets for which he chose to write.[5] The move confused readers and compromised his status as a religious guru among non-Catholics. S. Whipple wrote that he thought he knew who Muggeridge was, but he had to confess: "I cannot understand your recent conversion to Roman Catholicism. Perhaps it is not my business to understand it. I realize you have been influenced by the love Mother Teresa has demonstrated ... but, you have also for years rejected the institutionalized church."[6] D. Roe likewise wrote to say, "Considering statements you have made not all that long ago about the Catholic Church, your decision perplexes me."[7] The reason Roe felt an affinity with Muggeridge was because he thought they both "loathe[d]" the institutional church. His letter was an inquiry for explanation so that he could make sense of such conflicting ideas. In addition, another reader, who was at first inspired to write a letter after reading both *Something Beautiful for God* and *The End of Christendom*, had learnt by "word of mouth" that Muggeridge had become a Catholic. He had to admit, "At the moment, I am unable to reconcile this action with some of the things you wrote in these two books. It is not my intention to challenge your latest step of faith in any way ... but I would be most appreciative of hearing from you personally as to how this ... came to be."[8]

If the decision caused puzzlement in some, it evoked a deep disappointment in others. J. Woodbury put it most strongly when he sent his letter two weeks after learning Muggeridge was a Roman Catholic:

The ultimate obscenity of your apostasy is that you have destroyed the credibility of your life's work as a person who had the mental courage and intestinal fortitude to look squarely and unafraid into the smug face of people and institutions who have the ineffable

gall to suppose that they alone have a monopoly of wisdom to
direct men's minds and actions. Your invigorating cynical and
skeptical laughter at such arrogant presumption has now turned
to bitter ashes in the throats of those who thought you sincere in
that therapeutic mission.[9]

Woodbury's tumid letter is nonetheless insightful by its recognition that Muggeridge's credibility as a public figure was closely
tied to his iconoclastic reputation. He was popular because he
embodied so well the popular individualism that characterized the
anti-institutional spirit of postwar society. Much more than that,
people believed he was "sincere" in those sentiments. His conversion seemed to Woodbury a flat-out contradiction of his character.
Likewise, the Pennsylvanian fan R. Smith told Muggeridge, "I
always respected your openness and honesty as a Christian," but
now "I can only say how upset and disappointed I am at you and
your wife's decision."[10] A central reason for Smith's frustration was
that he believed the institutional structures of the Catholic
Church prohibited authentic faith. A personal relationship with
God could not depend on the mediator of a priest or pope, and so
Muggeridge's actions hampered his own spirituality. But perhaps
the worst outcome was the effect it would have on others: "you are
a rational figure, and many people may be led astray by your decision. Are you going to put your confidence and trust in God or in
a church?"[11] For readers such as these, Muggeridge's conversion
was less the fulfillment of a lifelong quest, and more a tragedy of
the divided self.[12]

Smith was apt to recognize the spiritual leadership that Muggeridge's readers ascribed to him. However, if fan mail is any indication, his conversion did more to narrow his readership than to
amplify his influence. As we have seen, Muggeridge exemplified what
it meant to embrace both the popular individualism of the 1960s and
1970s, and how one could maintain a Christian faith despite secularization arguments against it. That was what imbued him with
"authenticity" among so many readers of such a wide array of religious backgrounds. But by his joining institutional Christianity, his
readers began to question who he was. Anthony Giddens has made
the important observation that one's identity is deeply dependent on
"the capacity *to keep a particular narrative going*."[13] It is not just about

having a history of where one has been; an identity requires decisions and actions to link that history to an imagined future. Muggeridge was able to communicate a public image of anti-institutional Christian satirist to wonderful effect. Indeed, the narrative of his life was the commodity he packaged and sold in print. Nevertheless, entry into Rome, while fulfilling the utmost desires of his Catholic fans around the world, signalled an abrupt and unexpected redefinition of Malcolm Muggeridge. This was jarring to thousands of others. In short, his conversion broke the narrative that had animated his authenticity for readers around the world.

That can help to explain why Muggeridge received an increase in the number of letters from Catholics just as the total number of fan letters decreased. The sort of fans who had written to Muggeridge between 1966 and November of 1982 often did so for spiritual guidance because they, too, felt estranged from the churches even as they wished to continue practising their faith. They believed (sometimes *because* of Muggeridge) that institutional Christianity was in a state of irreversible decline that required a fundamental reformulation of what it meant to be a Christian. Muggeridge's readers saw his quasi-mystical expression of Christianity as an answer to what that might look like. Yet what did it mean now that he had joined the very thing he said was failing? For many, it meant they no longer saw Muggeridge as a kindred spirit who led a life parallel to their own. An unintended consequence that we can discern from Muggeridge's conversion was that it destabilized the textual community of readers around the world who, in the words of E. Harrington, made up his "apostolate."[14]

Destabilized, but not gone. Muggeridge's refigured religious identity attracted those who could appreciate his bona fide status as a Catholic thinker, just as it repelled those who did not. Yet, people sometimes couldn't care less about who wrote the books they read. What matters most is how it affected them at a particular moment in time. For Muggeridge's readers – whether or not they were Christian – the most common effect his books had was to inspire hope. It was in this spirit that one fan decided to write a letter to Muggeridge to say, "I have just finished reading *Jesus Rediscovered* at one sitting last night having only bought the book yesterday ... I really feel that you have shed a little light for me and that my life will have more meaning henceforward."[15]

This book has explored how ordinary readers around the world came to terms with religious, cultural, and social dynamics between 1966 and 1982. It has shown that Muggeridge's fans recognized him as a friend and kindred spirit whose life ran parallel to their own. In that process, Muggeridge became a surrogate cleric whom readers looked to as their trust in conventional religion declined. Through the emotional practices of reading and writing, they turned to Muggeridge for guidance and help as they wrestled with questions of faith and doubt, the role of the institutional church, permissiveness in society, the specter of decline and secularization, and the proper role of Christianity in social activism. He became an important source for their spiritual self-fashioning in a period that witnessed a fundamental redefinition of what it meant to be modern. These readers had taken for granted the "alternative paradigm" of a monolithic modernity that "humanity's future was radically individualist, expressive, anti-authoritarian, sexually libertarian, global, and, above all, secular."[16] Readers' acceptance of this narrative of a monolithic secular modernity fundamentally redefined how they thought about their religious lives in relation to the societies they inhabited. Even though readers instantiated parts of this narrative by exhibiting popular individualism and by remaining critical of institutional Christianity, its internalization nonetheless led to considerable emotional trauma as they grappled with the implications of this "seismic" shift for their lives of faith. Yet, Muggeridge, by his life story and apologetic writings, offered his Christian readers another alternative paradigm that gave confidence for lived religion in a secular age.

Scholars such as Callum Brown, Hugh McLeod, and Alana Harris have illustrated how analyses from below can enrich our understanding of religion in the postwar period. This book has built upon this trend by centralizing the lived religious history of ordinary readers. It has focused not only on the intellectual content of religious belief, but also upon the practical expressions of its emotional valences. This enables us to recognize more deeply the complexity that is not, and cannot be, counted in the litany of statistics showing that Christianity was losing social significance. Behind these numbers are stories – compelling stories – of how religion was lived, what it meant, and how it felt for people throughout the world. For this reason, this book has been preoccupied with approaching the question of religious change from the angle of the history of reading and the history of

emotions. Both of these fields have undergone significant development in recent years, and this study offers a small step in employing
them to make sense of a long-standing historiographical problem of
depicting the lived religious experience of ordinary people in the
1960s and 1970s. We have seen how fans used reading and writing as
emotional practices to mobilize and name inchoate thoughts and feelings, to communicate strongly felt attitudes to cultural and social
change, and as a medium that regulated their unsettled states of mind.
Remaining sensitive to these transient and complex dynamics within
their spiritual self-fashioning helps us to recognize the manifold ways
people conceived of, and experienced, religious belonging. It shows
that for these readers, their "religion [was] not fixed, unitary, or even
necessarily coherent. Rather, each person's religious practices and the
stories they use to make sense of their lives are continually adapting,
expanding or receding, and ever changing."[17] Here, that dynamic took
place in the form of a textual community shaped by shared concerns
across felt distances.

These distances – including the British Isles, North America, Australasia, among others – underscore the importance of analyzing post-
war religious change in a transnational perspective. Even though most
readers engaged with the British context (not to mention Muggeridge
himself), they felt themselves facing something that expanded beyond
borders. The fact that a comparative analysis of these letters confirms
remarkable convergences in their thoughts, feelings, and attitudes
should encourage future inquiry into how disparate intellectual and
emotional communities developed and spread. Muggeridge's letter
writers – nearly 2,000 of them – were old and young, rich and poor,
and intelligent and nescient, and had a dizzying array of unique life
experiences that inspired them to pick up a religious text, read it, and
write letters that, considered together, dwelt on a number of strikingly
similar themes. As we have seen, these religious questionings refracted
beyond the boundaries of conventional religion, revealing the ongoing interplay between Christianity, atheism, agnosticism, and an array
of world religions in the 1960s and 1970s.

This study also affirms recent scholarship that shows that internalized narratives were crucial for bringing about lasting historical
change during the 1960s and 1970s. While others have shown just
how influential this phenomenon was for religious and cultural
elites, this book has illustrated that it was pervasive among ordinary

readers, too. The most poignant expression of this phenomenon was their general acceptance that Christianity was in the midst of irreversible decline. While some of Muggeridge's readers met this with anticipation and excitement, it left most feeling doubtful, angry, anxious, or forlorn. Whatever the particular emotions of these readers, their letters reveal that Muggeridge's fans were not hapless victims of religious crises in the 1960s and 1970s. On the contrary, they actively participated in this history by choosing to reject religious authority or by fundamentally redefining their own spiritual character instead. Reading and writing were the tools they used to navigate new religious, cultural, and emotional terrains. Thus, these fans made their own history within this dynamic setting in complex and unexpected ways. Their active agency invites further attention to non-institutional expressions of religious belief and practice in the postwar period – especially among conservative Christians, which constituted many, though not all, of Muggeridge's readers.

Finally, this book has offered a snapshot of the profound influence of Malcolm Muggeridge. He appears occasionally in the historiography of postwar religious history, and many note his seemingly ubiquitous presence in the media during the 1950s, 1960s, and 1970s. Yet, apart from a few biographies and a small handful of journal articles and chapters, there is a general lack of sustained engagement with his life and work. Today, he is mostly remembered for his involvement in moral crusades like the Nationwide Festival of Light[18] and his conversion to Catholicism,[19] but these moments represent only a sliver of his place within the religious developments of the twentieth century. And, as this study has shown, his entrance into the Roman Catholic Church marked a significant shift in his reputation among those who recognized him as a kindred spirit after whom they could model their lives. When that happened, Muggeridge was seventy-nine years old. His Roman Catholic identity was only the final chapter of a storied life that exemplified the ambiguities, tensions, innovations, pains, and vitality of religion in the twentieth century. Then again, Christopher Hitchens was close to the mark when he said, "no serious person is without contradictions."[20] Muggeridge's fans related to him for that very reason. He was many things: author, satirist, gadfly, womanizer, contrarian, journalist, television personality, guru, Catholic convert … the list goes on. Yet, his chief significance for thousands of fans was that reading his books and writing him letters helped them to navigate the struggles of understanding themselves and the changing world they inhabited. One fan, M. Hardcastle, might have been speaking for thousands when he picked up pen and paper to tell Muggeridge, "[you are] a microcosm of us all; that in an articulated form you have expressed so well the dilemma of most of us in the twentieth century."[21]

# Appendix:
# Editions of Malcolm Muggeridge's Books,
# circa 1969–90

| Book Name | Language (Format) | Place of Publication | Publisher | Year |
|---|---|---|---|---|
| *Jesus* | English | London | Fontana | 1969 |
| *Rediscovered* | English | Garden City, NY | Doubleday | 1969 |
| | English | Wheaton, IL | Tyndale | 1969 |
| | English | Wheaton, IL | Tyndale | 1971 |
| | Italian | Milan, Italy | Rusconi | 1971 |
| | English | Wheaton, IL | Tyndale | 1972 |
| | English | London | Fontana | 1972 |
| | English | Wheaton, IL | Tyndale | 1974 |
| | English | New York | Doubleday | 1974 |
| | English | London | Collins | 1975 |
| | English | London | Collins | 1976 |
| | English | London | Collins | 1977 |
| | English | London | Collins | 1979 |
| | English | Garden City, NY | Doubleday | 1979 |
| | Dutch | Laren, Netherlands | Novapress | 1980 |
| | English | London | Collins | 1982 |
| | English | London | Collins | 1987 |
| | English (Audio Book) | Ashland, OR | Blackstone Audio Books | 1989 |
| *Something* | English | London | Collins | 1971 |
| *Beautiful* | English | New York | Ballantine Books | 1971 |
| *for God* | English | New York | Harper and Row | 1971 |
| | English | New York | Walker and Co. | 1971 |
| | Swedish | Stockholm, Sweden | Verbum | 1971 |
| | English | London | Fontana | 1972 |

| Book Name | Language (Format) | Place of Publication | Publisher | Year |
|---|---|---|---|---|
| | Italian | Bari, Italy | Paoline | 1972 |
| | German | Freiburg, Germany | Herder | 1972 |
| | German | Freiburg, Germany | Herder | 1973 |
| | English | New York | Ballantine Books | 1973 |
| | Polish | Warszawa, Poland | Instytut Wydawniczy Pax | 1973 |
| | Italian | Cinisello Balsamo, Italy | Edizioni Paoline | 1973 |
| | German | Freiburg, Germany | Herder | 1974 |
| | Korean | Soeul, South Korea | Sŏng Paoro Ch'ulp'ansa | 1974 |
| | Italian | Bari, Italy | Edizioni Paoline | 1974 |
| | German | Freiburg, Germany | Herder | 1975 |
| | Polish | Warszawa, Poland | Instytut Wydawniczy Pax | 1975 |
| | English | London | Collins | 1976 |
| | English | New York | Ballantine Books | 1976 |
| | German | Freiburg, Germany | Herder | 1976 |
| | Swedish | Stockholm, Sweden | Verbum | 1976 |
| | Japanese | Tokyo, Japan | Joshi Paurokai | 1976 |
| | Italian | Cinisello Balsamo, Italy | Edizioni Paoline | 1977 |
| | German | Freiburg, Germany | Herder | 1977 |
| | English | London | Collins | 1977 |
| | English | New York | Image Books | 1977 |
| | English | Garden City, NY | Doubleday | 1977 |
| | German | Freiburg, Germany | Herder | 1978 |
| | Finnish | Helsinki, Finland | Kirjapaja | 1978 |
| | German | Freiburg, Germany | Herder | 1979 |
| | Hungarian | Eisenstadt, Austria | Prugg | 1979 |
| | Norwegian | Oslo, Norway | Luther Forlag | 1979 |
| | German | Freiburg, Germany | Herder | 1980 |
| | English | London | Collins | 1980 |
| | German | Freiburg, Germany | Herder | 1982 |
| | German | Freiburg, Germany | Herder | 1984 |
| | English | New York | Walker and Co. | 1984 |
| | English | New York | Harper & Row | 1986 |
| | English | London | Collins | 1987 |
| | Italian | Cinisello Balsamo, Italy | Edizioni Paoline | 1988 |
| | English | San Francisco | Harper & Row | 1988 |
| | English | London | Collins | 1990 |
| | Italian | Torino, Italy | Edizioni Paoline | 1990 |
| *Paul: Envoy* | English | New York | Harper and Row | 1972 |
| *Extraordinary* | English | London | Collins | 1972 |
| | English | London | Fount Paperbacks | 1979 |

| Book Name | Language (Format) | Place of Publication | Publisher | Year |
|---|---|---|---|---|
| *Chronicles of* | English | London | Collins | 1972 |
| *Wasted Time:* | English | New York | William Morrow | 1973 |
| *The Green* | English | London | Collins | 1973 |
| *Stick* | English | London | Fontana | 1975 |
| | English | London | Fontana | 1981 |
| | English | New York | William Morrow | 1981 |
| | | | | |
| *Chronicles of* | English | London | Collins | 1973 |
| *Wasted Time:* | English | New York | William Morrow | 1974 |
| *The Infernal* | English | London | Fontana | 1975 |
| *Grove* | English | London | Fontana | 1981 |
| | English | New York | William Morrow | 1981 |
| | English | New York | Quill | 1982 |
| | | | | |
| *Jesus: The Man* | English | London | Collins | 1975 |
| *Who Lives* | English | London | Fontana | 1975 |
| | English | New York | Harper & Row | 1975 |
| | English | London | Collins | 1976 |
| | English | New York | Harper & Row | 1976 |
| | Dutch | Baarn, Netherlands | Ambo | 1976 |
| | German | Einsideln, Switzerland | Johannes-Verl. | 1980 |
| | English | New York | Harper & Row | 1987 |
| | | | | |
| *A Third* | English | Boston | Little, Brown and Co. | 1976 |
| *Testament* | English | London | Collins | 1976 |
| | English | New York | Ballantine Books | 1976 |
| | English | London | Collins | 1977 |
| | English | London | Collins | 1978 |
| | English | New York | Ballantine Books | 1983 |
| | English | Farmington, PA | Plough Publishing House | 1983 |
| | | | | |
| *Christ and the* | English | London | Hodder and Stoughton | 1977 |
| *Media* | English | Grand Rapids | Wm. B. Eerdmans | 1977 |
| | English | Grand Rapids | Wm. B. Eerdmans | 1978 |
| | English | Grand Rapids | Wm. B. Eerdmans | 1981 |
| | | | | |
| *Things Past* | English | London | Collins | 1978 |
| | English | New York | William Morrow | 1979 |
| | | | | |
| *Some Answers* | English | London | Methuen | 1982 |
| | English | London | Methuen | 1984 |

| Book Name | Language (Format) | Place of Publication | Publisher | Year |
|---|---|---|---|---|
| *Muggeridge: Ancient and Modern* | English | London | BBC Publications | 1981 |
| *Like It Was: The Diaries of Malcolm Muggeridge* | English English | London New York | Collins William and Morrow | 1981 1982 |
| *Vintage Muggeridge: Religion and Society* | English | Grand Rapids | Wm B. Eerdmans | 1985 |

*Conversion: A Spiritual Journey*
(US edition entitled *Confessions of a Twentieth-Century Pilgrim*)

| | | | | |
|---|---|---|---|---|
| | English | London | Collins | 1988 |
| | English | San Francisco | Harper and Row | 1988 |
| | English | London | Collins | 1989 |
| | English | London | Fount Paperbacks | 1989 |
| | Dutch | Baarn, Netherlands | Arbor | 1989 |
| | Spanish | Madrid, Spain | Rialp | 1990 |

# Notes

## INTRODUCTION

1 R.J. Slyfield to Malcolm Muggeridge, 26 November 1974, SC-004 95/13. Unless otherwise stated, the first name of Muggeridge's letter writers is obscured to protect privacy.

2 Ibid.

3 Ricœur, "Discussions: Ricoeur on Narrative," in *On Paul Ricoeur*, ed. Paul Wood (London: Routledge, 1991), 181.

4 Radway, *A Feeling for Books: The Book-of-the-Month Club, Literary Taste, and Middle-Class Desire* (Chapel Hill, NC: University of North Carolina Press), 13.

5 Muggeridge received approximately 20,000 fan letters in total between 1966 and 1982. The majority of these letters were prompted by Muggeridge's television and film appearances. About 10 per cent of the fan letters specifically discussed reading experiences. If the entire scope of his career is included, Muggeridge received roughly 25,000 fan letters. Thus, the vast majority of his fan mail was sent during the years under consideration here.

6 Ledger-Lomas, "Religion," in Andrew Nash, Claire Squires, and I.R. Willison, *The Cambridge History of the Book in Britain*, vol. 7: 393.

7 For twentieth-century Roman Catholic converts, see Schwartz, *The Third Spring*. This effect of Muggeridge joining the Roman Catholic Church upon his readers is explored in the conclusion of this study, below.

8 Though the "Religious Crisis of the 1960s" transcended linguistic boundaries, relatively few of Muggeridge's fan letters originated outside of Anglophone contexts. Tables o.1 to o.5 outline the demographics of Muggeridge's readers (17–21).

9　Taylor, *A Secular Age*, 3.

10　These developments are commonly repeated. See Field, *Secularization in the Long 1960s*; and Clements, *Surveying Christian Beliefs and Religious Debates in Post-War Britain*. See also, McLeod, *The Religious Crisis of the 1960s*.

11　See, for example, Gilbert, *The Making of Post-Christian Britain*; Wilson, *Religion in Secular Society*; and Chadwick, *The Victorian Church*. The thesis of secularization has grown in sophistication and is defended today by scholars like Steve Bruce and Tony Glendinning, who have produced an impressive number of studies. For a good expression of their position, see Bruce and Glendinning, "When was Secularization? Dating the Decline of British Churches and Locating its Cause," 107–26. See also Bruce, *God Is Dead: Secularization in the West*; *Religion in the Modern World*; *Secularisation: In Defense of an Unfashionable Theory*; and "Secularization and Church Growth in the United Kingdom," 273–96. See also Pollack, "Varieties of Secularization Theories and Their Indispensable Core," 60–79.

12　Many critics of classic accounts of secularization have made this observation. See Clark, "Secularization and Modernization: The Failure of a 'Grand Narrative,'" 161–94; and Morris, "Secularization and Religious Experience: Arguments in the Historiography of Modern British Religion," 195–219.

13　See Harris and O'Brien Castro, eds. *Preserving the Sixties: Britain and the "Decade of Protest"*; and McLeod and Ustorf, eds. *The Decline of Western Europe, 1750–2000*.

14　Marwick, *The Sixties: Cultural Revolution in Britain, France, Italy and the United States* (Oxford: Oxford University Press, 1998), 7.

15　McGuire, *Lived Religion*, 19.

16　See Clark, "Modernization and Secularization"; Morris, "Secularization and Religious Experience"; Peter Berger, ed., *The Desecularization of the World: Resurgent Religion and World Politics* (Grand Rapids, MI: Eerdmans, 1999); Cox, "Toward Eliminating the Concept of Secularisation," in *Secularisation in the Christian World*, 13–26; Erdozain, "'Cause is not Quite what it Used to Be,'" 377–400; McLeod, *The Religious Crisis of the 1960s*. Callum Brown is best known for his gendered analysis of secularization and refocusing the key period of religious change to the 1960s, which he understood as radical and abrupt. Brown, *The Death of Christian Britain*; *Religion and the Demographic Revolution*; "The Secularisation Decade: What the 1960s have done to the Study of Religious History," in *The Decline of Christendom in Western Europe*," 29–46; "Secularization, the

Growth of Militancy, 393–418; and "What was the Religious Crisis of the 1960s?," 468–79.

17  See Brewitt-Taylor, *Christian Radicalism in the Church of England*, 10–13; and "Christianity and the Invention of the Sexual Revolution in Britain, 519–46. See also Cohen, *Folk Devils and Moral Panics*; Donnelly, *Sixties Britain*; and Sandbrook's studies of postwar Britain, *Never Had It So Good*, *White Heat*, *State of Emergency* and *Seasons in the Sun*.

18  This trend is present across disciplines. For a good synthesis in literary studies, see Branch, "PostSecular Studies," in *The Routledge Companion to Literature and Religion*, 91–101. For religious studies, see McGuire, *Lived Religion*; and Ammerman, *Sacred Stories, Spiritual Tribes*. For history, see Brewitt-Taylor, *Christian Radicalism*; and Geiringer, *The Pope and the Pill*.

19  Ammerman, *Sacred Stories, Spiritual Tribes*, 8.

20  Brewitt-Taylor, *Christian Radicalism*, 10.

21  Field, "Another Window on British Secularization," 213.

22  Chapman, "Secularisation and the Ministry of John R. W. Stott," 496–513. See, especially, 498.

23  Grimley, "Law, Morality, and Secularisation," 725–41. See, especially, 739–40.

24  Brewitt-Taylor, "The Invention of a 'Secular Society'?," 327–50.

25  McLeod, *The Religious Crisis of the 1960s*, 240; Green, *The Passing of Protestant England*, 294.

26  Brewitt-Taylor, *Christian Radicalism*, 230.

27  This follows the call for greater focus on "individuals, the experiences they consider most important, and the concrete practices that make up their personal religious experience and expression." McGuire, *Lived Religion*, 4.

28  There are a growing number of exceptions to this. Hugh McLeod, Callum Brown, Alana Harris, and David Geiringer have each made innovative use of oral histories to uncover how ordinary people experienced the 1960s and 1970s. See McLeod, *The Religious Crisis*; Brown, *Becoming Atheist*; Harris, *Faith in the Family*; and, Geiringer, *The Pope and the Pill*. Another exception to this claim is Ian Jones, who shows how fears of decline shaped the "congregational mood" of parishioners in postwar Birmingham. His focus on six congregations throughout the Birmingham area invites a broader consideration of this phenomenon. See Jones, *The Local Church and Generational Change*, 52–72. Even though oral histories have revealed crucial undercurrents in this history, memories are filtered through subsequent experiences that may transform their meaning and significance for the subject. Contrariwise, fan mail to

Muggeridge, while not without its own methodological hazards, was often impulsive in its creation and thus not identical to the ad hoc rationalization that may be elicited from oral interviews aimed at recovering life histories years after the fact.

29 I use the term "lived religion" in the same sense as Meredith McGuire, Alana Harris, Nancy Ammerman, and Esther McIntosh; that is, to distinguish "the actual experience of religious persons from the prescribed religion of institutionally defined beliefs and practices" (McGuire, *Lived Religion*). This is not to say the lived religion of Muggeridge's readers was never in accord with the teachings of the churches they identified with – many were. Rather, this analytical framework helps to clarify the complex and unexpected ways Muggeridge's readers expressed their religious lives, which very often *did not* form under the guidance of the churches. See McGuire, *Lived Religion*, 12; McIntosh, "Living Religion," 383–96.

30 Nash, Squires, and Towheed, "Reading and Ownership," in Andrew Nash, Claire Squires, and I.R. Willison, *The Cambridge History of the Book in Britain*, 7: 231–2.

31 Ricœur, *Time and Narrative*, 3: 159.

32 Some important studies using fan mail include Cavicchi, "Fandom Before 'Fan,'" 52–72; McCusker, "Dear Radio Friend," 173–95; Neuhaus, "Is it Ridiculous for me to Say I Want to Write?," 115–37; Sawchuk, "C Wright Mills," 231–53; Simmons, "Dear Radio Broadcaster," 444–59; and Towler, *The Need for Certainty*.

33 Altick, *The English Common Reader*; Flint, *The Woman Reader*; Vincent, *Bread, Knowledge and Freedom*; and Rose, *The Intellectual Life of the British Working Classes*.

34 See McParland, *Charles Dickens's American Audience*, 64.

35 See Bates, "The fan letter correspondence of Willa Cather."

36 Jackson, "On Fans and Fan Mail."

37 See "A Connecticut Fan" to Malcolm Muggeridge, 28 April 1981, SC-004 124/4. Compared with the thousands of other letters he received, this one is not altogether remarkable from a researcher's perspective. It reads, "Dear sir, A few days ago I sent my respect + admiration for you on a card to Wm Morrow Co after reading your 2 vol. autobiography which I enjoyed so very much. Now I have just finished your splendid tribute to the saintly Mother Theresa [*sic*] of Calcutta, which is so lovely. You are a noble gentleman, sir! At daily mass, I ask God to bless you & your loved ones abundantly! A Connecticut fan." It is perhaps possible that Muggeridge was beginning to feel the draw of the Roman Catholic

Church, and this letter arrived at a crucial moment, but we cannot know for sure.

38 Pawley, "Beyond Market Models and Resistance," 75.

39 Nord, *Communities of Journalism*, 250.

40 Ryan, "One Reader, Two Votes," in Crone and Towheed, *The History of Reading*, vol. 3: 72.

41 Barton and Hall, eds., *Letter Writing as a Social Practice*, 2. See also Earle, ed., *Epistolary Selves*.

42 E.H. Carr, *What Is History?*, 30.

43 B. Meisenbach to Malcolm Muggeridge, December 1980, SC-004, 105/13.

44 D. Hunt to Malcolm Muggeridge, 20 March 1980, SC-004 105/3.

45 This phrasing was especially common. This one in particular is from N. Clark to Malcolm Muggeridge, August 1970, SC-004 22/15.

46 Margaretta Rook to Malcolm Muggeridge, 16 February 1969, SC-004 68/17.

47 Patrick [no last name given] to Malcolm Muggeridge, 28 January 1974, SC-004 10/26.

48 For overviews of this field, see Boddice, *The History of Emotions*; Matt and Stearns, eds., *Doing Emotions History*; Plamper, *The History of Emotions*; and Rosenwein and Cristiani, *What Is the History of Emotions?*

49 Scheer, "Are Emotions a Kind of Practice?" See also Plamper, *The History of Emotions*, 265–70; and Boddice, *The History of Emotions*, chap. 5.

50 Nancy Ammerman makes an important distinction about the role of agency in practice theory. She notes, "In sociology, 'practice theory' has emerged as an important mode of analysis, while in theology a 'theology of practice' has likewise emerged. The former tends to emphasize the habitual, everyday nature of practices and structures of power in which that activity occurs, while the latter tends to emphasize the voluntary intentional nature of activity and the ends toward which activity is directed. At the most basic level, a 'practice' is simply a cluster of actions given meaning by the social structure in which it is lodged and the people who occupy that social field. Either the habits of deliberate choices can be deemed 'practices,' depending on which theoretical lens one chooses" (Ammerman, *Sacred Stories, Spiritual Tribes*, 56). For Muggeridge's readers, reading and writing in the context of the 1960s and 1970s worked in both senses. They voluntarily strove to make sense of religious change in their own lives even as they took various "practices" for granted, such as methods of letter writing or the internalized narrative of religious decline that became, essentially, a kind of *doxa*.

51 Scheer, "Are Emotions a Kind of Practice?," 214.

52  Ibid., 216.

53  Ibid., 215.

54  See Orsi, *Between Heaven and Earth*, 2–3.

55  Rose, *Intellectual Life of the British Working Classes*, 1.

56  Anderson, *Imagined Communities*, 35.

57  This follows Barbara Rosenwein's encouragement that emotions be integrated into "regular" history. See Plamper, Reddy, Rosenwein, and Stearns, "History of Emotions," 260.

58  J.M. Raby to Malcolm Muggeridge, 6 August 1972, SC-004 88/6; 10 December 1974, SC-004 95/16; 4 February 1976, SC-004 98/9; 4 January 1978, SC-004 103/2; 29 January 1979, SC-004 102/1; 16 January 1980, SC-004 88/2; 26 May 1980, SC-004 105/5; 3 September 1980, SC-004 105/9; and 21 February 1982, SC-004 109/5.

59  Philips, *Contesting the Moral High Ground*, 100–27; Hunter, *Malcolm Muggeridge*; Wolfe, *Malcolm Muggeridge*; and Ingrams, *Muggeridge*. Other examples include studies of the BBC. See Briggs, *History of Broadcasting in the United Kingdom*; *The BBC*; Crisell, *An Introductory History of British Broadcasting*. See especially Grant, "An Historical Analysis of Biographical, Societal and Organizational Factors Shaping the Radio Career of Thomas Malcolm Muggeridge, 1948–1957."

60  Brown, *The Battle for Christian Britain*, 260.

61  Philips, *Contesting the Moral High Ground*, 103.

62  For example, he is not mentioned at all in either of Stefan Collini's penetrating studies of literary culture and critical debate in twentieth-century Britain. See *Common Reading* and *Common Writing*; Annan, *Our Age*, 167; and Stapleton, *Political Intellectuals and Public Identities*, 166–8.

63  Sandbrook, *White Heat*, 583. Interestingly, Sandbrook ignores Muggeridge altogether after 1969, when, as this study shows, his importance as a religious and cultural symbol peaked.

64  Ingrams, *Muggeridge*, 228.

65  Philips, *Contesting the Moral High Ground*, 104. In brief, *Gemeinschaft* and *Gesellschaft* refer to "community" and "society," respectively. Introduced by sociologist Ferdinand Tönnies in his 1887 study, *Community and Society*, *Gemeinschaft* describes the kinds of social bonds in which the good of the community takes precedence over that of the individual. By contrast, *Gesellschaft* refers to social relationships in which the individual takes precedence over the group as a collective.

66  Muggeridge, *Jesus: The Man Who Lives*, 11.

67  Philips, *Contesting the Moral High Ground*, 101–4.

68  Brewitt-Taylor, *Christian Radicalism*, 7.

69  Ibid., 7–9.

70  These formed the title of two lectures Muggeridge gave near the end of the 1970s, later published as *The End of Christendom*.

71  Muggeridge made this claim on many occasions, but for just one example, see William Buckley, interview with Malcolm Muggeridge, *Firing Line*, https://www.youtube.com/watch?v=_nHqyLfeFE.

72  One hundred fourteen letters were from people whose sex was not possible to discern. Readers often signed with their initials or provided only their last names. Within the context of Muggeridge's fans, it was normally not possible to conclude anything concrete about their reading experience based on their sex, or, contrariwise, anything about their sex based solely upon the content of their reading experience. Twenty-four letters were written by groups of people. Two of these were sent by a community of nuns and monks. Twenty-two of these letters were sent by couples who read the book together.

73  This is based on the 244 letter writers who shared their ages. Another 175 readers gave enough evidence to approximate an age, based on if they self-identified as a college student, a retired person, a parent with small children, or a parent with adult children. Three of these readers could be described as children or adolescent. Forty-three others were in their late teens or early twenties.

74  There were 104 clergy from at least nine different denominations, thirty-three nuns, eleven missionaries, seven monks, four canons, three rectors, three bishops, two curates, a monsignor, and a prioress. The remaining forty-five were those who worked on church staffs or for various parachurch organizations.

75  Seventy-eight fans were university students. There were also twenty-one professors at colleges and universities in Britain and the United States, including three others who worked as university administrators. Thus, readers connected to higher education made up over 5 per cent of Muggeridge's fans. Perhaps Muggeridge's small stint as rector of the University of Edinburgh had something to do with this. Other teachers outside of higher education number at thirty.

76  Forty fans described themselves as journalists, copywriters, editors, and authors or writers, which is perhaps not surprising given Muggeridge's profession.

77  Nineteen fans were medical doctors or scientists.

78  However, a closer look at the geographic breakdown of his fans shows that his readership was not nearly as global as this first figure suggests. Together, readers from Anglophone societies made up over 88 per cent

of all the fan mail he received. The 105 readers who did not include a
return address likely came from one of these settings. Muggeridge's
books were translated into other languages, and he did receive several
letters from people whose first language was not English. With a few
exceptions, the majority of readers in non-Western settings were British
citizens travelling abroad, living as expats, or working as Christian
missionaries.

79 For more on the fans who offered to translate Muggeridge's books, see
chapter 4.

80 Anonymous to Malcolm Muggeridge, 27 April 1979, SC-004 104/4.

81 G.M. Officer to Malcolm Muggeridge, 3 March 1973, SC-004 91/14.

82 Anonymous to Malcolm Muggeridge, 26 March 1974, SC-004 91/14.

83 Anonymous to Malcolm Muggeridge, 6 January 1981, SC-004 106/1.

84 R. Nathan to Malcolm Muggeridge, 24 April 1974, SC-004 104/4.

85 Ingrams, *Muggeridge*, 225.

86 E. Wilson to Malcolm Muggeridge, 19 June 1978, SC-004 103/9; 1 July
1979, SC-004 104/7; 10 November 1979, SC-004 104/11; 31 January 1980,
SC-004 105/1; 9 April 1980, SC-004 105/4; and 23 April 1982, SC-004
109/15.

87 H. Fern to Malcolm Muggeridge, 18 December 1972, SC-004 90/13.

88 Ibid.

89 A. Troia to Malcolm Muggeridge, January 1970, SC-004 74/9.

90 K. Downes to Malcolm Muggeridge, 6 November 1972, SC-004 89/15.

91 Anonymous to Malcolm Muggeridge, 3 January 1971, SC-004 80/8.

92 R. Stark to Malcolm Muggeridge, 7 July 1973, SC-004 92/6.

93 A. Crawford to Malcolm Muggeridge, 6 November 1970, SC-004 78/5.

94 R. Renton to Malcolm Muggeridge, 5 January 1971, SC-004 80/8.

### CHAPTER ONE

1 K. Williams to Malcolm Muggeridge, 25 July 1975, SC-004 97/2. Emphasis added.

2 Scheer, "Are Emotions a Kind of Practice?," 213.

3 Ibid.

4 Ibid.

5 E. Robinson, et al., "Telling Stories about Post-war Britain," 268.

6 Giddens, *Modernity and Self Identity*, 5.

7 Ibid., 215.

8 See Zhao and Biesta, "Lifelong Learning, Identity and the Moral
Dimension." This paper was later published as "The Moral Dimension

of Lifelong Learning: Giddens, Taylor, and the 'Reflexive Project of the Self."

9  E. Robinson, et al., "Telling Stories about Post-war Britain," 273.

10  Giddens, *Modernity and Self-Identity*, 3.

11  Ricœur, *Time and Narrative*, vol. 1: 54–71. The threefold mimesis Ricœur develops at length in *Time and Narrative* refers to the action when readers with prefigured notions about the world (Mimesis$_1$) interact with an already configured reality in the world of the text (Mimesis$_2$). The application of the text – whether through appropriation or rejection – has the potential to refigure the world of reader (Mimesis$_3$).

12  This theme is explored in Reddy, *The Navigation of Feeling*. William Reddy's analysis included the necessary existence of political regimes, which set the "normative emotions and the official rituals, practices, and emotives that express and inculcate them." However, as Rob Boddice has recently noted, emotives and emotional regimes function in cultural and social settings, too, without the direct influence of the state. See Boddice, *The History of Emotions*, 59–83.

13  Callum Brown has emphasized external causes for the religious dynamics of those years, paying special attention to the sexual revolution and its discourse. He sees the dynamics as a sharp and violent revolution that occurred quite unexpectedly. See Brown, *The Death of Christian Britain*. By contrast, Hugh McLeod has emphasized a more gradual decline, and pays special attention to internal dynamics within the churches themselves. McLeod, *The Religious Crisis of the 1960s*.

14  Indeed, not only was he among the first, he was among the few. The Italian translation did not sell very well. Only partial sales figures are available, but they are enough to extrapolate a general trend. One hundred seven copies sold in the first six months of 1973, forty copies in all of 1975, nine copies in the first six months of 1978, seven copies in the first six months of 1979, and eighteen copies in all of 1981. It is probably safe to assume that the Italian translation sold somewhere between five hundred and a thousand copies in its first ten years. Of course, sales figures do not tell us whether a book was read, or how much it might have moved people when it was, but letters from monks like V. Gargano do. See Muggeridge's records from his literary agents, David Higham Associates, in SC-004 19/4, 6, 10, 11, and 15. See also the appendix.

15  V. Gargano to Malcolm Muggeridge, 25 April 1971, SC-004 81/8.

16  Victoria I. to Malcolm Muggeridge, 4 September 1975, SC-004 97/6.

17  G. Flax to Malcolm Muggeridge, 6 June 1973, SC-004 92/3.

18  Ibid.
19  See Giddens, *Modernity and Self-Identity*, 78–9, 96, 186–7, and 215.
20  R. Groening to Malcolm Muggeridge, 29 June 1977, SC-004 101/5.
21  Ibid.
22  J. Ford to Malcolm Muggeridge, 17 February 1970, SC-004 22/13.
23  Ibid.
24  Ibid.
25  G. Evans to Malcolm Muggeridge, 25 July 1977, SC-004 101/8.
26  Malcolm Muggeridge to G. Evans, 29 July 1977, SC-004 101/8.
27  Malcolm Muggeridge, Entry for 23 August 1977, "'Data Day Diary' –
    1977; Weekly Appointments – 1979," SC-004 135/5.
28  Rev. D. Baker to Malcolm Muggeridge, 2 August 1977, SC-004 101/9.
29  Malcolm Muggeridge to Rev. D. Baker, 4 August 1977, SC-004 101/9.
30  Muggeridge's biographers make casual reference to the high number of
    visitors Muggeridge received in his home at Robertsbridge. Many of
    these were other journalists, friends, or professionals who met with him
    for work-related reasons. We know that at least some of them were his
    fans, too. See Ingrams, *Muggeridge*, 223.
31  D. Murphy to Malcolm Muggeridge, 18 October 1969, SC-004 22/11.
32  Ibid.
33  Ricœur, *Time and Narrative*, 1: 71.
34  Bangour Village Hospital opened in 1906 and closed in 2004. Its records
    are available at "Bangour Village Hospital," LHB44, Lothian Health Ser-
    vices Archive, University of Edinburgh, Edinburgh. According to the
    finding aid, most of the records predate Farquharson's letters to Mug-
    geridge. The "Register of Lunatics" ends in 1971. The first letter Mug-
    geridge received from Farquharson was in 1974.
35  T. Farquharson to Malcolm Muggeridge, 30 July 1974, SC-004 95/4.
36  Ibid.
37  Ibid.
38  T. Farquharson to Malcolm Muggeridge, 14 August 1974, SC-004 95/4.
39  A. Moriarty to Malcolm Muggeridge, n.d. [circa March 1970], SC-004
    22/13. Emphasis added.
40  The classic corrective is Larsen, *Crisis of Doubt*. Certainly, the "rational
    worldview" argument for religious decline was convincing for many;
    the error is to assume T.H. Huxley or J.A. Froude were normative exam-
    ples for a monolithic crisis of faith.
41  For example, see Taylor, *The Malaise of Modernity*.
42  McLeod, *The Religious Crisis of the 1960s*, 1; Marwick, *The Sixties*; Hast-
    ings, *A History of English Christianity*, 581; and Brown, *Religion and the*

*Demographic Revolution*. Marwick also makes this claim in "The International Context."

43  Stuart Taylor to Malcolm Muggeridge, 24 April 1981, SC-004 107/5.

44  M.J. Kett to Malcolm Muggeridge, 16 August 1976, SC-004 99/6.

45  Ibid.

46  J. Ford is discussed above, under "Kindred Spirits."

47  See, for example, Chartier, *The Cultural Uses of Print in Early Modern France*; and Rose, "How Historians Study Reader Response," in *Literature in the Marketplace*, 195–212.

48  See Pawley, "Beyond Market Models." While Pawley's focus is more so on the roles that institutions can have in the history of reading, her analysis is nevertheless helpful by navigating between what she calls the "market" models of reading (i.e., Robert Darnton's "communications circuit") and "resistance" models (i.e., Michel de Certeau's notion of "poaching"). Ricœur's threefold mimesis for understanding identity formation is similar in that it pays closer attention to the interactions between author, text, and reader. However, it avoids placing unwarranted emphasis on the reader as the sole source of meaning creation, or on the author as the "producer" of meaning, which the reader then "consumes." See also Ryan, "One Reader, Two Votes."

49  See, for example, Iser, *The Implied Reader*.

50  C. Hall to Malcolm Muggeridge, 19 January 1970, SC-004 22/13.

51  McLeod, *Religious Crisis*, 2, 140.

52  This was among the most important issues that Muggeridge's fans discussed in their letters and makes up the subject of the next chapter.

53  A. Brandow to Malcolm Muggeridge, 24 February 1970, SC-004 22/13.

54  Ibid.

55  Brewitt-Taylor, *Christian Radicalism*, 11.

56  McLeod, *Religious Crisis*, 104–7. For example, Methodist youth clubs in Britain reached a high point in 1962, with a membership of 114,211. Three years later, they had plummeted to under 90,000. This trend has continued in regards to Methodism generally. Since the mid-1960s, Methodist youth clubs hemorrhaged attendees at a considerable rate. By 2015, they recorded a yearly attendance figure of 200,000, or approximately 8 per cent of the total church attendance recorded by churches. Since 1980, that amounts to a 400,000-attendee drop, as well as a 4 per cent drop of the total share of church attendees for the thirty-five-year period. See "Church Attendance in Britain, 1980–2015," British Religion in Numbers, http://www.brin.ac.uk/figures/church-attendance-in-britain-1980-2015.

57  Hastings, *A History of English Christianity*, 545.

58  Ibid.

59  Muggeridge, *Jesus Rediscovered*, 55.

60  A. Lacey to Malcolm Muggeridge, 12 March 1982, SC-004 109/9.

61  Ibid.

62  To name just two examples: F. Harwood was eighty-three years old when he wrote a fan letter to Muggeridge. The only similarity between them was a shared working-class background, with a father who was politically active. However, Harwood was from British Colombia, and unlike Muggeridge, never lost his faith (F. Harwood to Malcolm Muggeridge, 26 September 1973, SC-004 92/16). Likewise, D.A. Zimmerman thought that her time in India was "remarkably similar" to that of Muggeridge's, with the exception that she had been there forty years afterwards. While Muggeridge stayed in India as a reporter, Zimmerman was in college studying abroad. They lived in quite different regions, with different dialects and with different customs (she was in Andhra Pradesh and Hyderabad, he was in Kerala and Calcutta), but she drew parallel experiences, however general they may have been (D.A. Zimmerman to Malcolm Muggeridge, 14 November 1971, SC-004 84/3).

63  D. Raymond to Malcolm Muggeridge, 12 November 1975, SC-004 97/15.

64  L.M. Wallace to Malcolm Muggeridge, 26 August 1981, SC-004 107/16.

65  Mary B. to Malcolm Muggeridge, 27 August 1974, SC-004 95/5. Emphasis added.

66  Hitchens, "A Hundred Years of Muggery."

67  M. Hardcastle to Malcolm Muggeridge, 17 March 1978, SC-4 102/4. In his letter, Hardcastle thanked Muggeridge first for introducing him to the works of Hugh Kingsmill and Christopher Booker, especially in regards to *The Neophiliacs*. It has been mentioned above that Muggeridge's home was often open to his fans who wanted to meet and chat. Booker enjoyed similar treatment. In the acknowledgement to *The Neophiliacs*, he writes, "The probability that I would one day write this book has been with me in one way or another, ever since I first read Malcolm Muggeridge's book *The Thirties* in 1953. It therefore gave me particular pleasure that, having met Malcolm and his wife Kitty many years later, I was able to write a part of *The Neophiliacs* while staying under their roof in Sussex; for all their hospitality and encouragement I am especially grateful." Booker, *The Neophiliacs*, 5. Hardcastle thought *The Neophiliacs* was "one of the most seminal books of recent years."

68  K. Crawford to Malcolm Muggeridge, n.d. [circa September 1973], SC-004 92/15. The paragraph Crawford had in mind on page 81 is: "I find it

strange that, knowing this, I should so often have inflicted upon myself the nausea of over-indulgence, and had to fight off the black dogs of satiety. Human beings, as Pascal points out, are peculiar in that they avidly pursue ends they know will bring them no satisfaction; gorge themselves with food, which cannot nourish and with pleasures, which cannot please. I am a prize example." Muggeridge, *Chronicles of Wasted Time*, 1: 81.

69  E. Kemp to Malcolm Muggeridge, 9 March 1970, SC-004 22/13.

70  Ibid.

71  E. Vellacott to Malcolm Muggeridge, 20 January 1970, SC-004 22/13.

72  Ibid.

73  Mrs J. Thiel to Malcolm Muggeridge, 5 January 1970, SC-004 22/13.

74  Ibid.

75  We do not know if Muggeridge ever responded to Vellacott, but cursory notes were scratched in the top margin of Thiel's letter that were presumably typed and then later sent to her: "Many thanks for Letter + for taking trouble to develop a carefully + clearly difference of view. We are agreed about problem but disagree about how to deal with it. To regard pleasure of sex as end rather than means, as it seems to me, is calculated to produce the very circumstances we agree in deploring." Malcolm Muggeridge to Mrs J. Theil, n.d., SC-004 22/13.

76  Ruth Graham to Malcolm Muggeridge, 17 December 1981, SC-004 17/12. Interestingly, it was reading *Chronicles of Wasted Time* that first inspired Billy Graham to invite Muggeridge to speak at the Lausanne Conference in 1974. In a letter to Muggeridge, Graham wrote, "During our recent holiday in Mexico, my wife and I read your book *Chronicles of Wasted Time*. I strongly recommended that the Chairman of the Program Committee at the Congress also read it, which he did. This book has made a profound impact on all of us. Therefore, at the Administrative meeting last week in Lausanne, I strongly recommended that you be invited to address the Congress. The invitation was unanimously approved that you be invited to address the Congress for thirty to thirty-five minutes on Monday night, July 22." Billy Graham to Malcolm Muggeridge, 8 April 1974, SC-004 17/12. Muggeridge's talk at the Lausanne Conference was characteristically despondent of current affairs. It was entitled, "Living through an Apocalypse," available at https://www.lausanne.org/content/lausanne-1974-documents.

77  H. Fern to Malcolm Muggeridge, 18 December 1972, SC-004 90/13.

78  S. Morgan to Malcolm Muggeridge, 2 February 1978, SC-004 103/2.

79  Ibid.

80 B. Moss to Malcolm Muggeridge, 12 March 1982, SC-004 109/9.

81 Moss did not name the exact titles of the works she read. However, she does refer to Wurmbrand's torture, so it is likely she read *Tortured for Christ*. She also mentioned reading Thomas Merton, but it is difficult to pinpoint which books she might have had in mind. Merton authored dozens of works, though his *Learning to Love: Exploring Solitude and Freedom* does refer to his relationship with his nurse, Margie Smith, which, like with Moss, precipitated an internal struggle about what to do.

82 B. Moss to Malcolm Muggeridge, 12 March 1982, SC-004 109/9.

83 Ibid.

84 Roof, *A Generation of Seekers*.

85 For felt distances, see Gammerl, "Felt Distances." Gammerl notes, "feelings were by no means limited to close interpersonal relationships … Emotions were both producers and products of proximity, as well as producers and products of distance. The customary contrast of rational distance with emotional closeness is plainly inadequate. Distanced relations could also have an emotional stamp upon them. Instead of emphasizing a categorical difference between close and distant relationships … different kinds of connection can have different emotional colourings … It follows from this that common assumption that emotions properly belong to close interpersonal relationships is without foundation" (199).

## CHAPTER TWO

1 Mark Chaves best expressed this argument in "Secularization as Declining Religious Authority." More recently it has been developed by Field, "Another Window on British Secularization," 190–218. See also Clements, *Religion and Public Opinion in Britain*, 11–43.

2 Davie, *Religion in Britain Since 1945*. See also the revised edition, *Religion in Britain: A Persistent Paradox*.

3 Muggeridge, *The Thirties*, 11.

4 The hate mail he received can be found in SC-004 34/19, 108/4, and 115/21.

5 Adrian Hastings also emphasizes that the dynamics of the 1960s were not unique to the church, but belonged to the total culture. "What happened in England was quite closely comparable to the pattern discernible in France, Germany, Australia, almost anywhere within the 'western' world. The social, intellectual, religious crisis of the 1960s was specific to no one particular religious tradition, nor to any one part of the world. More widely still, it was not even a specifically religious cri-

sis; it was rather one of the total culture, affecting many secular institutions in a way comparable to its effects on the churches. It was a crisis of the relevance ... of long-standing patterns of thought and institutions of all sorts in a time of intense, and rather self-conscious, modernization ... Suddenly the mood changed, neo-traditionalism crumbled in ridicule and the pendulum swung rather wildly to the other extreme, the glorification of the modern" (Hastings, *A History of English Christianity*, 581).

6  Philips, *Contesting the Moral High Ground*, 108.

7  Ibid., 109.

8  Kierkegaard had a particularly significant impact on Muggeridge's theology. They both were deeply committed to an anti-institutional vision of Christianity in which spiritual authenticity was determined by an existential decision to make a leap of faith against all evidence to the contrary. Indeed, Muggeridge's conversion to Christianity, despite his ardent belief in conventional Christianity's decline, was a robust expression of this. Kierkegaard was in vogue within intellectual circles, especially after the Second World War. However, George Pattison notes, interestingly, that Kierkegaard actually became less popular in Britain during the 1970s. This was, as we have seen, just as Muggeridge was reaching the peak of his theological reputation. It may be possible that Muggeridge in some ways served the role the Kierkegaard had years earlier and even succeeded in disseminating his expression of his ideas to a wider audience. Thus, Muggeridge's readers were receiving some of Kierkegaard's ideas even if they were not reading him themselves. See Pattison, "Great Britain: From 'Prophet of the Now' to Postmodern Ironist (and After)."

9  Quoted in Philips, *Contesting the Moral High Ground*, 126. The source of this quotation is Muggeridge, "Humour, Humility, and Faith," convocation address, St Francis Xavier University, 6 May 1979, Public Relations Records, RG 44/3/519, University Archives, Angus L. Macdonald Library, St Francis Xavier University, Antigonish, Nova Scotia.

10  Chaves, "Secularization as Declining Religious Authority," 749–74.

11  Field, "Another Window on British Secularization," 190–218.

12  See Chaves, "Secularization as Declining Religious Authority"; Field, "Another Window on British Secularization"; Clements, *Religion and Public Opinion in Britain*; Hoffmann, "Declining Religious Authority?," 1–25; Hoffmann, "Confidence in Religious Institutions and Secularization," 321–43; Kleiman, Ramsey, and Pallazo, "Public Confidence in Religious Leaders," 79–87; Rosen, *Transformation of British Life*, 47–51; and

Troughton, "Anti-Churchianity, Discursive Christianity, and Religious Change," 93–106.

13  Ben Clements in his study *Religion and Public Opinion in Britain* used five different surveys to trace religious change in Britain: the British Election Study (BES), 1963–2010; the British Social Attitudes (BSA), 1983–2012; the European Values Study (EVS), 1981–2008; the European Social Survey (ESS), 2002–2012; and the Eurobarometer (EB), 1970–2006. The BES included no questions on religious belief, focusing instead on behaving and belonging. The EVS and BSA included questions measuring belief, but since they both were begun in the early 1980s, they lie outside the scope of this study.

14  Troughton, "Anti-Churchianity."

15  For the Jesus People Movement, see Eskridge, *God's Forever Family*.

16  One of the premises of Chaves' argument is that religious beliefs are "socially efficacious only when they become mobilized and institutionalized as structures of authority." It is true that Muggeridge's fan mail displayed a wide array of shared experiences, emotions, and interpretations that indicates a global reading community. Even though they did not form an institutional entity, their private letters were nonetheless "socially efficacious" in the sense that they were the physical space in which ordinary readers around the world fundamentally redefined how they understood religious authority (Chaves, "Secularization as Declining Religious Authority," 770).

17  See E. Robinson, et al., "Telling Stories about Post-war Britain."

18  Hastings, *A History of English Christianity*, 545.

19  J. Robinson, *Honest to God*. See also Hastings, *A History of English Christianity*, 536–8; McLeod, *Religious Crisis*, 84–6; Machin, *Churches and Social Issues*, 176–7.

20  For the fiery debate that occurred after the publication of Robinson's book, see J. Robinson and Edwards, *The Honest to God Debate*.

21  Machin, *Churches and Social Issues*, 175–231.

22  The Second Vatican Council has attracted a great deal of scholarly attention. See O'Malley, *What Happened at Vatican II*. See also Bullivant, *Mass Exodus*; Harris, *Faith in the Family*; McLeod, *Religious Crisis*, 92–101; Hastings, *A History of English Christianity*, 519–31; and Napolitano, *Migrant Hearts and the Atlantic Return*, 34–7.

23  McLeod, *Religious Crisis*, 2. See also Bullivant, *Mass Exodus*, 183.

24  See Cummings, Matovina, and Orsi, eds., *Catholics in the Vatican II Era*. They note that "arguably the most understudied aspect of the lived history of [Vatican II], one that impacted Catholics in every corner of the

globe, is the way it shaped relations between Catholics of every background: priests, nuns, lay people, bishop." They continue, "All of these personal ties, many of them long standing, governed by inherited protocols, hierarchies, and expectations, were implicated in the others, so that to pull on any one strand in the web was to set all of them moving" (xviii–xix). Andrew Greeley makes a similar point in *The Catholic Revolution*. For how ordinary Catholic women responded to the Catholic Church's prohibition on birth control, see Geiringer, *The Pope and the Pill*.

25  Philips, *Contesting the Moral High Ground*, 41.

26  W. Rogers to Malcolm Muggeridge, 20 May 1971, SC-004 81/14.

27  S. Macartney to Malcolm Muggeridge, 23 May 1970, SC-004 22/14.

28  F.D. Meredith to Malcolm Muggeridge, 20 March 1966, SC-004 50/13. Citing the Parable of the Wheat and the Tares in Matthew 13 was especially common among Roman Catholics and High Church Anglicans who defended the necessity of the institutional church.

29  D.A.C. Blunt to Malcolm Muggeridge, circa February 1966, SC-004 50/10.

30  P. Henry to Malcolm Muggeridge, 14 August 1976, SC-004 99/6.

31  A. Tate to Malcolm Muggeridge, 3 February 1970, SC-004 22/13.

32  Ibid.

33  Ibid.

34  D.L.B. Howell to Malcolm Muggeridge, 28 May 1970, SC-004 22/14.

35  Ibid.

36  L. Furniss to Malcolm Muggeridge, 6 January 1982, SC-004 109/1.

37  Ibid.

38  S. Arthurs to Malcolm Muggeridge, 2 July 1969, SC-004 22/15.

39  Ibid.

40  Ibid.

41  N. Frost to Malcolm Muggeridge, 27 April 1971, SC-004 81/9.

42  M. Biersmith to Malcolm Muggeridge, 28 April 1978, SC-004 103/5.

43  I. Taylor to Malcolm Muggeridge, 19 October 1970, SC-004 22/14.

44  N. Green to Malcolm Muggeridge, 31 January 1966, SC-004 50/2.

45  [Illegible] to Malcolm Muggeridge, 29 January 1966, SC-004 50/2. Someone, presumably Muggeridge, spilled coffee or tea on the bottom quarter inch of this letter. Unfortunately, it smudged the signature making it impossible to identify the name.

46  W. Riccio to Malcolm Muggeridge, 30 September 1977, SC-004 101/16.

47  [Illegible] to Malcolm Muggeridge, 29 January 1966, SC-004 50/2.

48  J. Stewart to Malcolm Muggeridge, 23 May 1969, SC-004 22/14.

49  Ibid.

50  M. Hayes to Malcolm Muggeridge, 19 March 1966, SC-004 50/12.

51  Bullivant, *Mass Exodus*, 202–3.

52  Ibid., 203. For Bullivant's full discussion of the "Dogmatic Constitution on the Sacred Liturgy," see *Mass Exodus*, 133–88.

53  For more context on innovations in worship, see Pasture, "Christendom and the Legacy of the Sixties," 105–8. This was an important cause for the decline of churchgoing in the Netherlands, as well. See Van Rooden, "The Strange Death of Dutch Christendom."

54  McGuire, *Lived Religion*, 100.

55  Harris, "A Fresh Stripping of the Altars?" She notes that by 1980, however, a recognizable consensus formed in which the use of Latin in the liturgy diminished in importance when compared to more pressing issues of human life and sexuality. See also her *Faith in the Family*, 57–129.

56  Bullivant, *Mass Exodus*, 256.

57  T. John to Malcolm Muggeridge, 14 November 1980, SC-004 105/12.

58  Ibid.

59  Bullivant, *Mass Exodus*, 154.

60  Chapman, *Godly Ambition*. See also his "Secularisation and the Ministry of John R.W. Stott," 496–513.

61  Bebbington, *Evangelicalism in Modern Britain*.

62  C. Bartley to Malcolm Muggeridge, 30 January 1966, SC-004 50/4.

63  Ibid.

64  T. Kern to Malcolm Muggeridge, 1 February 1966, SC-004 50/5.

65  J.R. Percey to Malcolm Muggeridge, 28 July 1969, SC-004 22/11; C.J.H. Mill to Malcolm Muggeridge, 29 January 1966, SC-004 50/2; C.E. Pocknee to Malcolm Muggeridge, 29 January 1966, SC-004 50/2.

66  J.R. Percey to Malcolm Muggeridge, 28 July 1969, SC-004 22/11.

67  This contradicts Ian Hunter's claim that the reception of *Jesus Rediscovered* was largely cut along institutional lines. He wrote, "Whatever rejoicing may have been in heaven over a sinner who repents, there was none in the institutional church. In fact, the most withering criticism of *Jesus Rediscovered* came from ecclesiastical, not secular, quarters." Hunter, *Malcolm Muggeridge*, 232.

68  H. Waddams to Malcolm Muggeridge, 5 August 1970, SC-004 22/15.

69  Ibid.

70  One such person was a Detroit mechanic. The signature is difficult to decipher, but the fan does indicate he is the owner of an auto shop named "Walter's Pipe Shop." The store has since closed. He had read

*Jesus Rediscovered* and said, "I suppose it will become a great book for there are people like me who have learned thru trial & error that peace of mind & freedom from fear is only found thru that Inner peace one obtains from Christ's teachings. I have been raised with no religion, was never an atheist but rather an agnostic. I am probably still a poor Christian – Don't attend any Church – But am in a way successful. At any rate thanks again for what really served to confirm my own beliefs" ([Illegible] to Malcolm Muggeridge, 12 June 1970, SC-004 22/14). Another was sixty-three-year-old H. Swanson of Illinois. He wrote, "I find myself in complete agreement with your ideas and thoughts on the present state of organised religion. For most of my adult life I, too, was an agnostic, in fact, indifferent to any idea of God. Fortunate it has been for me that I had a spiritual awakening and developed a conscious contact with God. Not through the church, however, but as a simple gift of faith (H. Swanson to Malcolm Muggeridge, 21 November 1969, SC-004 22/11).

71 For example, the fifty-four-year-old Australian K. Parnell said, "I don't go to regular Church services anymore. Too much honkey-tonk. But I like to go into the Church & have it all to myself & feel at peace" (K. Parnell to Malcolm Muggeridge, July 1974, SC-004 95/2).

72 See Troughton, "Anti-Churchianity"; Nancy Brown to Malcolm Muggeridge, October 1969, SC-004 22/11; Charles Mylne to Malcolm Muggeridge, 4 July 1975, SC-004 97/1.

73 A. Smith to Malcolm Muggeridge, 19 August 1975, SC-004 97/4.

74 E. Kelly to Malcolm Muggeridge, 30 November 1969, SC-004 22/12.

75 Ibid.

76 Ibid.

77 J. Henderson to Malcolm Muggeridge, 27 January 1978, SC-004 103/1.

78 Derrick, "The Reception of C.S. Lewis in Britain and America," 277.

79 Christie and Gauvreau, *The Sixties and Beyond*, 15.

80 J. Buffield to Malcolm Muggeridge, 18 December 1970, SC-004 22/15.

81 Ibid.

82 E. Russell to Malcolm Muggeridge, 17 April 1967, SC-004 54/18.

83 Muggeridge, *Something Beautiful for God*, 48–9.

84 C. Mylne to Malcolm Muggeridge, 4 July 1975, SC-004 97/1.

85 Davie, "Europe: The Exception that Proves the Rules?," 68.

86 E. Harrington to Malcolm Muggeridge, 26 June 1976, SC-004 99/3.

87 K. Parnell to Malcolm Muggeridge, circa July 1974, SC-004 95/2; S. O'Brien to Malcolm Muggeridge, 4 July 1975, SC-004 97/1.

88 J. Johnson to Malcolm Muggeridge, circa December 1980, SC-004 105/14.

89  H. Gregory to Malcolm Muggeridge, 5 July 1977, SC-004 101/6.

90  E. Kelly to Malcolm Muggeridge, 30 November 1969, SC-004 22/12.

91  J. Kett to Malcolm Muggeridge, 16 August 1976, SC-004 99/6.

92  K. Williams to Malcolm Muggeridge, 25 July 1975, SC-004 97/2. J. Lisle to Malcolm Muggeridge, 4 June 1978, SC-004 103/9.

93  Karr, *Authors and Audiences*, 156.

94  For example, see the discussion of Methodist minister S. Arthurs, above.

95  J. Willey to Malcolm Muggeridge, 2 September 1975, SC-004 97/6.

96  Ibid.

97  Ibid.

98  E. Venner to Malcolm Muggeridge, 19 July 1974, SC-004 95/2.

99  B.P. Rosen to Malcolm Muggeridge, 7 June 1976, SC-004 99/1.

100  J. Kerrington to Malcolm Muggeridge, 2 May 1974, SC-004 94/18.

101  M.J. Harrison to Malcolm Muggeridge, 5 August 1980, SC-004 105/8.

102  Alex [no surname] to Malcolm Muggeridge, 26 January 1982, SC-004 109/2.

103  M. Hines to Malcolm Muggeridge, 28 March 1972, SC-004 87/8.

104  G. Althaus to Malcolm Muggeridge, 30 March 1963, SC-004 45/5.

105  Muggeridge, *Jesus: The Man Who Lives*, 4.

106  Enid [no last name] to Malcolm Muggeridge, 18 December 1976, SC-004 99/20.

107  Ibid.

108  See Booker, *The Seven Basic Plots*, 87–106.

109  H.P. Breuer to Malcolm Muggeridge, 27 April 1978, SC-004 103/5.

110  Ibid.

111  Ibid.

112  G. Jones to Malcolm Muggeridge, 9 December 1969, SC-004 22/12.

113  Ibid.

114  G. Jones to Malcolm Muggeridge, 22 January 1970, SC-004 22/13.

115  Ibid. Muggeridge's reply: "Dear [G.], Thanks. The subjects, in my opinion, most useful to a journalist are history & modern languages. But, of course, in the end where writing's concerned you can either do it or you can't. And only experience can show. Keep in Touch."

116  G. Jones to Malcolm Muggeridge, 8 June 1970, SC-004 22/14.

117  J. Adams to Malcolm Muggeridge, 2 September 1973, SC-004 92/13.

118  Ibid.

119  Ibid.

120  R. Kendrick to Malcolm Muggeridge, 17 June 1980, SC-004 105/6.

121 Ibid.

122 Brewitt-Taylor, *Christian Radicalism*, 153–7.

123 For example, see Christie and Gauvreau, Introduction to *Christian Churches and Their Peoples*, 3–8.

124 McGuire, *Lived Religion*, 187.

## CHAPTER THREE

1 D. Cooper to Malcolm Muggeridge, 10 February 1966, SC-004 50/6.

2 McLeod, *Religious Crisis*, 1.

3 Brewitt-Taylor, *Christian Radicalism*, 7.

4 Reddy, *Navigation of Feeling*. See also Boddice, *The History of Emotions*, 70–7.

5 Brewitt-Taylor, "From Religion to Revolution." See also Bingham, *Family Newspapers?*

6 I. Miller to Malcolm Muggeridge, 21 July 1973, SC-004 92/8.

7 B. Keiner to Malcolm Muggeridge, 27 October 1970, SC-004 22/15.

8 K. Thompson to Malcolm Muggeridge, 6 February 1970, SC-004 22/13.

9 F. Goodwin to Malcolm Muggeridge, 1 February 1966, SC-004 50/5.

10 Muggeridge, "The Sexual Revolution." See Brewitt-Taylor, "From Religion to Revolution."

11 I. Miller to Malcolm Muggeridge, 21 July 1973, SC-004 92/8.

12 Brewitt-Taylor, "Christianity and Sexual Revolution," 12–26.

13 N. Stone-Macdonald to Malcolm Muggeridge, 11 March 1974, SC-004 94/11.

14 T. Simpson to Malcolm Muggeridge, circa March 1978, SC-004 103/4.

15 L. Ransond to Malcolm Muggeridge, 17 December 1972, SC-004 90/13.

16 Ibid.

17 See Bruce and Glendinning, "When Was Secularization?," 107–26.

18 J. Heywood to Malcolm Muggeridge, 17 August 1973, SC-004 92/9.

19 F. Goodwin to Malcolm Muggeridge, 1 February 1966, SC-004 50/5.

20 M. Crewe to Malcolm Muggeridge, 25 May 1978, SC-004 103/8.

21 P. Harris to Malcolm Muggeridge, 19 July 1976, SC-004 99/5.

22 Ibid.

23 K. Wyndham to Malcolm Muggeridge, 16 May 1967, SC-004 54/28.

24 L. Smith to Malcolm Muggeridge, 19 December 1974, SC-004 95/15.

25 T. Stroud to Malcolm Muggeridge, 5 September 1975, SC-004 97/7.

26 Ibid.

27 R.E. Dean Jr to Malcolm Muggeridge, 18 June 1980, SC-004 105/6.

28 For a discussion of *sehnsucht*, see Scheibe, Freund, and Baltes, "Toward a Developmental Psychology of *Sehnsucht* (Life Longings)." According to Scheibe, Freund, and Baltes, there are six key characteristics of *sehnsucht*: "(a) utopian (unattainable) conceptions of ideal development; (b) a sense of incompleteness and imperfection of life; (c) a conjoint focus on the personal past, present, and future (tritime focus); (d) ambivalent emotions; (e) a sense of life reflection and evaluation; and (f) richness in symbolic meaning." Muggeridge's readers displayed all of these traits, though the most important ones for the present discussion include the first four.

29 See Brewitt-Taylor, *Christian Radicalism*, for the creation and promulgation of this "alternative paradigm" within the Church of England in the years leading up to the present study.

30 See also Erdozain, "Jesus and Augustine," 476–7.

31 C. Fink to Malcolm Muggeridge, 20 July 1978, SC-004 103/9.

32 Ibid.

33 B. Heffner to Malcolm Muggeridge, circa August 1981, SC-004 107/16.

34 M. Commell to Malcolm Muggeridge, 21 July 1981, SC-004 107/14.

35 J. Casella to Malcolm Muggeridge, 22 June 1971, SC-004 81/19.

36 R.J. Russell to Malcolm Muggeridge, ca. November 1976, SC-004 99/15.

37 Ibid.

38 See Hilliard, "Australia: Towards Secularisation and One Step Back," in *Secularisation in the Christian World*, 75–92.

39 Australian Bureau of Statistics, *Year Book Australia*, 2006, "Religious Affiliation," http://www.abs.gov.au/ausstats/abs@.nsf/46d1bc47ac9d0c7bca2 56c470025ff87/bfdda1ca506d6cfaca2570de0014496e!OpenDocument.

40 M. Vaughn to Malcolm Muggeridge, 10 June 1966, SC-004 51/8.

41 Brown, *Death of Christian Britain*, 165.

42 M. Vaughn to Malcolm Muggeridge, 10 June 1966, SC-004 51/8.

43 E. Poxon to Malcolm Muggeridge, 13 September 1970, SC-004 22/15.

44 Jones, *The Local Church and Generational Change*, 62–72.

45 Marwick, *The Sixties*, 7; Brown, *Death of Christian Britain*; McLeod, *Religious Crisis of the 1960s*, 84–6.

46 E. Poxon to Malcolm Muggeridge, 13 September 1970, SC-004 22/15.

47 Patrick [No last name] to Malcolm Muggeridge, 28 January 1974, SC-004 10/26.

48 S. Hands to Malcolm Muggeridge, 28 August 1980, SC-004 105/8.

49 D. Power to Malcolm Muggeridge, 23 December 1975, SC-004 97/17.

50 J. Savin to Malcolm Muggeridge, 1 November 1974, SC-004 95/11.

51 M. Horley to Malcolm Muggeridge, 19 September 1975, SC-004 97/10.

52 Ibid.
53 M. Vaughn to Malcolm Muggeridge, 10 June 1966, SC-004 51/8.
54 J. Halcomb to Malcolm Muggeridge, 3 February 1966, SC-004 50/5.
55 B. Fitzpatrick to Malcolm Muggeridge, September 1970, SC-004 22/11.
56 L. Lang-Sims to Malcolm Muggeridge, 17 December 1978, SC-004 103/11.
57 Ibid.
58 Ibid.
59 I. Taylor to Malcolm Muggeridge, 19 October 1970, SC-004 22/11.
60 R. Overall to Malcolm Muggeridge, 24 October 1976, SC-004 99/13.
61 Ibid.
62 Nash, "Believing in Secularisation," 530.
63 See Morris, "Enemy Within?," 177–200.
64 Scholars have faced similar challenges. William Gibson has noted the lack of consensus about the proper definition of secularization, let alone how it has played out in history. See Gibson, "Introduction: New Perspectives on Secularisation in Britain (and Beyond)," 431–8.
65 See, for example, Casanova, "The Secular and Secularisms," 1049–66. See also Chaves, "Secularization as Declining Religious Authority," 749–74; and Field, "Another Window."
66 Davie, *Religion in Britain Since 1945*.

## CHAPTER FOUR

1 Ammerman, *Sacred Stories, Spiritual Tribes*, 7.
2 This line of reasoning follows Eve Colpus's deft assessment that philanthropy functions "as part of the reflexive and communicative practices individuals used ... to make sense of the social, political and cultural changes in the world around them." Moreover, Muggeridge's readers affirm that charitable work served in "forging social relationships that extended familial and friendship bonds within the wider community." Colpus, *Female Philanthropy in the Interwar World*, 2, 6–7, 28, 62.
3 Prochaska, *Christianity and Social Service in Modern Britain*, 149.
4 Quoted in Prochaska, *Christianity and Social Service*, 151.
5 Woodhead, "Introduction," in *Religion and Change in Modern Britain*, 14.
6 Beveridge, *Voluntary Action*, 320. Quoted in Prochaska, *Christianity and Social Service*, 158–9.
7 Woodhead, "Introduction," in *Religion and Change in Modern Britain*, 15.
8 Geremek, *Poverty: A History*, 245.
9 Woodhead, "Introduction," in *Religion and Change in Modern Britain*, 10.

10  Rowntree and Lavers, *Poverty and the Welfare State*. See also Fink, "Welfare, Poverty and Social Inequalities," 271ff. Within intellectual circles, Marxist critics were concerned that welfare was in effect a bribe to the dispossessed to accept the legitimacy of government. Meanwhile, critics on the right thought that the welfare state was not helping consumers because it subsidized unprofitable sectors. Feminists also contended that the welfare state was patriarchal in its framework because it relegated women to pre-determined roles within the home. See Fawcett and Lowe, "Introduction," in *Welfare Policy in Britain*, 10–11.

11  Hampton, *Disability and the Welfare State in Britain*, 87; Brewitt-Taylor, *Christian Radicalism*, 213–16; Lowe, "The Rediscovery of Poverty," 602–11.

12  See Fink, "Welfare, Poverty and Social Inequalities," 271.

13  See E. Robinson, et al., "Telling Stories about Post-war Britain, 272.

14  See Fink, "Welfare, Poverty and Social Inequalities," 273.

15  Muggeridge thought the coming of the welfare state was a "nightmare" in which "all the faceless men, the men without opinions, have been posted in key positions for a bloodless take-over, and that no one is prepared to join a Resistance Movement in defense of freedom because no one remembers what freedom means." Quoted in Prochaska, *Christianity and Social Service*, 156–7.

16  Muggeridge, "The Importance of Being Beveridge."

17  *The Question Why*: "Poverty" [14 February 1972], SC-004 170/26. Other guests included economic experts Sir George Bolton and Peter Jay, social reformer Marion Stubbs, trade unionist Jimmy Reid, and politician Brian Griffiths.

18  Ibid.

19  Muggeridge, *Something Beautiful for God*, 27–8.

20  Ibid., 131–2.

21  J.C. Reid to Margaret [no last name given], 18 April 1974, SC-004 39/12. The English edition sold 167,648 copies domestically and overseas. The American edition sold just over 24,000 copies, and the Danish and Italian translations together sold about 7,000 copies. As a point of comparison, Fontana sold about 400,000 copies of C.S. Lewis's *Mere Christianity* by 1969. See Ledger-Lomas, "Religion," 398.

22  Ingrams, *Muggeridge*, 213.

23  See the appendix.

24  Ingrams, *Muggeridge*, 213.

25  P.E. John to Malcolm Muggeridge, 2 April 1986, SC-004 39/19.

26  W.G. Forker to Malcolm Muggeridge, 5 October 1972, SC-004 39/3.

27 Malcolm Muggeridge to W.G. Forker, 12 October 1972, SC-004 39/3.

28 See "Correspondence about nomination for Nobel Prize, 1967-1977," SC-004 39/2.

29 Most of the evidence available relates to his work in 1975 and before. There is at least one letter from Eileen Egan, in reply to a 1977 letter from Muggeridge, who was integral to the resubmission of Mother Teresa's name for the Nobel Peace Prize. See Eileen Egan to Malcolm Muggeridge, 11 February 1977, SC-004 39/2.

30 This was most noteworthy in the number of novitiates, which rose from 331 to 570.

31 See the reports for 1970, 1971, 1972–73, and 1973–74 for the International Association of Co-Workers of Mother Teresa in "International Association of Co-Workers of Mother Teresa Reports," SC-004 273/12. All of the reports make regular reference to distributing or showing *Something Beautiful for God* either in its documentary or book form to highlight the work of Mother Teresa and her organization.

32 Hitchens, "Christopher Hitchens on Mother Teresa (Interview)," *Free Inquiry Magazine* 16, no. 4 (Fall 1996), SC-004 273/10.

33 Hitchens, *The Missionary Position*, 46.

34 Michael Costigan, "Review of *Something Beautiful for God*, by Malcolm Muggeridge," SC-004 225/6. The clipping of this review was cut small enough that the place of publication is not listed in the Muggeridge Papers. It would seem that the review has not been digitized in any format, either, so it is difficult to track down the exact newspaper in which it appeared. A good guess would be the Melbourne-based Catholic publication the *Advocate*, which a Michael Costigan edited for many years. It would make sense that the *Advocate* would have wanted to include a review of *Something Beautiful for God* for their readers. Additionally, if the Michael Costigan who wrote the review was the same Michael Costigan who edited the *Advocate*, his remarks would make sense, too. He was a leader of the pro-life movement among Catholics during the 1960s and 1970s. All of the counter-examples he names were Roman Catholic social activists who did not find serious problems with using governmental authority to further social justice.

35 Mervyn Stockwood, "Review of *Something Beautiful for God*, by Malcolm Muggeridge," *Books and Bookmen* (June 1971): 52. SC-004 225/2.

36 Martin Smith, "Review of *Something Beautiful for God*, by Malcolm Muggeridge," *Brewarrina News* (23 February 1973). SC-004 225/6.

37 Lisa Hobbs, "Memories of Saint Blessing Calcutta," *Vancouver Sun* (28 October 1972), SC-004 225/2.

38  Muggeridge, *Something Beautiful for God*, 30–1.

39  Scheer, "Are Emotions a Kind of Practice?," 218.

40  Dr C. Vossen to Malcolm Muggeridge, 26 September 1974, SC-004 95/8.

41  Malcolm Muggeridge to Dr C. Vossen, 10 October 1974, SC-004 95/8.

42  S. Haddock to Malcolm Muggeridge, 26 July 1973, SC-004 92/8.

43  S. Haddock to Malcolm Muggeridge, 10 August 1973, SC-004 92/9.

44  C. Lake to Malcolm Muggeridge, 9 July 1969, SC-004 22/11.

45  Ibid.

46  M. Therese to Malcolm Muggeridge, 9 August 1972, SC-004 88/7.

47  W. Haines to Malcolm Muggeridge, 9 April 1971, SC-004 81/6.

48  M. Alperen to Malcolm Muggeridge, December 1973, SC-004 93/8.

49  W. Haines to Malcolm Muggeridge, 9 April 1971, SC-004 81/6.

50  M. Bracey to Malcolm Muggeridge, 10 September 1973, SC-004 92/15.

51  F. Loral to Malcolm Muggeridge, 30 October 1973, SC-004 93/4.

52  Anonymous to Malcolm Muggeridge, 19 June 1971, SC-004 81/19.

53  Lowes refers to working in development, but his name is also listed in
    the *United Nations System of Organizations and Directory of Senior
    Officials*, 77, 90.

54  See General Assembly Resolution 35/18, *Proclamation of the International
    Drinking Water Supply and Sanitation Decade* (10 November 1980), avail-
    able at https://www.refworld.org/docid/3b00f1a93c.html.

55  P. Lowes to Malcolm Muggeridge, 7 October 1982, SC-004 110/15.

56  Lowes shared a common religious focus as those "Golden Rule" Chris-
    tians explored by Nancy Ammerman in *Sacred Stores, Spiritual Tribes*,
    chap. 1.

57  P. Lowes to Malcolm Muggeridge, 7 October 1982, SC-004 110/15.

58  K. Thompson to Malcolm Muggeridge, 6 February 1970, SC-004 22/13.

59  K. Hutchison to Malcolm Muggeridge, 15 November 1980, SC-004
    105/12.

60  Michaela [no last name] to Malcolm Muggeridge, May 1980, SC-004
    105/5.

61  E. Ball to Malcolm Muggeridge, 11 April 1972, SC-004 87/12.

62  R. Clayden to Malcolm Muggeridge, 25 March 1972, SC-004 87/7.

63  M. McBride to Malcolm Muggeridge, 24 April 1978, SC-004 103/5.

64  S. Brackfield to Malcolm Muggeridge, 5 February 1972, SC-004 39/7.

65  Ibid.

66  Ibid.

67  K. Surin to Malcolm Muggeridge, 15 January 1973, SC-004 91/4; M.
    Williams to Kenneth Surin, 25 January 1973, SC-004 91/4.

68  M. Millenbach to Malcolm Muggeridge, 15 June 1977, SC-004 101/3.

69  Malcolm Muggeridge to M. Millenbach, 24 June 1977, SC-004 101/3.

70  C. Hall to Malcolm Muggeridge, February 1973, SC-004 91/10; J. Butters
    to Malcolm Muggeridge, February 1973, SC-004 91/10; J. Butters to Mal-
    colm Muggeridge, 11 April 1973, SC-004 91/18; C. Hall to Malcolm
    Muggeridge, 11 April 1973, SC-004 91/18; and B. Lowndes to Malcolm
    Muggeridge, 11 April 1973, SC-004 91/18.

71  M. Blake to Malcolm Muggeridge, 2 January 1972, SC-004 85/19.

72  A. Wintle to Malcolm Muggeridge, 15 May 1981, SC-004 107/8.

73  See "Teresa, Mother – Correspondence about Donations, 1977." SC-004
    39/22. Cross-referencing this file with the other boxes of fan mail from
    1977 shows that the secretary missed only two letters that mention
    donations, £100 each, to Mother Teresa.

74  G.L. Kane to Malcolm Muggeridge, 21 September 1971, SC-004 39/9.

75  W.H.P. Ager to Malcolm Muggeridge, 3 February 1972, SC-004 86/5.

76  M. Mart to Malcolm Muggeridge, 11 February 1973, SC-004 91/9.

77  Sister Martinia to Malcolm Muggeridge, 7 May 1971, SC-004 81/12; M.
    Nichols to Malcolm Muggeridge, 27 December 1971, SC-004 84/10.

78  For "emotional communities" see Barbara Rosenwein's now classic work
    *Emotional Communities in the Early Middle Ages.* See also Boddice, *The
    History of Emotions,* 77–83.

79  S. Girling to Malcolm Muggeridge, 8 May 1982, SC-004 110/1.

80  M. Klingber to Malcolm Muggeridge, June 1970, SC-004 22/14.

81  M. Choquette to Malcolm Muggeridge, 21 October 1974, SC-004 95/10.

82  Marian Williams to Fontana Distribution Department, 4 January 1975,
    SC-004 95/10.

### CHAPTER FIVE

1  See McGuire, *Lived Religion,* 208–13.

2  See Brown, "What Was the Religious Crisis of the 1960s?," 479. Brown
   notes: "the historian needs to put Christian conservatives back onto centre stage to better appreciate what the cultural revolution of the sixties
   was about and how religious history has evolved since then."

3  R. Blanks to Malcolm Muggeridge, 18 August 1980, SC-004 105/8. In her
   case, she read Muggeridge's *A Third Testament* because it dealt with Leo
   Tolstoy and William Blake.

4  J.W. Atkins to Malcolm Muggeridge, 14 February 1976, SC-004 98/13.

5  Field, *Secularization in the Long 1960s,* 229.

6  For example, see Heimann, "Christianity in Western Europe from the
   Enlightenment," 497–505. What follows will focus primarily on the

British context. Most of Muggeridge's readers were British, and it is that context that had the greatest impact in shaping Muggeridge himself.

7  See McLeod, *Religious Crisis*, 119–22. For this dynamic in Australia, see Chilton, *Evangelicals and the End of Christendom*. Chilton focuses specifically on how those in leadership positions in Australia engaged with the cultural and religious shifts of the 1960s and 1970s. One of these key shifts was in immigration and the decline of a collective Christian Britannic nationalism.

8  Field, "Religious Statistics in Great Britain: An Historical Introduction," *British Religion in Numbers*, http://www.brin.ac.uk/wp-content/uploads /2011/12/development-of-religious-statistics.pdf. In England and Wales alone, Muslims, Sikhs, and Hindus each experienced roughly a ten-fold increase in population between 1961 and 1981. The Muslim population increased from approximately 50,000 in 1961 to 553,000 in 1981, the Sikh population from 16,000 to 144,000, and the Hindu population from 30,000 to 278,000. We should be cautious about trusting raw figures of these groups, however. Clive Field has noted that statistics about "non-Christian faiths" are not altogether reliable because historically these groups (with Judaism excepted) have not attached a great deal of importance to counting themselves. See "Hindu, Muslim and Sikh Adherents," *British Religion in Numbers*, http://www.brin.ac.uk/figures /hindu-muslim-and-sikh-adherents. See also Peach and Gale, "Muslims, Hindus, and Sikhs in the New Religious Landscape of England." Peach and Gale make the important case that the influx of religiously diverse communities transformed the visual landscape of Britain, too. The creation of sites of worship for Hindus, Sikhs, and Muslims accentuated the reality of Britain's religious diversity. Also, Brewitt-Taylor, who otherwise downplays the role of immigration on transforming British culture in the early 1960s, says that "Immigration first became a general election issue in 1964, and the first Race Relations Act was not passed until 1965; it is only from the late 1960s, and almost certainly later, if even at all, that it becomes possible to talk of the decolonization of domestic British culture on any significant scale." Brewitt-Taylor, *Christian Radicalism*, 12.

9  Field, *Secularization in the Long 1960s*, 76.

10  See Peach and Gale, "Muslims, Hindus, and Sikhs," 469–90.

11  Mandler, *The English National Character*, 222.

12  Chapman, "The International Context of Secularization in England," 163–89.

13  Ibid., 179.

14  Maiden, "What Could Be More Christian Than to Allow the Sikhs to Use It?"

15 Parker and Freathy, "Ethnic Diversity, Christian Hegemony." They show that Christianity maintained a prominent position within this educational platform, itself based on the 1975 Birmingham *Agreed Syllabus of Religious Instruction*. The critiques from Christian conservatives were thus somewhat overstated. It is true that in some cases immigration caused religious fragmentation that could ignite reactionary movements within Christianity, what Peter Berger called "resurgent religion." Yet, that reaction to alternative belief systems was not typical, despite recent characterizations to that effect by Callum Brown. As Alister Chapman has demonstrated in his local study of Derby, multiculturalism could foster the creation of a new civil religion whereby diverse religious communities worked in concert, each mutually concerned for the good of society. Tolerance and various forms of appropriation were the norm; militant fundamentalism the exception. See Berger, *The Desecularization of the World*; Brown, *Religion and Society in Twentieth-Century Britain*, 297–314; and Chapman, "Civil Religions in Derby," 817–43.

16 Noonan, "Piety and Professionalism." See also Briggs, "Christ and the Media," especially 276–7. See also Brown, *The Battle for Christian Britain*, 256–83.

17 See Brewitt-Taylor, *Christian Radicalism*.

18 McLeod, "The 1960s," 264–5.

19 H. Salkin to Malcolm Muggeridge, 5 April 1970, SC-004 75/11.

20 E. Robinson, et al. "Telling Stories about Post-war Britain."

21 Giddens, *Modernity and Self-Identity*.

22 M. Ginsberg to Malcolm Muggeridge, February 1973, SC-004 91/24.

23 Ibid.

24 Ibid.

25 Bhagavad Gita, chapter 6, verse 32, quoted in M. Ginsberg to Malcolm Muggeridge, February 1973, SC-004 91/24.

26 M. Ginsberg to Malcolm Muggeridge, February 1973, SC-004 91/24.

27 E. Corfe to Malcolm Muggeridge, 1 November 1975, SC-004 97/14.

28 T. Halbert to Malcolm Muggeridge, 30 October 1966, SC-004 52/23.

29 See McLeod, *Religious Crisis of the 1960s*, 2.

30 See Brown, "The People of 'No Religion,'" 37–61.

31 Ibid., 60.

32 Brown notes that the typical person of no religion in the mid-twentieth century was young, white, and male. See Brown, "The People of 'No Religion,'" 58. For an attempt to classify varieties of atheism, see Sheard, "Ninety-Eight Atheists," 1–16.

33  H. Wilman to Malcolm Muggeridge, 30 September 1973, SC-004 92/17.
34  Ibid.
35  Quoted in Hunter, *Malcolm Muggeridge*, 225.
36  Muggeridge, *Christ and the Media*, 72.
37  E. Robinson et al., "Telling Stories about Post-war Britain," 276.
38  T.L. Williams to Malcolm Muggeridge, 15 August 1966, SC-004 52/4.
39  R. Poole to Malcolm Muggeridge, 12 June 1977, SC-004 101/2.
40  Ibid.
41  Hitchens, "A Hundred Years of Muggery."
42  The Bahá'í Faith underwent something of an evangelistic shift in the
    late 1930s under the leadership of Shoghí Effendí. Since then, it has
    launched several ambitious plans to grow their numbers. See Smith and
    Momen, "The Bahá'í Faith 1957–1988," 63–91. Poole's attempts to con-
    vert Muggeridge to the Bahá'í Faith may well have been the result of
    this larger project. This does not deny its fundamental teaching of the
    essential unity of all religions, but it does cause an attitudinal shift in
    how the more zealous of its adherents would interact with others out-
    side the Bahá'í Faith.
43  R. Poole to Malcolm Muggeridge, 12 June 1977, SC-004 101/2.
44  Malcolm Muggeridge to R. Poole, 21 June 1977, SC-004 101/2.
45  I.S. Stoby to Malcolm Muggeridge, 4 April 1977, SC-004 100/13.
46  Malcolm Muggeridge to I.S. Stoby, 23 May 1977, SC-004 100/13.
47  J.W. Atkins to Malcolm Muggeridge, 14 February 1976, SC-004 98/13.
48  J.W. Atkins to Malcolm Muggeridge, 18 June 1976, SC-004 99/2.
49  Ibid.
50  Ammerman, *Sacred Stories, Spiritual Tribes*, 127.
51  Brown, "Men Losing Faith."
52  R. Hunter to Malcolm Muggeridge, 26 May 1968, SC-004 61/11.
53  Ibid.
54  Malcolm Muggeridge to R. Hunter, 11 June 1968, SC-004 61/11.
55  R. Meeten to Malcolm Muggeridge, 18 August 1969, SC-004 61/11.
56  Ibid.
57  Ibid.
58  Malcolm Muggeridge to R. Meeten, 4 September 1969, SC-004 61/11.
59  See the examples of G. Evans and D. Baker in chapter 1.
60  T. Foster to Malcolm Muggeridge, 6 April 1974, SC-004 94/15.
61  Ibid.
62  Quoted in McLeod, *The Religious Crisis of the 1960s*, 131.
63  J. Knox to Malcolm Muggeridge, 13 January 1970, SC-004 22/13.

64  Ibid.
65  H. Hout to Malcolm Muggeridge, February 1973, SC-004 91/24.
66  Ibid.
67  Brown, "Men Losing Faith," 317–18.
68  P. Dawson to Malcolm Muggeridge, December 1971, SC-004 84/14.
69  Ibid.
70  Ibid.
71  Muggeridge, *Something Beautiful for God*, 27–8.
72  J. Baweden to Malcolm Muggeridge, 2 January 1972, SC-004 85/2.
73  Ibid.
74  Ibid.
75  Ibid.
76  L. Perigo to Malcolm Muggeridge, 15 September 1977, SC-004 101/14.
77  L.D. Hale to Malcolm Muggeridge, 9 August 1977, SC-004 101/9.
78  R. Dixon to Malcolm Muggeridge, 17 August 1970, SC-004 76/16.
79  Eisenstadt, "Multiple Modernities," 2. See also Brewitt-Taylor, *Christian Radicalism*.

## CONCLUSION

1   Ingrams, *Muggeridge*, 234.
2   Wolfe, *Malcolm Muggeridge*, 412.
3   Ibid., 409.
4   Muggeridge, *Something Beautiful for God*, 56.
5   Wolfe, *Malcolm Muggeridge*, 415.
6   S. Whipple to Malcolm Muggeridge, 14 March 1983, SC-004 113/12.
7   D. Roe to Malcolm Muggeridge, 19 February 1983, SC-004 113/13.
8   Frank [no last name] to Malcolm Muggeridge, 9 January 1983, SC-004 113/2.
9   J. Woodbury to Malcolm Muggeridge, 2 December 1982, SC-004 112/2.
10  R. Smith to Malcolm Muggeridge, 5 December 1982, SC-004 112/4.
11  Ibid.
12  Booker, *The Seven Basic Plots*, 173ff.
13  Giddens, *Modernity and Self-Identity*, 54.
14  E. Harrington to Malcolm Muggeridge, 26 June 1976, SC-004 99/3.
15  B. Harrild to Malcolm Muggeridge, December 1983, SC-004 114/22.
16  Brewitt-Taylor, *Christian Radicalism*, 10.
17  McGuire, *Lived Religion*, 210.

18 For the Nationwide Festival of Light, see Grimley, "Anglican Evangelicals and Anti-Permissiveness."

19 See, for example, Sandbrook, *White Heat*, 583. Interestingly, Callum
Brown describes Muggeridge as a Roman Catholic convert when discussing his frequent appearance on the BBC in the 1960s and 1970s. As
noted above, Muggeridge's conversion to Catholicism in 1982 was neither inevitable nor expected.

20 Hitchens, "A Hundred Years of Muggery."

21 M. Hardcastle to Malcolm Muggeridge, 17 March 1978, SC-004 102/4.

# Bibliography

## ARCHIVAL SOURCES

Wheaton College Special Collections, Wheaton, IL
Malcolm Muggeridge Papers (SC-004)

## PRINTED SOURCES

Abel-Smith, Brian, and Peter Townsend. *The Poor and the Poorest: A New Analysis of the Ministry of Labour's Family Expenditure Surveys of 1953–54 and 1960*. London: G. Bell and Sons, 1965.

Addison, Paul, and Harriet Jones. *A Companion to Contemporary Britain 1939–2000*. Malden, MA: Blackwell Publishing, 2005.

Altick, Richard. *The English Common Reader 1800–1900*, 2nd edition. Columbus: Ohio State University Press, 1998.

Ammerman, Nancy Tatom. *Sacred Stories, Spiritual Tribes: Finding Religion in Everyday Life*. Oxford: Oxford University Press, 2014.

Anderson, Benedict. *Imagined Communities: Reflections on the Origin and Spread of Nationalism*. London: Verso, 2006.

Annan, Noel. *Our Age: The Generation that Made Post-War Britain*. London: Harper Collins, 1990.

Atherstone, Andrew, and John Maiden, eds. *Evangelicalism and the Church of England in the Twentieth Century: Reform, Resistance, and Renewal*. Woodbridge: Boydell & Brewer, 2014.

Barker, Eileen, James A. Beckford, and Karel Dobbelaere, eds. *Secularization, Rationalism, and Sectarianism: Essays in Honour of Bryan R. Wilson*. Oxford: Clarendon Press, 1993.

Barton, David, and Nigel Hall, eds. *Letter Writing as a Social Practice*. Amsterdam: John Benjamins Publishing Company, 1999.

Bates, Courtney A. "The Fan Letter Correspondence of Willa Cather: Challenging the Divide between Professional and Common Reader." *Transformative Works and Cultures* 6 (2011). http://journal.transformativeworks.org/index.php/twc/article/view/221.

Bebbington, David. *Evangelicalism in Modern Britain: A History from the 1730s to the 1980s*. London: Routledge, 1989.

Bennett, Oliver. *Cultural Pessimism: Narratives of Decline in the Post Modern World*. Edinburgh: Edinburgh University Press, 2001.

Berger, Peter, ed. *The Desecularization of the World: Resurgent Religion and World Politics*. Grand Rapids: Wm. B. Eerdmans, 1999.

Bernard, R. Jerman. "Disraeli's Fan Mail: A Curiosity Item." *Nineteenth-Century Fiction* 9, no. 1 (June 1954): 61–71.

Bernstein, George L. *The Myth of Decline: The Rise of Britain Since 1945*. London: Pimlico, 2004.

Beveridge, William. *Voluntary Action: A Report on Methods of Social Advance*. London: G. Allen and Unwin, 1948.

Bingham, Adrian. *Family Newspapers? Sex, Private Life, and the British Popular Press, 1918–1978*. Oxford: Oxford University Press, 2009.

Boddice, Rob. *The History of Emotions*. Manchester: Manchester University Press, 2018.

Booker, Christopher. *The Neophiliacs: A Study of the Revolution in English Life in the Fifties and Sixties*. London: Collins, 1969.

– *The Seven Basic Plots: Why We Tell Stories*. New York: Continuum, 2003.

Brewitt-Taylor, Sam. "Christianity and the Invention of the Sexual Revolution in Britain, 1963–1967." *The Historical Journal* 60, no. 2 (June 2017): 519–24.

– *Christian Radicalism in the Church of England and the Invention of the British Sixties, 1957–1970*. Oxford: Oxford University Press, 2018.

– "From Religion to Revolution: Theologies of Secularisation in the British Student Christian Movement, 1963–1973." *Journal of Ecclesiastical History* 66, no. 4 (October 2015): 792–811.

– "The Invention of a 'Secular Society'? Christianity and the Sudden Emergence of Secularization Discourses in the British Media, 1961–4." *Twentieth Century British History* 24, no. 3 (2013): 327–50.

Briggs, Asa. *The BBC: The First Fifty Years*. Oxford: Oxford University Press, 1995.

– "Christ and the Media." In *Secularization, Rationalism, and Sectarianism: Essays in Honour of Bryan R. Wilson*, edited by Eileen Barker, James A.

Beckford, and Karel Dobbelaere, 267–86. Oxford: Clarendon Press, 1993.

– *The History of Broadcasting in the United Kingdom*, 5 vols. Oxford: Oxford University Press, 1961–95.

Brown, Callum. *The Battle for Christian Britain: Sex, Humanists and Secularisation, 1945–1980.* Cambridge: Cambridge University Press, 2019.

– *The Death of Christian Britain: Understanding Secularization, 1800–2000.* London: Routledge, 2000.

– "Men Losing Faith: The Making of Modern No Religionism in the UK, 1939–2010." In *Men, Masculinities and Religious Change in Twentieth-Century Britain*, edited by Lucy Delap and Sue Morgan, 301–25. London: Palgrave Macmillan, 2013.

– "The People of 'No Religion': The Demographics of Secularisation in the English-speaking world since c. 1900." *Archiv für Sozialgeschichte* 51 (2011): 37–61.

– *Religion and the Demographic Revolution: Women and Secularisation in Canada, Ireland, UK and USA since the 1960s.* Woodbridge: Boydell & Brewer, 2012.

– *Religion and Society in Twentieth-Century Britain.* London: Routledge, 2006.

– "The Secularisation Decade: What the 1960s have done to the Study of Religious History." In *The Decline of Christendom in Western Europe*, edited by Hugh McLeod and Wernert Ustord, 29–46. Cambridge: Cambridge University Press, 2003.

– "Secularization, the Growth of Militancy and the Spiritual Revolution: Religious Change and Gender Power in Britain, 1901–2001." *Historical Research* 80, no. 209 (August 2007): 393–418.

– "What Was the Religious Crisis of the 1960s?" *Journal of Religious History* 34, no. 4 (December 2010): 468–79.

Brown, Callum, and Michael Snape. *Secularisation in the Christian World: Essays in Honour of Hugh McLeod.* Farnham: Ashgate, 2010.

Bruce, Steve. *God Is Dead: Secularization in the West.* Malden, MA: Wiley Blackwell, 2002.

– *Religion in the Modern World: From Cathedrals to Cults.* Oxford: Oxford University Press, 1996.

– "Secularization and Church Growth in the United Kingdom." *Journal of Religion in Europe* 6, no. 3 (2013): 273–96.

– *Secularization: In Defense of an Unfashionable Theory.* Oxford: Oxford University Press, 2011.

Bruce, Steve, and Tony Glendinning. "When Was Secularization? Dating the Decline of the British Churches and Locating its Cause." *The British Journal of Sociology* 61, no. 1 (March 2010): 107–26.

Buckley, Reka. "The Emergence of Film Fandom in Postwar Italy: Reading Claudia Cardinale's Fan Mail." *Historical Journal of Film, Radio and Television* 29, no. 4 (2009): 523–59.

Bullivant, Stephen. *Mass Exodus: Catholic Disaffiliation in Britain and North America since Vatican II*. Oxford: Oxford University Press, 2019.

Burleigh, Michael. *Sacred Causes: The Clash of Religion and Politics from the Great War to the War on Terror*. New York: Harper Perennial, 2007.

Carr, E.H. *What Is History?* London: Penguin, 1961.

Casanova, José, "The Secular and Secularisms." *Social Research* 76, no. 4 (2009): 1049–66.

Cavicchi, Daniel. "Fandom Before 'Fan': Shaping the History of Enthusiastic Audiences." *Reception: Texts, Readers, Audiences, History* 6 (2014): 52–72.

Chadwick, Owen. *The Victorian Church*. London: Adam and Charles Black, 1972.

Chandler, Andrew. *The Church of England in the Twentieth Century: The Church Commissioners and the Politics of Reform, 1948–1998*. Woodbridge, 2006.

Chapman, Alister. "Civil Religions in Derby, 1930–2000." *Historical Journal* 59, no. 3 (2016): 817–43.

– *Godly Ambition: John Stott and the Evangelical Movement*. Oxford: Oxford University Press, 2012.

– "The International Context of Secularization in England: The End of Empire, Immigration, and the Decline of Christian National Identity, 1945–1970." *Journal of British Studies* 54 (January 2015): 163–189.

– "Secularisation and the Ministry of John R. W. Stott at All Souls, Langham Place, 1950–1970." *The Journal of Ecclesiastical History* 56, no. 3 (July 2005): 496–513.

Chartier, Roger. *The Cultural Uses of Print in Early Modern France*. Translated by Lydia G. Cochrane. Princeton: Princeton University Press, 1987.

Chaves, Mark. "Secularization as Declining Religious Authority." *Social Forces* 72, no. 3 (March 1994): 749–74.

Chilton, Hugh. *Evangelicals and the End of Christendom: Religion, Australia and the Crises of the 1960s*. Abingdon: Routledge, 2020.

Christie, Nancy, and Michael Gauvreau, eds. *Christian Churches and Their Peoples, 1840–1965: A Social History of Religion in Canada*. Toronto: University of Toronto Press, 2010.

- *The Sixties and Beyond: Dechristianization in North America and Western Europe, 1945–2000*. Toronto: University of Toronto Press, 2013.

Clark, J.C.D. "Secularization and Modernization: The Failure of a 'Grand Narrative.'" *Historical Journal* 55, no. 1 (2012): 161–94.

Clements, Ben. *Religion and Public Opinion in Britain: Continuity and Change*. New York: Palgrave Macmillan, 2015.

- *Surveying Christian Beliefs and Religious Debates in Post-War Britain*. London: Palgrave Macmillan, 2016.

Collini, Stefan. *Common Reading: Critics, Historians, Publics*. Oxford: Oxford University Press, 2008.

- *Common Writing: Essays on Literary Culture and Public Debate*. Oxford: Oxford University Press, 2016.

Collins, Marcus, ed. *The Permissive Society and its Enemies: Sixties British Culture*. London: Rivers Oram Press, 2007.

Colpus, Eve. *Female Philanthropy in the Interwar World: Between Self and Other*. London: Bloomsbury Academic, 2018.

Crisell, Andrew. *An Introductory History of British Broadcasting*. London: Routledge, 1997.

Crockett, Alasdair, and David Voas. "Generations of Decline: Religious Change in 20th-Century Britain." *Journal for the Scientific Study of Religion* 45 (2006): 567–84.

Crone, Rosalind, and Shafquat Towheed, eds. *The History of Reading, Volume 3: Methods, Strategies, Tactics*. New York: Palgrave, 2011.

Cummings, Kathleen Sprows, Timothy Matovina, and Robert A. Orsi, eds. *Catholics in the Vatican II Era*. Cambridge: Cambridge University Press, 2018.

Darnton, Robert. "First Steps Towards a History of Reading." *American Journal of French Studies* 23, no. 1 (1986): 5–30.

Davie, Grace. "Europe: The Exception that Proves the Rules?" In *The Desecularization of the World: Resurgent Religion and World Politics*, edited by Peter Berger, 65–83. Grand Rapids, MI: Wm B. Eerdmans, 1999.

- *Religion in Britain: Believing without Belonging*. Oxford: Wiley Blackwell, 1994.

- *Religion in Britain: A Persistent Paradox*. Second Edition. Oxford: Wiley Blackwell, 2015.

- *Religion in Britain Since 1945*. Oxford: Wiley Blackwell, 1994.

Delap, Lucy, and Sue Morgan, eds. *Men, Masculinities and Religious Change in Twentieth-Century Britain*. London: Palgrave Macmillan, 2013.

Derrick, Stephanie. "The Reception of C.S. Lewis in Britain and America."
    PhD dissertation, University of Stirling, 2013.

Dols, Chris. "Of Religious Diseases and Sociological Laboratories: Towards
    a Transnational Anatomy of Catholic Secularisation Narratives in West-
    ern Europe, 1940–1970." *Journal of Religion in Europe* 9 (2016): 107–32.

Donnelly, Mark. *Sixties Britain*. Harlow: Pearson Education Limited, 2005.

Earle, Rebecca. *Epistolary Selves: Letters and Letter-Writers, 1600–1945*. Alder-
    shot: Ashgate, 1999.

Edwards, David Lawrence, and John A.T. Robinson. *The "Honest to God"*
    *Debate: Some Reflections Reactions to the Book "Honest to God."* London:
    SCM Press, 2012.

Eisenstadt, S.N. "Multiple Modernities." *Daedalus* 129, no. 1 (Winter 2000):
    1–29.

Eliot, Simon, and Jonathan Rose, eds. *A Companion to the History of the*
    *Book*. Malden, MA: Wiley Blackwell, 2009.

Erdozain, Dominic. "'Cause is Not Quite What it Used to be': The Return
    of Secularisation." *English Historical Review* 77, no. 525 (2012):
    377–400.

– "Jesus and Augustine: The God of Terror and the Origins of European
    Doubt." *Journal of Religious History* 41, no. 4 (December 2017): 476–504.

– *The Soul of Doubt: The Religious Roots of Unbelief from Luther to Marx.*
    Oxford: Oxford University Press, 2015.

Eskridge, Larry. *God's Forever Family: The Jesus People Movement in America*.
    Oxford: Oxford University Press, 2013.

Fawcett, Helen, and Rodney Lowe, eds. *Welfare Policy in Britain: The Road*
    *from 1945*. London: Macmillan Press, 1999.

Field, Clive. D. "Another Window on British Secularization: Public Atti-
    tudes to Church and Clergy Since the 1960s." *Contemporary British History*
    28, no. 2 (2014): 190–218.

– *Britain's Last Religious Revival? Quantifying Belonging, Behaving, and Believ-*
    *ing in the Long 1950s*. New York: Palgrave, 2015.

– *Secularization in the Long 1960s: Numerating Religion in Britain*. Oxford:
    Oxford University Press, 2017.

Fink, Janet. "Welfare, Poverty and Social Inequalities." In *A Companion to*
    *Contemporary Britain, 1939–2000*, edited by Paul Addison and Harriet
    Jones, 263–80. Malden, MA: Blackwell Publishing, 2005.

Flint, Kate. *The Woman Reader, 1837–1914*. Oxford: Oxford University Press,
    1995.

Francis, Leslie J., and Peter W. Brierley, "The Changing Face of British
    Churches, 1975–1995." In *Leaving Religion and the Religious Life*, edited by

Mordechai Bar-Lev and William Shaffir, 159–84. Greenwich, CT: JAI Press, 1997.

Gammerl, Benno. "Felt Distances." In *Emotional Lexicons: Continuity and Change in the Vocabulary of Feeling 1700–2000*, 177–200. Oxford: Oxford University Press, 2014.

Garnett, Jane, Matthew Grimley, Alana Harris, William Whyte, and Sarah Williams, eds. *Redefining Christian Britain: Post-1945 Perspectives*. London: SCM Press, 2007.

Geiringer, David. *The Pope and the Pill: Sex, Catholicism and Women in Post-War England*. Manchester: Manchester University Press, 2018.

Gelfgren, Stefan. "Virtual Churches, Participatory Culture, and Secularization." *Journal of Technology, Theology, and Religion* 2, no. 1 (2011).

Geremek, Bronislaw. *Poverty: A History*. Translated by Agnieszka Kolokowska. Oxford: Blackwell, 1994.

Gibson, William. "Introduction: New Perspectives on Secularisation in Britain (and Beyond)." *Journal of Religious History* 41, no. 4 (2017): 431–8.

Giddens, Anthony. *Modernity and Self-Identity: Self and Society in the Late Modern Age*. Stanford: Stanford University Press, 1991.

Gilbert, Alan D. *The Making of Post-Christian Britain: A History of Secularization of Modern Society*. London: Longman, 1980.

Gill, Robin. *The "Empty" Church Revisited*. Farnham: Ashgate, 2003.

Grant, Myrna. "An Historical Analysis of Biographical, Societal and Organizational Factors Shaping the Radio Career of Thomas Malcolm Muggeridge, 1948–1957," PhD dissertation, Northwestern University, 1986.

Greeley, Andrew. *The Catholic Revolution: New Wine, Old Wineskins, and the Second Vatican Council*. Berkeley: University of California Press, 2004.

Green, Simon. *The Passing of Protestant England, c. 1920–1960*. Cambridge: Cambridge University Press, 2011.

Grimley, Matthew. "Anglican Evangelicals and Anti-Permissiveness." In *Evangelicalism and the Church of England in the Twentieth Century: Reform, Resistance, and Renewal*, edited by Andrew Atherstone and John Maiden, 319–39. Woodbridge: Boydell & Brewer, 2014.

– "Law, Morality, and Secularization: The Church of England and the Wolfenden Report, 1954–1967." *Journal of Ecclesiastical History* 60 (2009): 725–41.

Halsey, A.H. *The Decline of Donnish Dominion: The British Academic Professions in the Twentieth Century*. Oxford: Clarendon Press, 1995.

Hampton, Jameel. *Disability and the Welfare State in Britain: Changes in Perception and Policy, 1948–79*. Bristol: Policy Press, 2016.

Harris, Alana. *Faith in the Family: A Lived Religious History of English Catholicism, 1945–82*. Manchester: Manchester University Press, 2013.

– "A Fresh Stripping of the Altars?" In *Catholics in the Vatican II Era*, edited
by Kathleen Sprows Cummings, Timothy Matovina, and Robert A. Orsi,
245–74. Cambridge: Cambridge University Press, 2018.

Harris, Trevor, and Monia O'Brien Castro, eds. *Preserving the Sixties: Britain
and the "Decade of Protest."* London: Palgrave Macmillan, 2014.

Hastings, Adrian. *A History of English Christianity 1920–2000*. London: SCM
Press, 2001.

– ed. *A World History of Christianity*. Grand Rapids, MI: Wm. B. Eerdmans,
1999.

Hayward, Jennifer. *Consuming Pleasures: Active Audiences and Serial Fictions
from Dickens to Soap Opera*. Lexington: University of Kentucky Press,
1997.

Heimann, Mary. "Christianity in Western Europe from the Enlightenment."
In *A World History of Christianity*, edited by Adrian Hastings, 458–507.
Grand Rapids, MI: Wm. B. Eerdmans, 1999.

Hilliard, David. "Australia: Towards Secularisation and One Step Back." In
Callum Brown and Michael Snape, *Secularisation in the Christian World:
Essays in Honour of Hugh McLeod*, 75–92. Farnham: Ashgate, 2010.

Hitchens, Christopher. "A Hundred Years of Muggery," *Weekly Standard*, 5
May 2003.

– *The Missionary Position: Mother Teresa in Theory and Practice*. London:
Verso, 1995.

Hobsbawm, Eric. *The Age of Extremes*. New York: Vintage Books, 1994.

Hoffman, John. "Confidence in Religious Institutions and Secularization."
*Review of Religious Research* 39, no. 4 (1998): 321–43.

– "Declining Religious Authority?" *Review of Religious Research* 55, no. 1
(2013): 1–25.

Hornsby-Smith, Michael P. *Roman Catholics in England: Studies in Social
Structure since the Second World War*. Cambridge: Cambridge University
Press, 1987.

Hunter, Ian. *Malcolm Muggeridge: A Life*. Nashville: Thomas Nelson Publishing Company, 1980.

Ingrams, Richard. *Muggeridge: The Biography*. London: Harper Collins, 1995.

Iser, Wolfgang. *The Implied Reader: Patterns of Communication in Prose Fiction
from Bunyan to Beckett*. Baltimore: Johns Hopkins University Press, 1974.

Jerman, Bernard R. "Disraeli's Fan Mail: A Curiosity Item." *Nineteenth-
Century Fiction* 9, no. 1 (June 1954): 61–71.

Jones, Ian. *The Local Church and Generational Change in Birmingham, 1945–2000*. Woodbridge: Boydell & Brewer, 2012.

Karr, Clarence. *Authors and Audiences: Popular Canadian Fiction in the Early Twentieth Century*. Montreal and Kingston: McGill-Queen's University Press, 2000.

Katznelson, Ira, and Gareth Stedman Jones, eds. *Religion and the Political Imagination*. Cambridge: Cambridge University Press, 2010.

Kleiman, Michael, Nancy Ramsey, and Lorella Pallazo. "Public Confidence in Religious Leaders." *Review of Religious Research* 38, no. 1 (1996): 79–87.

Koestler, Arthur, ed. *Suicide of a Nation?* New York: Macmillan, 1964.

Ledger-Lomas, Michael. "Religion." In *The Cambridge History of the Book in Britain, Vol. VII*, edited by Andrew Nash, Claire Squires, and I.R. Wilson, 392–426. Cambridge: Cambridge University Press, 2019.

Lee, Lois. *Recognizing the Non-Religious: Reimagining the Secular*. Oxford: Oxford University Press, 2015.

Lockhart, Alastair. "Religious and Spiritual Mobility in Britain: The Panacea Society and Other Movements in the Twentieth Century," *Contemporary British History* 29, no. 2 (2015): 155–78.

Lowe, Rodney. "The Rediscovery of Poverty and the Creation of the Child Poverty Action Group, 1962–68," *Contemporary Record* 9, no. 3 (Winter 1995): 602–11.

Lynch, Gordon. "Living with Two Cultural Turns: The Case of the Study of Religion." In *Social Research after the Cultural Turn*, edited by S. Roseneil and S. Frosh, 73–92. London: Palgrave, 2012.

Machin, G.I.T. *Churches and Social Issues in Twentieth-Century Britain*. Oxford: Oxford University Press, 1998.

Maiden, John. "The Emergence of Catholic Charismatic Renewal 'In a Country': Australia and Transnational Catholic Charismatic Renewal." *Studies in World Christianity* 25, no. 3 (2019): 274–96.

– "What Could Be More Christian Than to Allow the Sikhs to Use It?" In *Christianity and Religious Plurality*, edited by Charlotte Methuen, Andrew Spicer, and John Wolffe, 399–411. Woodbridge: Boydell and Brewer, 2015.

Mandler, Peter. *The English National Character: The History of an Idea from Edmund Burke to Tony Blair*. New Haven: Yale University Press, 2006.

Marwick, Arthur. "The International Context." In *The Permissive Society and its Enemies: Sixties British Culture*, edited by Marcus Collins, 169–84. London: Rivers Oram Press, 2007.

– *The Sixties: Cultural Revolution in Britain, France, Italy and the United States, c. 1958–1974*. Oxford: Oxford University Press, 1998.

Matt, Susan J., and Peter N. Stearns, eds. *Doing Emotions History*. Urbana: University of Illinois Press, 2014.

McCusker, Kristine M. "'Dear Radio Friend': Listener Mail and the *National Barn Dance*, 1931–1941." *American Studies* 39, no. 2 (Summer 1998): 173–95.

McGuire, Meredith B. *Lived Religion: Faith and Practice in Everyday Life*. Oxford: Oxford University Press, 2008.

McIntosh, Esther. "Living Religion: The Fluidity of Practice." *International Journal of Philosophy and Theology* 79, no. 4 (2018): 383–96.

McLeod, Hugh. "The 1960s." In *Religion and the Political Imagination*, edited by Ira Katznelson and Gareth Stedman Jones, 254–74. Cambridge: Cambridge University Press, 2010.

– "The Long March of Religious History: Where have We Travelled since the Sixties, and Why?" In *Religion as an Agent of Change*, edited by Per Igesman Leiden: Brill, 2016.

– *The Religious Crisis of the 1960s*. Oxford: Oxford University Press, 2007.

McLeod, Hugh, and Werner Ustorf, eds. *The Decline of Christendom in Western Europe, 1750–2000*. Cambridge: Cambridge University Press, 2003.

McParland, Robert. *Charles Dicken's American Audience*. Lanham: Lexington Books, 2010.

Methuen, Charlotte, Andrew Spicer, and John Wolffe, eds. *Christianity and Religious Plurality*. Woodbridge: Boydell and Brewer, 2015.

Mittmann, Thomas. "The Lasting Impact of the 'Sociological Moment' on the Churches' Discourse of 'Secularization' in West Germany." *Journal of Religion in Europe* 9 (2016): 157–76.

Morgan, D. Densil. *The Span of the Cross: Christian Religion and Society in Wales 1914–2000*. Cardiff: University of Wales Press, 1999.

Morris, Jeremy. "Enemy Within? The Appeal of the Discipline of Sociology to Religious Professionals in Post-War Britain." *Journal of Religion in Europe* 9 (2016): 177–200.

– "Secularization and Religious Experience: Arguments in the Historiography of Modern British Religion." *The Historical Journal* 55, no. 1 (2012): 195–219.

Muggeridge, Malcolm. *Christ and the Media*. London: Hodder and Stoughton, 1976.

– *Chronicles of Wasted Time, Vol. 1: The Green Stick*. London: Collins, 1972.

– *Chronicles of Wasted Time, Vol. 2: The Infernal Grove*. London: Collins, 1973.

– *The End of Christendom*. Grand Rapids: Wm. B. Eerdmans, 1980.

– "The Importance of Being Beveridge." *Punch*, 6 January 1954.

– *Jesus: The Man Who Lives*. London. Collins, 1975.

– *Jesus Rediscovered*. New York: Doubleday & Company, 1969.

– *Like It Was: The Diaries of Malcolm Muggeridge*. New York: Morrow, 1982.

– *The Most of Malcolm Muggeridge*. New York: Simon and Schuster, 1969.

– "The Sexual Revolution." *New Statesman*, 2 April 1965.

– *Something Beautiful for God: Mother Teresa of Calcutta*. London: Collins, 1971.

– *A Third Testament*. Boston: Little, Brown and Co., 1976.

– *The Thirties: (1930–1940) in Great Britain*. London: Fontana, 1971.

Napolitano, Valentina. *Migrant Hearts and the Atlantic Return: Transnationalism and the Roman Catholic Church*. New York: Fordham University Press, 2016.

Nash, Andrew, Claire Squires, and I.R. Willison, eds. *The Cambridge History of the Book in Britain*, vol. 7, *The Twentieth Century and Beyond*. Cambridge: Cambridge University Press, 2019.

Nash, David. "Believing in Secularisation: Stories of Decline, Potential, and Resurgence." *Journal of Religious History* 41, no. 4 (December 2017): 505–31.

Nelson, Elizabeth. *The British Counter-Culture 1966–73: A Study of the Underground Press*. Basingstoke: Palgrave MacMillan, 1989.

Neuhaus, Jessamyn. "'Is it Ridiculous for me to Say I Want to Write?': Domestic Humor and Redefining the 1950s Housewife Writer in Fan Mail to Shirley Jackson." *Journal of Women's History* 21, no. 2 (Summer 2009): 115–37.

Noonan, Caitriona. "Piety and Professionalism: The BBC's Changing Religious Mission (1960–1979)." *Media History* 19, no. 2 (2013): 196–212.

Nord, David Paul. *Communities of Journalism: A History of Newspapers and Their Readers*. Urbana: University of Illinois Press, 2000.

O'Malley, John W., S.J. *What Happened at Vatican II?* Cambridge, MA: Harvard University Press, 2010.

Orsi, Robert. *Between Heaven and Earth: The Religious Worlds People Make and the Scholars Who Study Them*. Princeton: Princeton University Press, 2004.

Ortolano, Guy. "'Decline' as a Weapon in Cultural Politics." In *Penultimate Adventures with Britannia: Personalities, Politics and Culture in Britain*, edited by William Roger Louis, 201–214. London: I.B. Taurus, 2005.

– *The Two Cultures Controversy: Science, Literature, and Cultural Politics in Postwar Britain*. Cambridge: Cambridge University Press, 2009.

Parker, Stephen G., and Rob J.K. Freathy. "Ethnic Diversity, Christian Hege-

mony and the Emergence of Multi-Faith Religious Education in the
1970s." *History of Education* 41, no. 3 (May 2012): 381–404.

Parsons, Gerald, and John Wolffe, eds. *The Growth of Religious Diversity in
Britain from 1945*, 3 vols. London: Routledge, 1993.

Pasture, Patrick. "Christendom and the Legacy of the Sixties: Between the
Secular City and the Age of Aquarius." *Revue d'Histoire Ecclésiastique* 99,
no. 1 (2004): 82–117.

Pattison, George. "Great Britain: From 'Prophet of the Now' to Postmodern
Ironist (and After)." In *Kierkegaard's International Reception, Tome I, North-
ern and Western Europe*, edited by Jon Stewart, 237–69. Farnham: Ashgate,
2009.

Pawley, Christine. "Beyond Market Models and Resistance: Organizations as
a Middle Layer in the History of Reading." *Library Quarterly: Information,
Community, Policy* 79, no. 1 (January 2009): 73–93.

Peach, Ceri, and Richard Gale. "Muslims, Hindus, and Sikhs in the New
Religious Landscape of England." *The Geographical Review* 93, no. 4 (October 2003): 469–90.

Philips, Paul T. *Contesting the Moral High Ground: Popular Moralists in Mid-
Twentieth Century Britain*. Montreal and Kingston: McGill-Queen's Press,
2013.

Plamper, Jan. *The History of Emotions: An Introduction*. Translated by Keith
Tribe. Oxford: Oxford University Press, 2012.

Plamper, Jan, William Reddy, Barbara Rosenwein, and Peter Stearns. "The
History of Emotions: An Interview with William Reddy, Barbara Rosenwein, and Peter Stearns." *History and Theory* 49, no. 2 (May 2010): 237–65.

Pollack, Detlef. "Varieties of Secularization Theories and Their Indispensable Core." *The Germanic Review: Literature, Culture, Theory* 90, no. 1
(2015): 60–79.

Price, Leah. "Reading: The State of the Discipline." *Book History* 7 (2004):
303–20.

Priest, Robert. *The Gospel According to Renan: Reading, Writing, and Religion
in Nineteenth Century France*. Oxford: Oxford University Press, 2015.

Prochaska, Frank. *Christianity and Social Service in Modern Britain: The Disin-
herited Spirit*. Oxford: Oxford University Press, 2006.

Radway, Janice. *A Feeling for Books: The Book-of-the-Month Club, Literary Taste,
and Middle-Class Desire*. Chapel Hill, NC: University of North Carolina
Press, 1997.

Reddy, William. *The Navigation of Feeling: A Framework for the History of
Emotions*. Cambridge: Cambridge University Press, 2001.

Ricœur, Paul. *Time and Narrative*, 3 vols. Chicago: University of Chicago Press, 1984–88.

Riis, Ole, and Linda Woodhead. *A Sociology of Religious Emotion*. Oxford: Oxford University Press, 2010.

Robinson, Emily, Camilla Schofield, Florence Sutcliffe-Braithwaite, and Natalie Thomlinson. "Telling Stories about Post-war Britain: Popular Individualism and the 'Crisis' of the 1970s." *Twentieth Century British History* 28, no. 2 (2017): 268–304.

Robinson, John. *Honest to God*. London: SCM Press, 1963.

Roof, Wade Clark. *A Generation of Seekers: The Spiritual Journeys of the Baby Boom Generation*. New York: Harper Collins, 1993.

Rose, Jonathan. "The History of Education as the History of Reading." *History of Education* 46, nos. 4–5 (July–September 2007): 595–605.

– "How Historians Study Reader Response." In *Literature in the Marketplace: Nineteenth-Century British Publishing and Reading Practices*, edited by John O. Jordan and Robert L. Patten, 195–212. Cambridge: Cambridge University Press, 1995.

– *The Intellectual Life of the British Working Classes*, 2nd edition. New Haven: Yale University Press, 2010.

Rosen, Andrew. *The Transformation of British Life, 1950–2000: A Social History*. Manchester: Manchester University Press, 2003.

Rosenwein, Barbara H. *Emotional Communities in the Early Middle Ages*. Ithaca, NY: Cornell University Press, 2006.

– *Generations of Feeling: A History of Emotions, 600–1700*. Cambridge: Cambridge University Press, 2016.

– "Worrying about Emotions in History." *The American Historian Review*, 107 no. 3 (June 2002): 821–45.

Rosenwein, Barbara H., and Riccardo Cristiani. *What Is the History of Emotions?* Cambridge: Polity Press, 2018.

Rowntree, Benjamin Seebohm, and George Russell Lavers. *Poverty and the Welfare State: A Third Social Survey of York Dealing Only with Economic Questions*. London: Longmans Green, 1951.

Ryan, Barbara. "One Reader, Two Votes: Retooling Fan Mail Scholarship." In *The History of Reading*, vol. 3, edited by Rosalind Crone and Shafquat Towheed, 66–79. New York: Palgrave, 2011.

– "Teasing out Clues, Not Kooks: *The Man Nobody Knows* and *Ben-Hur.*" *Reception: Texts, Readers, Audiences, History* 5 (2013): 9–23.

Sandbrook, Dominic. *Never had it So Good: A History of Britain from Suez to the Beatles*. London: Abacus, 2005.

- *Seasons in the Sun: The Battle for Britain, 1974–1979.* London: Allen Lane, 2012.
- *State of Emergency: The Way We Were, 1970–1974.* London: Penguin, 2011.
- *White Heat: A History of Britain in the Swinging Sixties.* London: Abacus, 2007.

Sawchuk, Kim. "C Wright Mills: A Political Writer and his Fan Mail." *Canadian Journal of Communication* 26, nos. 2–3 (2001): 231–53.

Scheer, Monique. "Are Emotions a Kind of Practice (And Is That What Makes Them Have A History)? A Bourdieuian Approach to Understanding Emotion." *History and Theory* 51 (May 2012): 193–220.

Scheibe, Susanne, Alexandra B. Freund, and Paul B. Baltes. "Toward a Developmental Psychology of *Sehnsucht* (Life Longings): The Optimal (Utopian) Life." *Developmental Psychology* 43, no. 3 (2007): 778–95.

Schwartz, Adam. *The Third Spring: G.K. Chesterton, Graham Greene, Christopher Dawson, and David Jones.* Washington, DC: Catholic University of America Press, 2005.

Shanks, Michael. *Stagnant Society.* London: Penguin Books, 1961.

Sheard, Matt. "Ninety-Eight Atheists: Atheism among the Non-Elite in Twentieth Century Britain." *Secularism & Nonreligion* 3, no. 6 (2014): 1–16.

Shonfield, Andrew. *British Economic Policy since the War.* London: Penguin Books, 1958.

Simmons, Charlene. "Dear Radio Broadcaster: Fan Mail as a Form of Perceived Interactivity." *Journal of Broadcasting & Electronic Media* 53, no. 3 (2009): 444–59.

Smith, Peter, and Moojan Momen. "The Bahá'í Faith 1957–1988: A Survey of Contemporary Developments." *Religion* 19 (1989): 63–91.

Snow, C.P. *The Two Cultures and the Scientific Revolution.* Cambridge: Cambridge University Press, 1959.

Spencer, Gregory Horton. "The Relationship Between Christian Conversion and the Rhetoric of Malcolm Muggeridge," PhD dissertation, University of Oregon, 1985.

Stapleton, Julia. *Political Intellectuals and Public Identities in Britain Since 1850.* Manchester: Manchester University Press, 2001.

Stolz, Jörg, Judith Könemann, Mallory Schneuwly Puride, Thomas Engleberger, and Michael Krüggeler, eds. *(Un)Believing in Modern Society: Religion, Spirituality, and Religious-Secular Competition.* London: Ashgate, 2015.

Taylor, Charles. *The Malaise of Modernity*. Toronto: House of Anansi Press, 1991.

– *A Secular Age*. Cambridge, MA: Belknap Press, 2007.

Tombs, Robert. *The English and Their History*. New York: Alfred A. Knopf, 2015.

Tomlinson, Jim. "Inventing 'Decline': The Falling behind of the British Economy in the Postwar Years." *The Economic History Review* 49, no. 4 (Nov. 1996): 731–57.

– *Politics of Decline: Understanding Post-war Britain*. Harlow: Longman, 2000.

Towler, Robert. *The Need for Certainty: A Sociological Study of Conventional Religion*. London: Routledge & Kegan Paul, 1984.

Troughton, Geoff. "Anti-Churchianity, Discursive Christianity, and Religious Change in the Twentieth-Century." *Journal of New Zealand Studies* NS17 (2014): 79–87.

United Nations. *United Nations System of Organizations and Directory of Senior Officials*. New York: Office for Inter-Agency Affairs and Co-Ordination, 1976.

Van Rooden, Peter. "The Strange Death of Dutch Christendom." In Callum Brown and Michael Snape, *Secularisation in the Christian World: Essays in Honour of Hugh McLeod*, 175–96. Farnham: Ashgate, 2010.

Vincent, David. *Bread, Knowledge and Freedom: A Study of Nineteenth-Century Working Class Autobiography*. London: Methuen, 1982.

Webster, Peter. *Archbishop Ramsay: The Shape of the Church*. Farnham: Ashgate, 2015.

Whipple, Amy C. "Speaking for Whom? The 1971 Festival of Light and the Search for the 'Silent Majority.'" *Contemporary British History* 24, no. 3 (2010): 319–39.

Wiener, Martin. *English Culture and the Decline of the Industrial Spirit*. Cambridge: Cambridge University Press, 1981.

Wilson, Bryan. *Religion in Secular Society: A Sociological Comment*. London: C.A. Watts & Co., 1966.

Wolfe, Gregory. *Malcolm Muggeridge: A Biography*. Grand Rapids: Wm. B. Eerdmans, 1995.

Wolffe, John. *The Churches and the British Broadcasting Corporation, 1922–1956: The Politics of Religion in Broadcasting*. Canterbury: SCM Press, 1984.

Wood, Paul, ed. *On Paul Ricœur: Narrative and Interpretation*. London: Routledge, 1991.

Woodhead, Linda, ed. *Religion and Change in Modern Britain*. London: Rout-
    ledge, 2012.

Zemmin, Florian, Colin Jager, and Guido Vanheeswijck, eds. *Working with* A
    Secular Age: *Interdisciplinary Perspectives on Charles Taylor's Master Narra-
    tive*. Berlin: De Gruyter, 2016.

Zhao, Kang, and Gert Biesta. "Lifelong Learning, Identity and the Moral
    Dimension: The 'Reflexive Project of the Self' revisited." Paper presented
    at the 38th Annual SCUTREA Conference, 2–4 July 2008, University of
    Edinburgh.

# Index

*The letter* t *following a page number denotes a table*